The reformation of the parishes

The clergy were central to the initial outbreak and direction of the Reformation. The reformed movement had gained much of its impetus from hostility towards the clerical estate and this intensity of feeling had a devastating effect on the clergy in the first decades of the evangelical movement. The status and authority of the clergy had been transformed by the Reformation and this book looks at how they emerged from this traumatic experience – not subdued and demoralised but as a new respected professional elite.

Each chapter in the book looks at a different aspect of the transformation process, illustrating clearly that this process of reconstruction was the work of more than one generation or church. The chapters range from case studies as diverse as pre-Reformation England and Scotland; The development of the ministry in established Lutheran and Catholic cultures in Germany and Lower Austria; Geneva, the fulcrum of emerging new concepts of the ministry; and the new missionary Calvinist churches in France and the Netherlands. As a cohesive whole, the studies show how destructive criticism gave way to a recognition of the crucial role that the clergy would play in inculcating the essentials of the new faith.

This book draws original conclusions about this crucial phase in the clergy's history and provides the first comprehensive analysis of the reformed ministry throughout Europe. It will be essential reading for scholars of early modern Europe and Reformation Studies.

Andrew Pettegree is Lecturer in Modern History at the University of St Andrews.

The reformation of the parishes
The ministry and the Reformation in town and country

Edited by Andrew Pettegree

Manchester University Press
Manchester and New York

distributed exclusively in the USA and Canada by St Martin's Press

Copyright © Manchester University Press 1993

While copyright in the volume as a whole is vested in
Manchester University Press, copyright in individual chapters
belong to their respective authors, and no chapter may be
reproduced wholly or in part without the express permission in
writing of both author and publisher

Published by Manchester University Press
Oxford Road, Manchester M13 9PL, UK
and Room 400, 175 Fifth Avenue,
New York, NY 10010, USA

Distributed exclusively in the USA and Canada
by St. Martin's Press. Inc., 175 Fifth Avenue, New York, NY 10010, USA

British Library Cataloguing-in-Publication Data

A catalogue record for this book is available from the British Library

Library of Congress Cataloging-in-Publication Data applied for

ISBN 0 7190 4005 1 *hardback*

Phototypeset by Intype, London
Printed in Great Britain by Biddles Ltd, Guildford and King's Lynn

Contents

CONTENTS

Notes on Contributors

ANDREW PETTEGREE is Lecturer in Modern History at the University of St Andrews.

CAROL EDINGTON is British Academy Post-Doctoral Fellow in the Department of Scottish History, University of St Andrews.

BEAT KÜMIN is a Research Fellow at Magdalene College, Cambridge.

BRUCE GORDON was until recently Research Fellow at the Institute for European History in Mainz. He is now training for the ministry at Knox College, University of Toronto.

SCOTT DIXON, formerly a research student at the University of Cambridge, is now Fellow of the Centre for Renaissance and Reformation Studies at the University of Toronto.

WILLIAM G. NAPHY, formerly a research student at the University of St Andrews, is now Research Assistant on the J. H. Oldham Biography project at New College, Edinburgh.

KARIN MAAG is the Sir Harold Mitchell Postgraduate Fellow at the University of St Andrews.

PENNY ROBERTS is Lecturer in History at the University of Warwick.

NOTES ON CONTRIBUTORS

RICHARD FITZSIMMONS, formerly a research student at the University of St Andrews, teaches history at Strathallan School.

ANDREW SPICER, formerly a research student at the University of Southampton, teaches history at Stonyhurst College.

RONA JOHNSTON, formerly a research student at Oxford University, now holds a Theodor Heuss Research Fellowship at the Institut für Europaische Geschichte, Mainz.

Preface

This book was first conceived as a result of a series of informal conferences held in the University of St Andrews in the summer vacations of 1991 and 1992. Having gathered together a group whose interests were primarily in the field of the European Reformation, it seemed a logical development to explore these common interests in a rather more disciplined and co-ordinated fashion, and in particular to focus on the clergy, one of the central issues of the first generation of evangelical agitation and the group whose status and way of life were most spectacularly under threat. Although my principal thanks must be to the contributors who have engaged these issues, this project has also benefited materially from the colleagues in St Andrews who attended our meetings, and contributed their comments and criticism to the discussion: James Cameron, Jane Dawson, John Guy, Bruce Lenman, Roger Mason, and Hamish Scott. I am once again grateful to Julian Crowe of the St Andrews University Computer Laboratory for his help in rendering computer discs into a compatible format. I also wish to acknowledge our debt to the anonymous reader for Manchester University Press, who contributed detailed and thoughtful remarks at an early stage, and to Jane Thorniley-Walker, who has seen our volume into production with all possible despatch, and encouraged many of the contributors by her informed interest in their work.

ADMP
St Andrews, December 1992

ix

Abbreviations

AEG	Archives d'Etat de Genève
ARG	*Archiv für Reformationsgeschichte*
Bèze, *Correspondance*	*Correspondance de Théodore de Bèze*, ed. Hippolyte Aubert, Henri Meylan et al. (Geneva, 1960–)
BHR	*Bibliothèque d'Humanisme et Renaissance*
BN	Bibliothèque Nationale, Biblioteca Nacional
BCRH	*Bulletin de la Commission Royale d'Histoire*
BPU	Bibliothèque publique et Universitaire Geneva
BSHPF	*Bulletin de la Société de l'Histoire du Protestantisme Français*
CH	*Church History*
CO	*Calvini Opera*
CR	*Corpus Reformatorum*
EHR	*English Historical Review*
HJ	*Historical Journal*
JEH	*Journal of Ecclesiastical History*
NAK	*Nederlands Archief voor Kerkgeschiedenis*
NNBW	*Nieuw Nederlandsch biografisch woordenboek*
P & P	*Past and Present*
RC	Registres du Conseil de Genève (Mss. at AEG)

RCP	*Registre de la Compagnie des Pasteurs de Genève*, ed. R. M. Kingdon, J.-F. Bergier et al. (Geneva, 1964–)
RGP	Rijks Geschiedkundige Publicatiën
RHPR	*Revue d'Histoire et Philosophie Religieuses*
RSCHS	*Records of the Scottish Church History Society*
RV	*Acta der provinciale en particuliere synoden gehouden in de noordelijke Nederlanden gedurende de jaren 1572–1620*, ed. J. Reitsma and S. D. van Veen (8 vols, Groningen, 1892–99)
SCH	Studies in Church History
SCJ	*Sixteenth Century Journal*
StAZ	Staatsarchiv Zürich
STS	Scottish Text Society
TRE	*Theologische Realenzyklopädie*
WMV	*Werken der Marnix-Vereeniging*

1

The clergy and the Reformation: from 'devilish priesthood'[1] to new professional elite

Andrew Pettegree

How did the clergy survive the Reformation? To pose the question in this way is not, I think, to overdramatise the traumatic nature of the challenge posed to religious professionals by the new evangelical movement of the sixteenth century. The first estate of the mediaeval church could not have expected to have emerged unscathed from such a wide-ranging movement of reform, but in fact the Reformation challenged the clergy in every way: in their income, their social status, and in their claim to that special access to spiritual remedies which marked them off from the laity and gave them their separate standing. One influential German historian has characterised this assault on clerical pretensions as the central binding force of the Reformation: to him the Reformation was first and foremost an uprising against the clergy (*ein Aufstand gegen die Priester*).[2] And this was an insurrection which seemed likely in the first decade of evangelical reform to change fundamentally and for all time the relationship between the laity and religious professionals.

And yet the clergy did survive; transformed, but with their social prestige and claims to a special status very largely intact. The clerical groups which emerged from this process were certainly very different: much smaller, less differentiated by function than their mediaeval counterparts and better educated, but certainly not broken by the experience of evangelical criticism. Indeed the end of the Reformation century saw the emergence in several parts of Europe of a new sort of clergy, characterised by a professional esprit de corps and elitism, and confident in the possession of a unique expertise; in this respect it is fair to talk of them as one of

1

the new emerging professions, at least in embryo.[3] The clergy was transformed by the Reformation, but not defeated.

The essays which make up this volume are all designed to engage various aspects of this process of criticism, reform, and transformation. Progress towards these new parameters was never uniform: indeed different parts of Europe reflected the quite different expectations which lay people had of those who in the mediaeval world had played a vital mediating role in their quest for salvation. In many respects the transformation of the clerical estate would reflect the wider forces of change at work in society. But if there was one lesson which would emerge it was that – however subtly redefined – the clergy had succeeded in defending their claims to a special place in society.

Notwithstanding the evidence that can be advanced for wide-ranging criticism it is clear that anticlericalism was not endemic through Europe on the eve of the Reformation. One of the lessons learned from recent scholarship is that we must differentiate more carefully between relatively well organised churches such as England where the parochial clergy seem by and large to have retained the respect of their parishioners, and the altogether much less satisfactory position in large parts of central Europe.[4] Here the condition of the clerical estate, from the immensely wealthy but largely secularised ecclesiastical hierarchy to a numerous, impoverished, highly varied clerical proletariat, gave cause for real concern. Estimates of the size of the clerical order vary: from a relatively modest 1.5 per cent of the population in pre-Reformation England to a staggering (and quite unsustainable) 10 per cent in some German cities.[5] These raw statistics also conceal an immense variety of status and function. There was a considerable difference between the fully ordained priest and those on the fringes of the profession in minor orders, and within the priesthood between the beneficed parish minister and those who performed a range of (generally less well remunerated) auxiliary functions. These differences were reflected in a similar disparity of income and economic status. This led, inevitably, to a restless search for additional sources of income which might bring marginal economic security to the hapless curate, or great wealth to an ecclesiastical prince or landlord. The result was an increasing commercialisation of spiritual functions, where each sacrament or clerical service had its appropriate fee.[6]

The consequence, not least of this economic imperative, was that the clergy was an all-pervasive presence in many late mediaeval communities. It rubbed up against the laity and intruded into their everyday lives in a number of irritating ways; the great diversity within the clerical estate also produced an often underrated potential for internecine strife. The need for some sort of reform was widely recognised. Attempts at reform, whether in the conciliar movement or Observant branches of monasticism, reached back deep into the Middle Ages.[7] But certainly this was given a fresh impetus and a new turn by the new intellectual movements of the fifteenth and sixteenth centuries. Whatever the relationship between Humanism and Reformation – and some of the church's most passionate defenders might lay equal claim to be schooled in the new movement – Humanism certainly brought a new rigour and breadth of discussion to an intellectual community which spread quite naturally across national boundaries. The clergy were not exempt from this process of criticism and examination. Both their theological and economic status – as in Conrad Summerhert's influential treatise questioning the spiritual basis of tithe – were subjected to a searching re-evaluation.[8] Such intellectual debate blended insensibly into the casual but corrosive literary anticlericalism of works like Brant's *Ship of Fools*, which enjoyed a vogue alongside more measured scholarly literature in the prestigious Humanist sodalities of southern Germany.[9]

Such a climate of criticism was clearly not confined to Germany. Carol Edington's essay in this volume is an example of how conventional, stereotypical criticism of abuses in the church could be infused with a more pointed and coherent agenda by humanist influences. Humanism brought a new vigour to calls for an educated, preaching clergy, and lay critics were not afraid to point up the connection between church levies and the services lay people demanded of the clergy in return.[10] Both these currents of thought were of course well represented in the work of Erasmus, the quintessential representative of northern Humanism. His *Enchiridion*, the *Handbook of the Christian Soldier*, included an excoriating denunciation of superstitious practices which acted as a substitute for true belief and the godly life. By implication this work, published in 1505 but only truly in vogue a decade later, also promoted a highly influential vision of the active lay vocation with

3

its emphasis on the spiritual life as against the external ceremonies of the church.

All of this helped create an intellectual climate in which criticism of the church was wide-ranging and intellectually respectable; a circumstance which could not but influence the intellectual context in which the German controversies ignited by Luther would be conducted. In all of this Luther himself is a somewhat ambiguous figure.[11] But the fact that he was undoubtedly a striking example of success within the old church, and that he set considerable store by his status as a doctor of theology, should not disguise the strong anticlerical tone of many of his early writings. The years when he was pursuing his own intellectual emancipation from scholastic theology were also years of great bitterness against a clerical hierarchy which had met his call for reasoned debate with the demand for unconditional recantation: his sense of alienation issued in writings of extraordinary vituperation. The misuse of the Gospel, the exploitation of spiritual power, the neglect of the preaching office in favour of a shameless traffic in benefices, lands, and spiritual remedies, all were the subject of a pitiless condemnation as Luther emphasised the gulf which had grown up between him and the 'damnable and horrible priesthood of the papists'.[12]

It was therefore no surprise that as Luther developed his alternative theological agenda he should turn his back on the church as the traditional mediator of salvation. It is important to realise that both the theological cornerstones of Luther's teaching, Justification by Faith and the call for teaching based on the Pure Gospel, carry an implicit anticlerical message: the first by removing the priest as a necessary element in the salvation process, the second by its implicit judgement on pre-Reformation scholastic theology.[13] And it was this second theme which found the broadest resonance in the towns and cities across the Empire. Whatever the liberating appeal of Luther's concept of Justification to fellow clerics and the theologically literate, it was the concept of the Pure Gospel, especially when contrasted with the teachings and practices of the local clergy, which spoke most directly to the concerns of lay folk who saw in the evangelical movement the vehicle for their most pressing spiritual and secular concerns.[14] All across Germany calls for reform were linked with the call for the *Rein Evangelium*.[15] And this was a movement which Luther appeared to endorse as, despairing of a self-generating reform

4

within the clerical estate, he increasingly came to see the laity as the major springboard of evangelical renewal. For a time he seemed even prepared to argue that an uncorrupted laity possessed a superior access to wisdom, and certainly an equal claim to salvation: the central message of his most difficult, and most explicitly anticlerical theological concept, the priesthood of all believers.

How far Luther's more esoteric theological concepts influenced the Reformation movement is a debated question. Arguably the real impact of the Reformation message lay in more basic appeals to lay interests and concerns. In their eagerness to broaden the appeal of the new movement the new evangelical preachers did not scruple to touch upon long-standing lay grievances, even at the cost of spreading unclarity about the central theological message.[16] The result, evident from the contemporary pamphlet literature, was to subject the clerical estate to a sustained battering. In contrast to theology, the attacks on clerical immunities and privileges were something which could engage all strata of urban and lay societies. In the towns the call for ministers who would teach 'the Pure Gospel' was central to demands for reform, in a movement which, as recent research has shown, found broad support among the middle levels of the urban population.[17] But the urban patriciates also had much to gain, once initial anxieties about the movement's potential for destabilising the delicate social balance had been overcome. In particular, town councils perceived in the new movement the opportunity to remove from the church exemptions and privileges which had long been a source of irritation; in this respect the Reformation formed part of a continuing and longer-term movement to subject all the life of the city to lay control.[18] Here city magistracies were greatly emboldened by the claim, first advanced in the Zurich disputation of 1523, that in putting into practice demands for Gospel preaching the council might take upon itself the task of arbitrating conflicting claims to spiritual truth: a striking, even revolutionary thrust against the clergy's claim to any exclusive expertise in interpreting the Word of God. This was a position with which Luther briefly and rashly seemed to associate himself, notably in his 1523 tract, that a *Christian Assembly has the right to judge all teaching*.[19]

The same concern that the priest should be subjugated to the specific needs of the local community was evident as the Reformation spread out into the countryside.[20] It has justly been remarked that country people understood Luther's teaching as it applied not to salvation but to pastoral provision, and in this the villagers had their own agenda, notably an insistence that clerical levies on their income and goods should be applied to the provision of a resident preaching ministry. If countryfolk thirsted equally after the *Rein Evangelium*, they also sought freedom from a wide range of customary impositions with which they were burdened, and which frequently poisoned the relationship with their priest or clerical landlord. Large areas of southern Germany witnessed early attempts to put this agenda into practice, culminating in widespread demands for an elective ministry in 1525, the year of the Peasants' War.

How damaging this multifaceted assault on the clerical estate must have been is evident in the turmoil of the first evangelical decade. The effect of crumbling morale was seen first and foremost in rapidly declining numbers, as members of the old clerical orders declared for the new movement or abandoned their vocations altogether. The first victims were generally the regular clergy. Erasmus noted a flight from the monasteries in 1524, and in the German towns the religious houses were inevitably an early target for reforming councils eager to settle old scores and establish their authority.[21] It was also clear that the church would no longer be able to sustain such a vast range of clerical personnel, given that the theological foundation of their particular functions had been so thoroughly undermined. As William Naphy makes clear here in his study of Geneva, one of the most striking aspects of the new system was the sharp decrease in the numbers of clergy employed: in the case of Geneva a reduction from some hundreds to no more than a dozen.[22] All across central Europe a mass of regular and secular clergy were forced in middle life to seek alternative employment as their clerical functions were abruptly terminated. The more fortunate and influential received pensions, but many did not. What became of them is seldom clear: possibly they found employment in nearby Catholic territories, or even in handicrafts, but for the many with no skills outside their former clerical functions the prospects must have been grim indeed.

The hardship faced by this first generation of victims was the worst the clergy would experience. For in truth, the Reformation would offer a redefinition of clerical functions, rather than a blanket condemnation. Luther's initial confidence in the superior judgement of the laity, which had led him briefly to commit theology to the judgement of the community, proved to be fleeting. If the radical disturbances at Wittenberg during his absence in 1522 had not convinced him of the dangers of the unregulated search for Gospel principles, then the Peasants' War brought this home with a vengeance. Luther's violent reaction against the excesses of the peasants was a turning point for the Reformation. Hereafter when he and his supporters among the reformers spoke of lay authority, it was to the natural leaders of society that they turned, the city magistrates and the princes.[23]

In this context the mature Luther had no doubt of the need for a separate ministerial group. Even in the *Christian Assembly* of 1523, Luther had recognised the need for preachers and teachers, since the Christian community cannot unprompted perceive the word of God. It was therefore necessary to appoint from among the community those whom God had endowed with understanding and abilities. In the light of the experience of 1525, Luther was even more clear that the choice of appropriate persons should be resigned to those of mature judgement, the civil magistrates. By the time he came to write his *Deutsche Messe* (1526), Luther was persuaded that the laity was not mature enough for major changes such as an elective priesthood.

In truth Luther's ecclesiology fell far short of what one might regard as a coherent system. It was left to others, notably Melanchthon and Bugenhagen, to elaborate a coherent theology and scheme of church-building. Their work made clear that once the first rash of viturperative criticism had passed, the recognition of the need for trained personnel was universal, at least in the Reformation mainstream. The belief that the gift of inspired prophecy might be shared by the untrained layman was from this point the exclusive property of those radical groups which Luther now denounced as 'false brethren'.[24] This trend should not be at all surprising. One of the most potent charges against the clergy in the pre-Reformation period had been that of ignorance; the recognition of the need to improve standards of education had been at the heart of most pre-Reformation reforming endeavours, now given new point by the criticisms of the Humanist movement. In this respect efforts to reform the clergy were a reflection of wider social trends. After all, a principal factor in the success of Humanism had been a belief in and respect for learning, an aspiration also reflected in the steady growth of university education in the centuries before the Reformation.[25] The universities were increasingly regarded as a necessary training ground for the emerging secular professions, such as the law; this represented the laicisation of education, rather than its rejection. We can regard this long-term erosion of the clerical monopoly of learning as one of the underlying causes of the sixteenth-century reform movement, and it was through their own access to learning that the laity were able to impose and insist on higher standards for the clergy. This same respect for learning ensured a place for trained specialists in the post-Reformation churches. It ran much deeper than the attack on book-learning that characterised the reaction against scholastic theology in the opening years of the evangelical movement.

But where were such clerical specialists to be found? Inevitably in the first years communities were forced to look to the only bodies with the appropriate expertise, that is the existing clergy. All studies of the first generation of evangelical preachers and parish ministers agree that they were substantially drawn from the existing clerical professions: either the local parish priest accepting new responsibilities or a former religious happy to accept parish employment in the new evangelical context.[26] The essential conservatism of this parish Reformation stands in marked contrast to the radical expectations aroused by the most visionary of the early Reformation pamphlets. But as the studies here suggest, pragmatic solutions of this nature were often reasonably successful in satisfying parochial needs.[27]

By the time that the Reformation became established in the Reformed churches of Switzerland, the leaders of the new churches, mostly men of the second generation, had had time to ponder a more considered theological response to the problems of church organisation and ministry. In particular they had been able to consider how to reconcile the conflicting claims of calling and training within the context of an evangelical ministry. In the case of John Calvin there is little doubt of the emphasis he placed on the importance of a theologically-trained ministry. Calvin had a conviction of the value of education which was both intuitive – a reflection of his own background and scholarly training – and theological. To Calvin the importance of the preaching office arose directly from his understanding of the primacy of scripture. The message of scripture was God's own revelation of his will. Not only was the message handed on by the preacher the Word of God, but it possessed the authority of God himself. Since the preacher is the servant of that message it is necessary that he should know the Bible well; in order to be a teacher he must first have been a disciple.[28]

This perception did not give the minister an unlimited authority. Although he was under a clear responsibility to preach the word boldly, a responsibility Calvin himself exercised to the frequent embarrassment of his local auditors, he had also to live up to the Word. The preacher himself must be obedient to the teaching he was urging on his congregation. In this respect it was no accident that the *Ecclesiastical Ordinances* laid as much stress on morals and behaviour as on educational qualifications, or that Calvin's search for men who could live up to these standards led to the premature departure of almost all the men appointed to the ministry in the early years of the Genevan Reformation.[30]

In Zurich, reformers reached largely cognate conclusions from somewhat different premises. The Zurich church settlement was built on Zwingli's view of the church as a mixed assembly of the good and evil. In this context the ministry played a necessary role in bringing the Word of God before the people and calling them to repentance and faith. Such repentance was only possible when the people learn of God through the preaching of the Word. These conclusions were heartily endorsed by Heinrich Bullinger, who shared in full the Humanist conviction of the teachable nature of faith.[31]

A minister therefore possessed a double function: to preach the Word, and to oversee the spiritual health of the community. This in turn imposes a double obligation: a minister must be educated, so as to avoid false doctrine, but also of exemplary life, so as to set a moral example. This, as in Geneva, set a high standard, somewhat unrealistic in the context of sixteenth-century Zurich, a city state with a large rural hinterland of parishes all of which had to be staffed. In managing the clergy Bullinger took a humane view of what might be expected of the under-educated rural clergy, which could only gradually be brought up to the standard required.[32] The situation was very different in Geneva, a small city state with an insignificant rural territory and a seemingly endless supply of highly qualified refugees. William Naphy's essay in this volume demonstrates the extent to which by 1546 Calvin had succeeded in creating a ministerial cadre the like of which was probably never equalled throughout Europe. With the co-operation of lay sympathisers in the consistory Calvin was able to embark on the sort of active supervision of morals which in the disparate communities of the Zurich territory proved wholly impracticable.[33]

It is interesting to speculate how this abnormal experience, plainly unattainable in the larger Reformed states, might have coloured Calvin's view of the ministry as expressed in his writings and sermons. Certainly the strains which would be evident when these largely ideal precepts were applied in very different geographical and political situations became apparent as Reformed Protestantism began to spread beyond the borders of Switzerland in the middle years of the sixteenth century. In France and the Netherlands, England and Scotland, the new churches that emerged in these decades faced a quite different situation. In the case of England and Scotland, the new regime faced problems familiar from Germany in the first half of the century, of staffing a large number of churches with a limited cadre of qualified individuals. In France and the Netherlands the exercise of a preaching ministry posed quite different problems, since in the first decade at least churches were established only in the teeth of fierce opposition from the local powers, and in conditions of considerable danger. The qualities demanded of men who ministered in these circumstances were very different. Here the need for a firm sense of inner calling clearly took precedence over formal education. The first generation of ministers who served in these 'churches under the cross', and not infrequently paid for their bravery with their lives, included a considerable number from comparatively humble social backgrounds: a throwback to the artisan ministers of the first German generation.[34] Men of this sort were often preferred for strictly practical reasons: an artisan preacher could more easily blend into the background and avoid detection, and even on occasions continue with his occupation, thus lessening the financial strain on congregations which were usually small and possessed only limited resources.[35]

These considerations of course no longer applied when church-forming took place in freedom, or under the protection of the state power, as was the case in England and Scotland, and at intervals in both France and the Netherlands. In these periods of often rapid church-building the qualities demanded of a minister were rather different. Important city churches now looked for men who would be an ornament to their pulpits: ideally men with both the education and social background to command the respect of the local community.

This led, inevitably, to a degree of tension between ministers of the first and second generation, in situations where changes in the political climate permitted former secret congregations to organise in public.[36] But normally there would be room for both, for in every case where the attempt was made to organise a Reformed church on a national basis the most pressing problem was a dearth of qualified ministers. The immediate need was tackled variously in the new churches of the late sixteenth century. In England the Elizabethan regime briefly employed a policy of ordaining anyone who presented themselves, regardless of their qualifications or (not unusually) total lack of the same.[37] The new Scottish Calvinist church meanwhile made use of a large number of former notaries and schoolmasters.[38] In France, a church like Troyes which could rely on a succession of highly trained ministers sponsored by Geneva and other Swiss centres was rather the exception than the rule. Outside the strategic urban centres favoured in this way the French Huguenot congregations were plagued by men of patently inadequate qualifications or obvious insincerity who thrust themselves into ministerial positions.[39] As in the Netherlands local congregations were all too easily convinced that any sort of ministry was preferable to none at all.[40]

Faced with such a rapidly evolving situation, the new Calvinist churches were forced very quickly to develop institutions by which to regulate the appointment and conduct of this ministerial cadre. Here again the precepts laid down by Calvin offered little relevant guidance. Although Calvin expressed a clear preference for an educated ministry, he made no specifications as to how that education should be conducted, nor indeed the process by which a minister should be chosen. The *Institutes* noted somewhat vaguely that the choice should not be against the wishes of the local congregation, but Calvin was equally clear that such an important decision should not be left to the fickle favour of the 'unbridled multitude'.[41] The procedures adopted in the new Calvinist

11

churches in fact evince a severe practicality. The regulation of ministerial conduct was generally delegated to the synod and its local equivalent, the classis or *colloque*; the classis meanwhile also undertook to monitor the theological progress of both candidates for the ministry and those already in post.[42] This form of in-service training, which took the form of an exposition by turns of a passage of scripture under the correction of colleagues from other churches in the locality, represented a sensitive response to the situation where many of those appointed inevitably fell far short of an ideal standard. And it seems to have worked remarkably well. A recent study of the classis of Dordrecht, admittedly one of the best organised of the Dutch churches, credits the classical exercises with the production of a generation of highly qualified ministers, much in demand in other parts of Holland, at least a decade before university training became the norm.[43]

The lack of concern for university education is at first sight surprising. After all, the Geneva Academy had been founded in 1559 with the specific aim of providing well-trained ministers in accordance with Calvin's ideal.[44] The same needs and aspirations are evident in the foundation of Leiden University in 1575, the Huguenot Academies in France, and new colleges in several well-established universities: the statutes of Emmanuel College, Cambridge (1585) read very much as if what was intended was the foundation of a Protestant seminary.[45]

Nevertheless there remained a considerable gulf between these pious aspirations and reality on the ground. Most universities retained the essential character of the mediaeval institutions, with little change to their basic institutional structure or curriculum to take account of the practical skills required by aspirant ministers. Even in the new institutions there remained a clear difference in intention between those who envisaged the Protestant Academies as places of professional training and those who hankered after the prestige and greater drawing power of more conventionally organised universities. Thus the magistrates of godly Geneva were not unaware that by adorning their new Academy with a Law Faculty they would increase the number of wealthy noble students they could attract to their city.[46]

For all of these reasons progress towards a graduate clergy was fitful. The normal pattern seems to have been a generational one: in the first two decades of any new church, the overwhelming priority was to provide some sort of ministry to replace the former Catholic priesthood with men who recognised a loyalty to the new church even if their level of formal educational attainment was low. The length of this transitional period depended in part on the size of the territory and the availability of suitable local training institutions. In the Lutheran territories investigated by Scott Dixon one sees a steady progress towards a graduate clergy, which nevertheless took the best part of fifty years to become fully established. In the Netherlands it was the early years of the seventeenth century before a graduate clergy was the norm, a circumstance which in part reflected the difficulties which beset the University of Leiden in its formative years.[47] Even in England the point at which most parish clergy could boast university qualifications comes later than is often recognised.[48]

And despite the increasing emphasis on the need for theological training, it is remarkable how frequently the practical demands of the ministry were cited when congregations sought new ministers. The need for a strong voice, for instance, was repeatedly mentioned as a prerequisite for appointment.[49] This is not surprising, perhaps, in view of the importance attached to regular preaching, and the need to command the attention of an audience for an hour or more in large unheated buildings; but a corrective, nevertheless, against historians ignoring the mundane factors which could be crucial to an effective preaching ministry in sixteenth-century circumstances.

This notwithstanding, all the churches studied here show steady progress towards a ministerial body with more formal qualifications, subjected to stricter controls, and a more formal examination process before they embarked on their ministry. This was by no means a negative development from the point of view of the clergy. Stricter regulation and higher qualifications brought with them a certain enhancement of social status, and gave the clergy a more solid basis for their claim to a position of special respect in the community. No longer was it possible to regard ministers with the contempt often heaped on their uneducated, semi-literate predecessors.

One can discern some significant straws in the wind from an early stage. Whereas in Strasburg the early stages of the Reformation had been accompanied by the demand that the resident clergy should become citizens, a symbolic demolition of their claims to a special caste status, by 1551 the Geneva Council felt obliged to ban the ministers from speaking at the General Assembly: clearly it was no longer possible for the magistrates to tolerate the influence which these articulate and well-educated men were able to exercise on civic affairs.[50] In Geneva as in Strasburg, the ministers made full use of their control of the pulpit, which it is worth reminding ourselves was generally the sole means of regular communication between the city elite and the general public. The magistrates were well aware how powerful a weapon this could be, and in many cities attempted to exercise control over how the ministers exercised their preaching office, but seldom with total success.[51] All over Europe, the magistrates arrayed on their benches below the preacher would occasionally get to hear some unpleasant home truths. Such conflict was not the norm, but it was inevitable that the emergence of a generation of articulate and well-educated preaching ministers would recover for the clergy much of the moral authority which had been so compromised by the first evangelical assault. In this respect the search for a qualified preaching ministry was a distinctly double-edged sword.

If this was the case in the towns, it was perhaps even more pronounced in the countryside. It has justly been remarked that the best qualified and most talented clergy would inevitably graduate to the larger, more prestigious urban churches.[52] This was certainly true, but as some measure of educational qualification became the norm, even the least talented of this new clerical cadre would have been significantly more educated than their parishioners. The introduction of a generation of parish priests with university education could only enhance the degree of separation from the local community. These new men were also more often outsiders than local men, often appointed by the state or an outside patron.[53] The fact that they brought with them a now legitimate family only reinforced the extent to which they were a new presence in the community. Inevitably these changes brought with them certain tensions. If parishioners questioned by the systematic German visitations were on the whole satisfied with their pastors, disputes could still flare over financial matters, particularly where the minister's greater family responsibilities led to new and unfamiliar financial exactions. Many parish incomes were simply insufficient to meet the needs and expectations of the new ministerial breed, and parishioners objected to the imposition of new tithes which did not have the sanction of tradition.[54] Such a situation often required the intervention of the state to reconcile the practical need for an adequate income with the theological necessity of a resident pastor, which in almost all Reformed churches ruled out the pre-Reformation compromise of holding more than one benefice.[55] Improvement of the standards of the clergy therefore often involved a certain degree of rationalisation of parish boundaries, if the same effect could not be achieved by reallocation of redundant church funds.

All of this was necessary to make the ministry once again an attractive career option. That it succeeded is evident in the degree to which clerical service became a dynastic occupation. In several countries a surprisingly high proportion of the second generation of Reformed ministers were themselves the product of clerical households.[56] It also emphasised the extent to which ministers and the state were natural partners in the work of state building, social control, and the generalisation of administrative structures which characterised this period of consolidation. This process, sometimes referred to as confessionalisation, could proceed only by a process of co-operation between government and church, since the minister was a natural focus of authority in the community, and in some communities almost the only literate individual.[57] In return the state lent its weight to developing ministerial efforts to ensure doctrinal orthodoxy and general compliance to its moral teachings.[58] The difficulties of securing effective control over the quality of clerical services and religious life where this partnership was not operating effectively is clear from the contribution of Rona Johnston in this volume.[59] In the Habsburg lands of Lower Austria it proved quite impossible to begin the work of reformation in places where lay patrons were in a position to prevent Catholic clergy even from entering their churches. The renovation of religious life in this context necessarily went hand in hand with the effective exercise of authority on the part of the state.[60]

It was this partnership which might finally be said to have put the seal on the clerical renaissance so evident by the end of the Reformation century. By the early seventeenth century the ministry was a profession to be sought after, not just by sons of the manse; members of the merchant classes and even the gentry now sought to place their younger sons in appropriate benefices.[61] In some senses the Reformation must have seemed to have changed remarkably little, with the same clear differentiation between a privileged clerical elite and a less favoured clerical proletariat which we have observed as characteristic of the pre-Reformation church re-emerging in many countries. And yet this was only part of the story. For all the continued importance attached to social status in the hunt for benefices, the aristocratic character of the pre-Reformation church (particularly the prominence enjoyed by the nobility in the higher reaches of the clerical hierarchy) was not re-established. The new Protestant churches remained to a large extent dominated by urban, bourgeois values.[62] This was a fundamental shift, which reflected the fact that the challenge of the Reformation had involved the working out of a new relationship between clergy and laity, which required the clergy as an occupational group to justify and if necessary redefine the rationale behind their claims to a special place in society. The clergy, whether Catholic or Protestant, certainly now functioned in a more demanding intellectual climate, one which reflected the dual expectations of both lay society and their own professional superiors that they provided their parishioners with real theological leadership. That they had to a large extent succeeded in meeting this challenge is a certain endorsement of the changes brought about by the evangelical agitation.[63] But it was also a reflection of a widespread understanding of a continuing need for an occupational group with special expertise who could assist and guide lay people in their fumbling quest to divine the mysteries of God and the afterlife.

Notes

1 The description comes from Martin Luther's *The Misuse of the Mass* (1521), one of his most excoriating denunciations of the papal priesthood. *Luther's Works*, ed. Jaroslav Pelikan and Helmut Lehmann (55 vols, St Louis/Philadelphia, 1958–86), XXXVI p. 199.

2 Hans-Jürgen Goertz, *Pfaffenhaß und groß Geschrei. Die reformatorischen Bewegungen in Deutschland, 1517–1529* (Munich, 1987).

3 Wilfrid Prest (ed.), *The Professions in Early Modern England* (London, 1987).

4 On England Peter Heath, *The English Parish Clergy on the Eve of the Reformation* (London, 1969). Beat Kümin, chapter 3, below.

5 The figure for England from Rosemary O'Day, 'The Anatomy of a Profession: The Clergy of the Church of England', in Prest, *Professions in Early Modern England*, pp. 30–1. For Germany, Bernd Moeller,

'Religious Life in Germany on the Eve of the Reformation', in Gerald Strauss (ed.), *Pre-Reformation Germany* (London, 1972), p. 29.

6 Discussed in Robert Scribner, 'Anticlericalism and the German Reformation', in his *Popular Culture and Popular Movements in Reformation Germany* (London, 1987), pp. 243–56. The reactions of the authorities and laity to this sort of commercialisation are well described by Anton Störmann, *Die städtischen Gravamina gegen den Klerus am Ausgang des Mittelalters und in der Reformationszeit* (Münster, 1916).

7 An introduction in Stephen Ozment, *The Age of Reform, 1250–1550* (New Haven, 1980). Bruce Gordon, *Clerical Discipline and the Rural Reformation* (Zürcher Beiträge zur Reformationsgeschichte, 1992), pp. 23–36, emphasises the seriousness of pre-Reformation reform efforts in Switzerland, and their utter failure. The crippling restrictions on bishops' freedom of action on which many reforming efforts foundered are described in Francis Rapp, *Réformes et Reformation à Strasbourg. Eglise et Société dans le diocèse de Strasbourg (1450–1525)* (Paris, 1974).

8 Heiko Oberman, *Masters of the Reformation. The Emergence of a new Intellectual Climate in Europe (Cambridge, 1981)*, pp. 115–22.

9 The literature on Brant listed in A. G. Dickens, *The German Nation and Martin Luther* (London, 1974), p. 25. On the sodalities, Phillip Bebb, 'Humanism and Reformation: The Nürnberg *Sodalitas* Revisited', in Phillip N. Bebb and Sherrin Marshall (eds), *The Process of Change in Early Modern Europe* (Athens, OH, 1988), pp. 59–79.

10 Chapter 2, below.

11 On Luther's ambiguous relationship with Humanism see A. G. Dickens, 'Luther and the Humanists', in P. Mack (ed.), *Politics and Culture in Early Modern Europe* (Cambridge, 1987), pp. 199–213. Dickens emphasises Luther's debt to Humanist scholarly techniques. Recent scholarship has been inclined to point up the mediaeval cast of Luther's mind. See particularly Heiko Oberman, *Luther. Man between God and the Devil* (New Haven, 1989).

12 For example the *Treatise on Good Works* (1520), *The Misuse of the Mass* (1521), as well as the more obvious *Babylonian Captivity, Christian Nobility*, and *On the Papacy in Rome* (all 1520). The quotation from *The Misuse of the Mass, Luther's Works*, XXXVI p. 199.

13 Goertz, *Pfaffenhaß*, pp. 84–8.

14 This following Heinrich Richard Schmidt, *Reichstädte, Reich und Reformation* (Stuttgart, 1986), against the earlier tradition of Ozment and Moeller, who emphasise the liberating impact of Justification. Steven Ozment, The *Reformation in the Cities* (New Haven, 1975). Bernd Moeller, 'Luther und die Städte', in *Aus der Lutherforschung* (Cologne, 1983), pp. 9–26; id., 'Was wurde in der Frühzeit der Reformation in den deutschen Städten gepredigt?', *ARG*, 75 (1984), 176–93.

15 Schmidt, *Reichstädte*.

16 A point neatly made by Thomas Brady, *Turning Swiss. Cities and Empire, 1450–1550* (Cambridge, 1985), pp. 153–5.

17 All recent research on the urban Reformation has emphasised the primary importance of pressure from below. Günther Vogler, 'Imperial

City Nuremberg, 1524–1525: The Reform Movement in Transition', in R. Po-Chia Hsia (ed.), *The German People and the Reformation* (Ithaca, 1988), pp. 33–49; Rainer Postel, *Die Reformation in Hamburg, 1517–1528* (Quellen und Forschungen zur Reformationsgeschichte, 52, 1986); R. W. Scribner, 'The Reformation as a Social Movement', in *Popular Culture and Popular Movements*, pp. 145–74.

18 Scribner, 'Anticlericalism', p. 245, and 'Civic Unity and the Reformation in Erfurt', *Popular Culture and Popular Movements*, pp. 185–216. Postel, *Reformation in Hamburg*, pp. 157–81.

19 *Luther's Works*, XXXIX pp. 301–14.

20 Here, most influentially, Peter Blickle, *The Communal Reformation* (Eng. trans., London, 1992). For an illuminating local case study Franziska Conrad, *Reformation in der bäuerlichen Gesellschaft. Zur Rezeption Reformatorischer Theologie im Elsass* (Stuttgart, 1984).

21 Erasmus to Willibald Pirckheimer. *Corpus documentorum inquisitionis haeriticae pravitatis neerlandicae*, ed. P. Fredericq (5 vols, Ghent/The Hague, 1889–1902), IV p. 284. The Netherlands authorities responded with a succession of edicts establishing severe punishments for renegade monks. Alastair Duke, 'The Origins of Evangelical Dissent in the Low Countries', in his *Reformation and Revolt in the Low Countries* (London, 1990), p. 9.

22 Chapter 6, below.

23 Helga Robinson-Hammerstein, 'Luther and the Laity', in her *The Transmission of Ideas in the Lutheran Reformation* (Dublin, 1989), pp. 26–9.

24 M. U. Edwards, *Luther and the False Brethren* (Stanford, 1975).

25 R. Emmet McLaughlin, 'Universities, Scholasticism and the German Reformation', *History of Universities*, 9 (1990), 1–43. Lewis Spitz, 'The Importance of the Reformation for the Universities: Culture and Confessions in the Critical Years', in James M. Kittelson and Pamela Transue (eds), *Rebirth, Reform, Resilience: Universities in Transition 1300–1700* (Columbus, OH, 1984), pp. 42–67.

26 R. W. Scribner, 'Principle and Practice in the German Towns: Preachers and People', in Peter Newman Brooks (ed.), *Reformation Principle and Practice* (London, 1980), pp. 95–117. Reprinted in *Popular Culture and Popular Movements*, pp. 123–43. Martin Brecht, 'Herkunft und Ausbildung der protestantischen Geistlichen des Herzogtums Württemberg im 16. Jahrhundert', *Zeitschrift für Kirchengeschichte*, 80 (1969), 165–6. The important part played by former religious in the first generation of Dutch Reformed preachers is remarked by Richard Fitzsimmons, chapter 9, below.

27 See chapters 4 and 5, below.

28 A useful introduction to these themes is T. H. L. Parker, *Calvin's Preaching* (Edinburgh, 1992), pp. 1–47.

29 For the inflammatory nature of Calvin's sermons see William Naphy, 'Calvin and the Consolidation of the Genevan Reformation' (St Andrews University Ph.D. thesis, 1993), chapter 5. An example in Alastair Duke, Gillian Lewis, and Andrew Pettegree (eds), *Calvinism in Europe, 1540–1610. A Collection of Documents* (Manchester, 1992), pp. 30–4.

30 *The Ecclesiastical Ordinances* in P. E. Hughes (ed.), *The Register of the Company of Pastors of Geneva in the time of Calvin* (Grand Rapids, 1966), pp. 35–49. See esp. 35–9. Naphy, chapter 6 below.
31 See the helpful introduction in Gordon, *Clerical Discipline*, pp. 36–72. Cf. Pamela Biel, *Doorkeepers at the House of Righteousness. Heinrich Bullinger and the Zurich Clergy 1535–1575* (Zürcher Beiträge zur Reformationsgeschichte, 15, 1992).
32 Gordon, *Clerical Discipine*, pp. 109–93.
33 Chapter 6, below.
34 For the Netherlands see the lists collected in E. M. Braekman, 'Theological Training of Reformed Ministers of the Low Countries', in H. de Ridder-Symoens and J. M. Fletcher (eds), *Academic Relations between the Low Countries and the British Isles, 1450–1700* (Ghent, 1989), pp. 83–91. Fitzsimmons, chapter 9 below. For the brief existence of an artisan ministeriat in Ernestine Saxony, Susan Karant-Nunn, *Luther's Pastors. The Reformation in the Ernestine Countryside* (Transactions of the American Philosophical Society, 69, 8, 1979), p. 11.
35 The case of Antwerp, where the church clearly preferred the ministry of the artisan van der Heyden over the more educated Haemstede, is discussed in my *Emden and the Dutch revolt. Exile and the Development of Reformed Protestantism* (Oxford, 1992), pp. 59–65.
36 See, for instance, Caspar Coolhaes's comments on his former artisan colleagues quoted by Richard Fitzsimmons, chapter 9 below.
37 O'Day, 'Clergy of the Church of England', p. 42.
38 James Kirk, 'Recruitment to the Ministry at the Reformation', in his *Patterns of Reformation* (Edinburgh, 1989), pp. 96–153.
39 Penny Roberts, chapter 8 below. A selection of the worst cases of ministers who intruded themselves into positions with French churches may be found in the Roll of vagrant and deprived ministers, compiled at each of the French national synods. See John Quick, *Synodicon in Gallia Reformata* (2 vols, London, 1692), I pp. 46–7, 74.
40 The case of Arnold de Steur, in Richard Fitzsimmons's discussion of Holland, chapter 9, below.
41 John Calvin, *Institutes of the Christian Religion*, ed. J. T. McNeill (Library of the Christian Classics, 20, 21, 1960), II pp. 1064–6. The actual procedures adopted in Geneva left little room for congregational participation. See the records of the calling of Jean Fabri in 1549: *RCP* I pp. 61–3.
42 For France, Quick, *Synodicon*, vol. 1, pp. 13–14 (Synod of Poitiers, 1560). For the Netherlands, *Classicale Acta, 1573–1620. Particuliere synode Zuid-Holland I: Classis Dordrecht, 1573–1600*, ed. J. P. van Dooren (RGP, 49, 1980).
43 John P. Elliott, 'Protestantization in the Northern Netherlands, a Case Study: The Classis of Dordrecht, 1572–1640' (Columbia University Ph.D. thesis, 1990), chapter 3.
44 Karin Maag, chapter 7. See also Gillian Lewis, 'The Geneva Academy', in Alastair Duke, Gillian, Lewis and Andrew Pettegree (eds), *Calvinism in Europe* (Cambridge, 1993).

THE REFORMATION OF THE PARISHES

45 'Thus in establishing this college we have set before us this one aim, of rendering as many persons as possible fit for the sacred ministry of the word and the sacraments; so that from this seminary the Church of England might have men whom it may call forth to instruct the people and undertake the duty of pastors.' Quoted by Rosemary O'Day, *The English Clergy. The Emergence and Consolidation of a Profession, 1558–1642* (Leicester, 1979), p. 134.

46 Below, chapter 7.

47 Described in my article, 'Coming to Terms with Victory: Calvinist Church-building in Holland, 1572–1590', in Duke, Lewis, and Pettegree, *Calvinism in Europe*. Many Dutch ministers were so suspicious of the new institution that they preferred to send their sons to schools abroad. It was only with the foundation of the States College in 1593 that the university began to fulfil an effective training role.

48 O'Day, 'Clergy of the Church of England', pp. 44–8.

49 Examples cited by Roberts, chapter 8, Fitzsimmons, chapter 9, and Spicer, chapter 10. See particularly Maag, chapter 7, note 33.

50 Bernd Moeller, 'Kleriker als Bürger', *Festschrift für Hermann Heimpel* (2 vols, Göttingen, 1972), II pp. 195–224. William Naphy, 'Calvin and the Consolidation of the Genevan Reformation', chapter 4.

51 The Strasburg magistrates repeatedly forbade the ministers to criticise the secular authorities in their preaching: Lorna Jane Abray, *The People's Reformation. Magistrates, Clergy and Commons in Strasburg 1500–1598* (Oxford, 1985), pp. 60–1.

52 Ian Green, ' "Reformed Pastors" and *Bons Curés*: The Changing Role of the Parish Clergy in Early Modern Europe', in W. J. Sheils and Diana Wood (eds), *The Ministry: Clerical and Lay* (SCH, 26, 1989), pp. 266–7, 271–2.

53 Gordon, *Clerical Discipline*. Dixon, chapter 5.

54 Scott Dixon, chapter 5, stresses resistance to non-traditional levies.

55 Of course by stressing the close bond between a minister and his community the Reformation churches effectively dealt with one of the most persistent problems of the pre-Reformation church, that of non-residence. In the Dutch church there was simply no ministry without a calling to a particular church, and both French and Dutch churches treated it as a serious offence when a minister attempted to move from his parish without permission. See the provisions of the French Ecclesiastical Discipline (1559) in *Histoire Ecclesiastique des Eglises Réformées au Royaume de France* (2 vols, Toulouse, 1882), I, pp. 105–7. In this climate non-residency rates of 30 per cent or more, commonplace in Europe before the Reformation, were simply inconceivable.

56 Gordon, chapter 4, and Dixon, chapter 5. O'Day, *English Clergy*, pp. 161–2. Michael Roberts, 'The Swedish Church', in his *Sweden's Age of Greatness, 1632–1718* (London, 1973), p. 164. A similar phenomenon is remarked by Andrew Spicer in the French exile congregations: below, chapter 10.

57 Ian Green, ' "Reformed Pastors" and *Bons Curés*', pp. 254–7. For examples of the same process at work in Catholic countries, O. Hufton,

20

'The French Church', in W. H. Callahan and D. Higgs (eds), *Church and Society in Catholic Europe of the Eighteenth Century* (Cambridge, 1979). Rona Johnston, chapter 11 below.

58 The campaign for greater doctrinal uniformity is evident in the emphasis placed on catechising. On catechising, Strauss, *Luther's House of Learning. Indoctrination of the Young in the German Reformation* (Baltimore, 1978); Ozment, *Reformation in the Cities*, chapter 4; Roberts, 'Swedish Church', pp. 162–3; Ian Green, ' "For Children in Yeeres and Children in Understanding": The Emergence of the English Catechism under Elizabeth and the Early Stuarts', *JEH*, 37 (1986), 397–425. For an overview, John Bossy, *Christianity in the West, 1400–1700* (Oxford, 1987), pp. 118–20.

59 Chapter 11, below.

60 The whole confessionalisation debate is comprehensively aired in Heinz Schilling (ed.), *Die reformierte Konfessionalisierung in Deutschland – Das Problem der 'Zweiten Reformation'* (Schriften des Vereins für Reformationsgeschichte, 195, 1985).

61 Green, ' "Reformed Pastors" and *Bons Curés*', p. 270. O'Day, 'Clergy of the Church of England', pp. 50–9.

62 Moeller, 'Kleriker als Bürger'. Heinz Schilling, 'The Rise of Early Modern Burgher Elites during the Sixteenth and Seventeenth Centuries', in his *Religion, Political Culture and the Emergence of Early Modern Society* (Studies in Medieval and Reformation Thought, 50, 1992), pp. 135–87. Henry Heller emphasises the aristocratic character of the pre-Reformation church. Heller, *The Conquest of Poverty. The Calvinist Revolt in Sixteenth-Century France* (Studies in Medieval and Reformation Thought, 35, 1986).

63 This against a historiographical tradition which increasingly now stresses the 'failure' of the Reformation. See Gerald Strauss, 'The Reformation and its Public in an Age of Orthodoxy', in Hsia, *The German People and the Reformation*, pp. 194–214.

2

'To speik of Preistis be sure it is na bourds': discussing the priesthood in pre-Reformation Scotland[1]

Carol Edington

As Sir David Lindsay of the Mount explained to the audience at the first performance of his *Satyre of the Thrie Estatis* (1552), to speak of the clergy in the sixteenth century was no laughing matter. What Lindsay had in mind here was the possible action of an outraged Kirk against its critics: 'Thay will burne men now for rackles words' (2774). In fact, despite periodic anti-heresy legislation, religious persecution in pre-Reformation Scotland was sporadic and relatively slight. Lindsay's words represent not so much the historical reality as a dramatic ploy: with a nod and a wink he hints at things left unsaid, at ecclesiastical oppression and clerical hypocrisy.

This example nicely suggests a second sense in which a discussion of the priesthood may be termed no laughing matter. For the historian attempting to assess the significance of literary texts, such a discussion is fraught with problems, methodological and practical. Recent debate on the extent and vitality of anticlerical feeling in sixteenth-century England has to some degree turned on conflicting evaluations of well-known literary texts.[2] A principal feature, and it might be argued an important weakness of this discussion, has been a tendency to concentrate on the extent to which literary depictions of the clergy coincide with contemporary reality. Defining 'reality', however, is not always a straightforward business. In addition to the reality of what went on in the parishes, there is also the reality of the author's perceptions to consider and, finally, the reality of the language and ideas embodied in the texts themselves. As well as assessing the extent to which these overlap, a more subtle critique must also acknowledge and analyse each on its own terms, for while it is obviously quite inadequate to regard literary depictions of clerical vice as straightforward historical representation of contemporary fact, the border between historical study and literary criticism is, in the context of sixteenth-century society, a largely artificial one. Treated with appropriate care and an understanding of the generic conventions within which they operate, literary sources offer some highly suggestive clues regarding contemporary attitudes towards the church and its personnel. Indeed, it is tempting to go further and argue that literature is a source no historian can safely ignore. It does not, after all, exist in a vacuum isolated from other social processes, nor is it simply a 'mirror', passively reflecting current ideas and attitudes. On the contrary, literature participates in a dynamic social process. Possessing a reality – or identity – of its own, it is also capable of generating its own series of assumptions and expectations.

Of course, literature as a source is not without its problems: texts produce a multiplicity of readings, each with a different meaning for individuals in different cultural contexts. A balanced approach is one which recognises that while the literature of the past can be illuminated by our own understanding of, say, economics, psychology, or the dynamics of gender, there is equally a need to appreciate the cultural, social, and political contexts which conditioned a line of thought or mode of expression. Aiming to recover, so far as is possible, that cultural context shared by both author and audience, this study will see how far a number of important pre-Reformation Scottish texts can help address questions concerning lay attitudes towards the priesthood on the eve of the Reformation.

Such a study must also recognise that it is not only the texts which can generate problems. The church's numerous servants hardly constitute a monolithic body and the notion of 'the priesthood' itself is not necessarily straightforward. The great prelates at the top of the ecclesiastical hierarchy had precious little in common with those in minor orders, men who actually served in the parishes and who probably identified more closely with the laity to whom they ministered.[3] It is important to bear such differences in mind and to recognise their implications for an analysis of the literary discussion of the priesthood.

It must be admitted that literary texts present the historian with additional hazards: there are, for instance, numerous practical difficulties concerning the dating, authorship and reception of any particular text. In addition, dealing with the pre-Reformation period poses its own snags. While in any case confessional boundaries were far from clear-cut, the attitude of an increasingly hostile ecclesiastical establishment frequently served to encourage ambiguity and ambivalence. Examples of many of these problems are found in the work of Sir David Lindsay of the Mount (1486–1555). A household servant at the court of James IV, herald and later Lyon King of Arms under James V, Lindsay – in so far as such an ill-defined and unofficially unrecognised position can be said to have existed – also acted as court-poet. Between 1526 and 1542, he composed at least eight works for the Stewart court. Of these, none survive in their original form, our texts deriving from editions published only after his death. This is also largely true for his later works. Only two – *The Tragedie of the Late Cardinal Beaton* and *Ane Dialogue betuix Experience and ane Courteour* (more conveniently known as *The Monarche*) – survive as published before 1555.[4] Clearly, questions of dating and audience are extremely problematic. Arguably, however, they are less relevant to the earlier poems, poems clearly written for the edification and amusement of the Scottish court. Given that three such works, *The Dreme of Schir Dauid Lyndesay* (1526), *The Complaynt* (1530), and *The Testament, and Complaynt, of our Soverane Lordis Papyngo* (1530), all incorporate a vigorous commentary on the Kirk and its clergy, this in itself raises some interesting questions concerning the discussion of religious affairs on the eve of the Reformation.

That Lindsay chose court poetry as a vehicle for the discussion of religious issues possesses implications not only for the works themselves but also for our understanding of the political scenario in which and for which they were written. A recent study of the English court suggests that literature was viewed as a powerful weapon in furthering the cause of reform and there is no reason to doubt the existence of similar opinions north of the border.[5] In Scotland, as elsewhere, the pre-Reformation period was characterised by an often intense debate over the problems thrown up by church reformers both orthodox and heretical. Experience taught such men that, to have any hope of success, obtaining the support of the secular authority – the godly prince or magistrate – was vital. This lesson was not lost upon those in Scotland who, for differing reasons, hoped to advance their position with the king and hence to influence a religious policy the future direction of which was by no means certain. This is not the place for a detailed examination of the factional divisions of the 1530s, but it is clear that there existed a small yet significant group of men (many of whom, like Lindsay, remained faithful to the Catholic church) who were anxious to persuade James V of the benefits of ecclesiastical reformation.[6] The persuasive value of literature in this battle for the heart and mind of the king, surely obvious to all, could only have been further reinforced in Lindsay's mind during a visit to the English court in 1535, a visit which coincided with Thomas Cromwell's vigorous propaganda campaign and the enthusiastic employment of sermons, pamphlets, and plays for evangelical ends.

A Scottish example of such evangelical persuasion is the play performed before James V and his queen in 1540 as part of that year's Epiphany celebrations.[7] Our knowledge of the drama – unfortunately slight – is derived solely from the notes of the English commissioner on the Borders, Sir William Eure, who heard of it from two Scottish Protestants who, with more optimism than accuracy, presented it as evidence of James V's enthusiasm for an ecclesiastical settlement along English lines.[8] While there are many differences between the two, the 1540 drama is sufficiently similar to Lindsay's *Ane Satyre of the Thrie Estatis* for his authorship never to have been seriously doubted.[9] Both plays 'shewed the great abusion of busshopes, Prelattes [and] Abbottes', and although the very brief description of the 1540 performance makes it extremely difficult to draw firm conclusions, it is clear that in attacking clerical promiscuity together with an excessive interest in temporal possessions, the satire drew on some long-established traditions. Whatever the provenance of the Epiphany drama, its performance confirms the idea that court literature – however stereotyped – was being employed in a real attempt to engage the support of the king for religious reform, particularly for a reform of the clergy. Indeed, at least a decade before this, Lindsay was using his verse to exhort the government to 'haue Ee' unto the Spiritual Estate (*The Complaynt*, 412). As we shall see, the reassessment of the clergy discussed in this type of court circle owed much to the ideals of Erasmian Humanism. But, in addition, the fact that this debate was conducted through what was a very traditional court literature gave the discourse its own very distinctive voice.

What might best be termed the 'literary anticlericalism' of

25

this debate was clearly a real phenomenon. It was also a specialised one. Not only was it conducted within its own confined circle – literary, educated, and courtly – it also possessed its own conventions and language. It is not enough, therefore, simply to lay bare the political context in which an author wrote. Equally vital is the identification of the different modes of expression available to a writer and the ways in which these were manipulated by him. For example, while it has in the past been commonplace to catalogue the problems dogging the pre-Reformation Kirk, citing as evidence some of the more lively works of the period, these have not necessarily been seen for what they are: a highly stylised form of writing owing much to long-established generic traditions.[10] The depraved cleric – of whatever ecclesiastical rank – was a common mediaeval *topos*, a long-favoured target of the satirist's pen. Satire – a term notoriously difficult to define – presents a deliberate caricature of the absurdities and miseries of the human condition, drawing heavily on such techniques as parody, burlesque, and, particularly in Scotland, on flyting, a vicious collection of alliterative invective. With its readily comprehended stereotypes and 'in-jokes', satirical literature has its own history and traditions and these must be understood if we are fully to appreciate the literary anticlericalism of much of Lindsay's work.

Another important literary form, again extremely common in the late Middle Ages, was the complaint. Whether or not this can be reckoned a genre in its own right or should more accurately be seen as an element of the satirical tradition is debatable but, like satire, it too can present a twentieth-century audience with a potentially distorted picture of contemporary opinion.[11] With its otherworldly stress upon the transitory nature of earthly experience and its emphasis on human misery, the complaint (like all human activity itself) was firmly located within a divine cosmological framework. All the woes of the mediaeval world were clearly perceived to proceed from human sin and frailty. Consequently, literary discussions of worldly problems were couched very largely in abstract, ethical terms pinpointing postlapsarian human weakness as the root cause of any problem in contemporary society. To modern ears, this type of moralising can sound banal to the point of irrelevance. But sincere as it was serious, it enjoyed a long-lived popularity and played a significant role in the discussion of clerical affairs. Concentrating on universal moralities in this way tended to preclude a rigorous examination of the priestly office (in any case an analysis hardly to be expected in verse) and hence to obscure points of real theological difference. Arguably, this helped accommodate discontent within the established church and, at a time when many were cautiously feeling their way to an understanding of their faith, this surely represented a more comfortable discourse.

Examining those poems Lindsay used as a vehicle for his ideas on church reform and on the clergy in particular illustrates not only his debts to a conventional literary anticlericalism but, equally important, his departures from tradition. Such departures provide a telling insight into his perceptions of the clergy and may suggest some of the ways in which literary sources can be used to gauge contemporary attitudes towards the church. Lindsay's early works are heavily dependent on conventional ideas and vocabulary. Articulated in abstract, ethical language, his complaints against the clergy are directed almost exclusively against standards of personal morality. For example, in his earliest extant work, *The Dreme* (1526), we find a savage denunciation of simony, avarice, pride, sensuality, and ambition (979–87). In a way characteristic of the complaint, the importance of universal moralities is paramount. Thus, in his 'Exhortatioun to the Kyngis Grace', Lindsay offers no specific suggestions for church reform but focuses instead upon an ultra-traditional, allegorical advocacy of the cardinal virtues. Nevertheless, the clerical vices considered in this poem – 'Couatyce, Luste, and ambysioun' – provide a good starting point for considering those attitudes which, put forward by one author, offer a clue to a climate of opinion existing within at least some influential circles of the Scottish court.

Attacking the practice of simony and the misuse of ecclesiastical revenue, *The Dreme* does offer a slightly more specific yet still extremely formulaic denunciation of clerical 'couatyce'. Instead of effecting a tripartite division of income for the upholding of the Kirk, for the upkeep of church property, and for alms, 'the Patrimonie and rent' is spent 'On cartis, and dyce, on harlotrie and huris' (200 & 207). In *The Testament of the Papyngo* (1530), we find clerical avarice more bitterly attacked. The poem opens with a humorous parody of the 'fall-of-princes' type tale when a vain and boastful papyngo (parrot) ignores good counsel and meets her death. As she lies in mortal agony, there appear on the scene a Pye, Reuin, and Gled (Magpie, Raven, and Kite), identified respectively as an Augustinian prior, a monk, and a friar. The three avow their concern for the Papyngo's spiritual welfare, but it is immediately apparent that their sole interest lies in her 'gudis naturall' (658). This indictment of clerical avarice reaches a climax when, in a scene of shocking brutality, the three birds reveal their true carrion nature and 'Full gormondlyke' devour the Papyngo's corpse (1149). This particular attack on clerical greed represents a departure from Lindsay's more common, more conventional, attacks on the upper echelons of the ecclesiastical hierarchy. Here, he comments on the situation in the parishes where the 'wyffis of the village cryis, with cair' (712). This example nicely illustrates the importance of traditional – ethical – forms of expression and their potential for creating a distorted picture. In fact, the real and underlying problem in this instance was not ethical but institutional – the system of appropriations whereby the revenues of the parish were appropriated by various religious institutions such as cathedrals, monasteries, collegiate churches, and universities. By the sixteenth century, the revenues of 86 per cent of all parish churches had been appropriated, and by 1560 only 148 remained independent.[12] Arrangements to serve the appropriated parishes involved the installation of a vicar. However, failure to provide the majority of vicars with an adequate stipend meant that they were rarely of the highest calibre and economic necessity forced many to exploit what was their most readily available source of extra income – their parishioners. Teinds (which formed part of the appropriated income) were rigorously exacted, often resulting in acrimonious litigation, and on top of this the average parishioner faced numerous and strident demands for mortuary dues and other 'voluntary' offerings. Lindsay's later works, *Ane Satyre* (1552) and *The Monarche* (1554), both incorporate similar criticism of the church's economic exploitation of the poor and even the well-worn imagery cannot blunt the ferocity of his attack:

> Christ did command Peter to feid his scheip,
> And so he did feid thame full tenderlye.
> Off that command thay take bot lytill keip,
> Bot Christis scheip thay spolye petuouslye,
> And with the woll thay cleith thame curiouslye.
> Lyk gormand wolfis, thay tak of thame thare fude,
> Thai eit thair flesche, & drynkis boith mylk & blude.
>
> (*The Monarche*, 4799–805)

Similar outrage is expressed in the tale of a rapacious vicar who, as each member of a family dies, claims his mortuary dues and leaves the orphaned children destitute, a story which is repeated almost verbatim in both works. The literary representation of specific incidents raises valid questions concerning the actual experience of parishioners in the pre-Reformation period. At least one parallel to this episode is to be found in the case brought by Nicholas Wilkieson, vicar of St Cuthbert's, Edinburgh, against the widow of David Ravy in 1546 but this type of pursuit through the church courts does not seem to have been that common.[13] Nevertheless, Lindsay does seem to be tapping a real sense of discontent and, when in 1559 the Provincial Council of the church addressed the question of death duties, it was in part 'to put an end to the clamour and murmurs of grumblers at morturies'.[14]

Lindsay was skilful in recognising this aspect of the church's concern and, in stressing the need for economic reform, he did more than appeal to Christian sensibility. In a manner calculated to alarm, he also raised the spectre of popular discontent which such practices might engender. In *The Testament of the Papyngo*, for example, he deliberately evokes the humble audience familiar with economic exploitation, successfully utilising another traditional mediaeval literary concept, the *vox populi vox Dei* idea. This long-established notion of the poor as in some way nearer to God (inspired both by the example of Christ's own poverty and his treatment of society's outcasts), exercised a powerful appeal on the popular and literary imagination throughout the Middle Ages and we find several examples of it in Lindsay's works. *The Testament of the Papyngo* provides an interesting instance of how Lindsay exploited the conventions of the tradition. The poem opens with Lindsay disowning his usual courtly audience:

> Quharefor, because myne mater bene so rude
> Off sentence, and of Rethorike denude,
> To rurall folke myne dyting bene directit,
> Far lemit frome the sicht of men of gude.
>
> (64–7)

This is, of course, a poetic commonplace designed to elicit a rueful smile from the audience and to prepare them for some harsh home truths. Yet, by appealing to the humble classes of society, Lindsay's statement of popular grievances attains added force. Not only does his portrayal of the straight-talking poor suggest they have right on their side, but the threat of popular discontent – a hugely disturbing concept to the early modern mind – is subversively insinuated into the courtly environment when, in the second half of the poem, the Papyngo, her moral consciousness heightened by imminent death, is credited with knowledge of 'the vulgare pepyllis Iudgement' and invited to explain why the clergy are held in such low esteem (765). The *vox populi* tradition imparts added authority to her words, allowing Lindsay to launch a vitriolic attack on the worldliness of the church, one which in reality owes little to the 'vulgar people' but which allows Lindsay to distance himself from the debate.

Another example of the way in which Lindsay manipulates the *vox populi* tradition is found in *Ane Satyre of the Thrie Estatis* when the character of the poor man articulates a bitter attack upon the consistorial courts. Incredibly lengthy and ultimately fruitless, his attempts to sue a neighbour over the death of his horse provide a convincing illustration of what was a very real grievance. However, in reality, it was not the poor and dispossessed who conducted such suits but rather lairds and burgesses, men very much like Lindsay himself.[15] Here the long-established associations of a well-known tradition lead Lindsay to substitute a more familiar, more persuasive, ultimately more threatening, spokesman for what was surely his own cause.

Of those clerical vices identified in *The Dreme*, it was lust which, at first sight, seems to have excited the most striking criticism. Again, it is a criticism which occurs throughout the corpus of Lindsay's work – particularly in respect of the higher clergy. *The Dreme* attacks prelates who misuse their revenues to clothe their mistresses and provide for their bastards (209–12), while *The Testament of the Papyngo* describes how Dame Chastitie was driven from the church by Lady Sensuall. The idea is reworked in *The Monarche* (4419–22), while in *Ane Satyre*, this ungodly union is presented in dramatic form with Spiritualitie welcoming the wanton Dame (4741–4). Again, satire at the expense of sexually immoral churchmen was a common literary motif and, although promiscuity was far from unknown amongst the Scottish episcopate, it need not be taken too seriously as precise criticism. Typological figures are being employed within a traditional framework, one particularly suited to Lindsay's essentially moralistic, didactic critique.

While still hugely traditional, there is possibly a greater degree of precision in Lindsay's criticisms of clerical 'ambysioun', particularly as it relates to the long-established involvement of churchmen in secular affairs. *The Dreme* describes clerics who 'seruit wardlie Prencis insolent' in Hell (192) while in *The Complaynt* Lindsay launches a further attack upon the worldly ambition of churchmen. Albeit far from novel, such criticism would have found a receptive audience in sixteenth-century Scotland where the lives of many leading churchmen were noted for their worldliness. Of course, involvement in secular affairs and matters of state had always been part and parcel of high clerical office but the situation was clearly exacerbated by the Crown's dubious manipulation of ecclesiastical patronage to provide for royal servants and family members alike. However, although *The Complaynt* is the most overtly autobiographical of Lindsay's works and his protest is made with specific reference to James V's minority, this is surely best seen as a general criticism of the worldly cynicism of churchmen rather than as a specific commentary on ecclesiastical affairs.[16] This also seems true of Lindsay's most damning indictment of clerical ambition, his depiction of David Beaton in a work written shortly after the Cardinal's assassination in 1547. Here, Lindsay relies on the familiar 'fall-of-princes' genre, introducing the ghostly figure of Beaton himself to recite his tale of overweening pride brought low. The account of a prelate 'Quhilk rang so lang, and so tryumphantlie, / Syne in the dust, doung doun so dulefullie' and, who, seeing the error of his ways, counsels his colleagues to 'Put nocht your hope into no warldly gude' also stresses the transitory nature of earthly authority in a manner highly characteristic of the complaint (272–3, 320). Clearly, Lindsay's treatment of his subject matter is to a large extent conditioned by generic convention. Nevertheless, the supplication Beaton makes to his 'brether Prencis of the Prestis' is not altogether tradition-bound. Alongside the conventional plea to leave off gambling and whoring, Beaton also stresses the need for bishops to preach. As we shall see, this concern with preaching becomes an increasingly dominant feature of Lindsay's work. Here he condemns those bishops who leave the task to the 'syllie frieris':

> For, and thay planelie schaw the veritie,
> Than wyll thay want the Byshope charitie
>
> *(The Tragedie of the Cardinal*, 313–15)

These lines reappear almost verbatim in *Ane Satyre of the Thrie Estatis* written some four years later (750–2). However, Lindsay's attitude towards the friars is not as consistent as this might suggest and, for this reason, merits further consideration.

As the rapacious bird-friar in *The Testament of the Papyngo* illustrates, Lindsay readily satirised the mendicant orders. Like his later criticisms of their privileges, their craven reluctance to denounce malpractice and their idolatry, this owes a great deal to a long-standing tradition of anti-mendicant literature first forged in the heat of the thirteenth-century conflict between the secular clergy and the friars.[17] Its appeal was not, however, limited to ecclesiastical polemic and mediaeval lay literature concerned with the topic exhibits an antifraternal approach very similar to that found in more learned treatises.[18] In pre-Reformation Scotland, the tradition found lively and widespread expression. Works as diverse as William Dunbar's *How Dunbar was desyred to be ane Freir*, George Buchanan's *Somnium, Palinodes* and *Franciscanus* (the last based on Dunbar's earlier work), and the Earl of Glencairn's *Friar of Loretto* testify to its popularity. It is, however, Lindsay's departures from this tradition and the explanation for this which are particularly intriguing. While the examples we have already considered reveal his debt to antifraternal convention, on other occasions, Lindsay adopts a less hostile tone. Why should this be so? One explanation may be that the friars constituted a particularly vital aspect of the religious life in pre-Reformation Scotland, the scale of donations and endowments made to them suggesting considerable popular support.[19] Underlying the friars' success was the vigour of their preaching and, although Lindsay's later works suggest he believed the secular clergy should be the active preachers in the community, he acknowledges mendicant activity in this sphere. This assuredly explains the occasional ambivalence of his early works. While *The Dreme* describes how virtue has been largely driven from the spiritual estate and 'Deuotion is fled vnto the freris' (982), in *The Testament of the Papyngo*, we find admiration and criticism delicately juxtaposed:

War nocht the precheing of the beggyng freiris,
Tynt [lost] war the faith amang the Secularis.

(1036–37)

Later, Lindsay's opinion hardened. His criticisms are more frequently expressed and, in *Ane Satyre*, he presents a bitterly twisted
version of his earlier idea: on this occasion, the 'Deuotioun' who
hides himself amongst the friars is in reality the character Flatterie
under an assumed name. Acknowledging still that friars do preach,
thereby making good the deficiencies of the secular clergy, he now
– as in *The Tragedie of the Cardinal* – undermines this with charges
of flattery:

Als God hes lent to them sic graces,
That Bishops puts them in thair places
Out-throw thair Dioceis to preiche,
Bot ferlie nocht, howbeit thay fleiche [flatter]:

(*Ane Satyre*, 747–50)

Lindsay's return to the vocabulary of traditional anti-mendicant
satire suggests his growing concern with the priestly function of
preaching, a concern which was echoed elsewhere in pre-Reformation Scotland. In this respect, it seems clear that Lindsay's
commentary on the clergy was not conditioned by literary tradition
alone but by other ideological factors. It has been argued that
anticlericalism in the English church, deeply rooted in the pre-
Reformation texts of such authors as Langland and Wycliff, received
an important boost from both Humanist and Protestant writers.[20]
Although such distinctions are by no means clear cut, in Lindsay's
early works traditional criticisms are similarly blended with a more
innovative critique: perhaps the most striking characteristic of
these early poems is their thoroughly Humanist complexion.[21] The
tone of Lindsay's Humanism is typically Erasmian. Theologically
conservative, it focuses for the most part upon questions of moral
behaviour. Lindsay rarely touches upon matters of doctrine, but
launches instead upon a moral critique of the church's failings
addressed, again in typical Humanist fashion, to the king. But,
while the Humanist agenda which Lindsay set before the Scottish
court was in itself relatively novel, it is significant that the traditional literary conventions he employed served as an entirely
appropriate vehicle for the expression of his ideas. Satire, 'the
sharpest of Erasmian reformatory tools', is often cited in this

respect but of equal if not greater significance here is the complaint genre, the ethical thrust of which perfectly complements the moral emphasis inherent in his Humanist critique.[22] Significantly though, Lindsay was not content merely to rehash well-worn stereotypes for the amusement of his audience, he eagerly promoted a Humanist-inspired programme of education, preaching, and spiritual reform.

Viewing education as the key to spiritual regeneration is typical of Humanist thinking. It lies at the heart of the advice proffered by the Reuin in *The Testament of the Papyngo*: 'thame promoue that war moste sapient' (1031). Ironically, the Reuin himself serves only as an example of the type of clerical ignorance which is so bitterly denounced again and again in Lindsay's work. In *Ane Satyre of the Thrie Estatis*, for example, Spiritualitie, unlearned, if not actually illiterate, is made to confess never having read the New Testament (2919–22). Lindsay's point here is not really to further the *studia humanitatis*, but to deplore the clergy's ignorance as to the nature of their 'true vocation'. Here we have the nub of Lindsay's quarrel with the spiritual estate, religious and secular, prelate and parson. As represented by him, they have no consideration for the welfare of their flock, and indeed positively stand between them and eternal salvation. In blunt terms, Lindsay outlines the duties of the priesthood:

> To Preche with vnfenyeit intentis,
> And trewly vse the Sacramentis,
> Efter Christis Institutionis,

> *(The Complaynt, 415–17)*

The preaching of the Gospel and the administration of the sacraments according to Christ's institution were rapidly emerging as characteristic demands of the Lutheran church and Lindsay seems here to echo the Confession of Augsburg formulated that same year. Although Lindsay's words are not in themselves unorthodox and hardly constitute conclusive proof of a commitment to Lutheran beliefs, they do suggest that the spirit of the Lutheran Reformers was beginning to exert a subtle influence on his ideas and to inform the language in which he expressed himself.[23] What we can say with greater certainty is that such passages illustrate not only concern for standards of personal morality – a concern which was in any case highly conditioned by traditional literary genres – but also a keen interest in the priestly office as a whole.

Of the two functions of the ordained priesthood, it was preaching – perhaps the key issue of the pre-Reformation period – which claimed the greater part of Lindsay's attention. From Pope to parson, churchmen are condemned for their worldliness, for their failure to preach and for the spiritual neglect of the population.[24] Christ instructed disciples only to preach:

> None vther office he to thame gaif.
> He did nocht bid thame seik nor craif
> Cors presentis, nor offerandis,
> Nor gett Lordschipis of temporall landis.
>
> (*The Monarche*, 4477–80)

Elsewhere, Lindsay acknowledges that temporal endowment and the payment of teinds are important aspects of the ecclesiastical system. Interestingly, however, they are firmly tied to the issue of preaching: 'The law is plaine: our teinds suld furnish teichours' (*Ane Satyre*, 2936). This idea, repeated several times in Lindsay's work, points to a situation in which an increasingly self-confident sector of the Scottish laity were voicing their own demands and expectations, asking not how they might serve the church but how the church should serve them.

Although Lindsay attacks all ranks of the clerical estate for their failure to preach, his principal quarrel is with the bishops. In *The Monarche*, he claims that the reluctance of prelates to preach explained why 'the peple now abhor thame' (4494). His satire was not without foundation. A lack of learning and failure to preach was recognised by the three Provincial Councils (1549, 1552, and 1559), all of which prescribed measures to deal with the situation.[25] A series of acts was passed aimed at raising the intellectual standards of the clergy at all levels and stress was laid upon the necessity of preaching 'seing that the preaching of the Gospel is no less necessary to Christian commonwealth than lecturing thereon'.[26] This statute went on to state that preaching was 'the principal duty of the bishops', but, in recognition of the existing situation, permitted prelates to entrust the duty to 'fit persons'. However, ten years later in 1559, the Council insisted that bishops preach in person at least four times a year, only elderly churchmen over the age of fifty and 'not hitherto . . . accustomed to preach' being allowed to delegate the responsibility.[27] Such a solution had been suggested by Lindsay in *The Monarche* when he argued that, if bishops could not fulfil this responsibility, they should pay for a suffragan until their death enabled the appointment of 'ane perfyte precheour' (4861). The similar solutions proposed by Lindsay and the church authorities point to one approach to the problem; another was to be found in the actions of reforming town councils which, even before 1560, were installing godly preachers. Clearly the issue was fundamental to lay expectations of the priesthood and, as such, received sensitive treatment in the literary discussion.

Within Lindsay's later works, we detect an attempt to go beyond the traditional ethical analysis of problems be they in the body politic or the Catholic church. Here, notably in *Ane Satyre of the Thrie Estatis*, Lindsay offers a more sophisticated, recognisably more modern, examination of social and religious problems, occasionally prescribing viable remedies dependent upon the action of secular administrations rather than the eradication of human sin or granting of divine grace. The reasons behind this shifting outlook – discernible in attitudes towards both church and state – are complex and not really the concern of this analysis except as they possess implications for a literary discussion of the clergy.[28] Of course, this more specific commentary existed alongside or even within a more generalised commentary on universal ethics and blistering criticism of the personal standards of churchmen remained an essential feature of Lindsay's work. In *Ane Satyre*, for example, churchmen are denounced in familiar terms:

> As for our reverent fathers of Spiritualitie,
> Thay ar led be Couetice and cairles Sensualitie

(2446–7)

The examination of Spiritualitie, the Abbot and the Parson vividly conveys the extent of their moral degeneracy. It is an examination, however, which relies heavily upon three very traditional clerical stereotypes: the proud bishop, the gluttonous monk, and the worldly parson. Thus Spiritualitie prides himself upon exacting his financial dues and acting in all respects like a temporal lord – with the important exception that, as he can not marry, he has several mistresses (3346–71). The Abbot congratulates himself upon keeping his monks in luxury and upon providing for his paramours and bastards (3394–409). His boast that 'Thair is na Monks from Carraill to Carraill / That fairs better and drinks mair helsum Aill', draws heavily on traditional notions of monastic gluttony.[29] The

Parson meanwhile brags of his skill at games and of his fine attire (3411–19). In particular, he flaunts his 'round bonats . . . now four nuickit' (3416). This comment, however, was more topical than typical as only three years previously the Provincial Council, attempting to eradicate such vanity, had stipulated that round birettas should be worn.[30] Similarly, while the Council had decreed that wool – not silk – was to be worn by clerics, Lindsay's Prioress wears a silk kirtle beneath her habit (3651–6).[31]

Lindsay's attitude towards the female religious life is particularly interesting for the way in which traditional satire is blended with a more pointed commentary specifically relevant to the controversies of the Reformation. In *The Testament of the Papyngo*, he criticises 'The sillye Nonnis' for succumbing to the blandishments of Ryches and Sensualitie. These are themes which resurface both in the 1540 Epiphany drama and in *Ane Satyre* (908). In the later work, however, the acquisitive and promiscuous Prioress arouses a poignant blend of outrage and understanding as she curses her friends whose greed compelled her to take the veil. She herself considers the religious life unnecessary and should have preferred honest matrimony (3672–4). This is supported by the legislative action at the core of the play which goes on to advocate the dissolution of Scotland's nunneries (the revenues being used to support a College of Justice in the north of the country).

Lindsay's attitude to the whole issue of clerical marriage is highly suggestive. In traditional enough fashion, he pokes fun at the randy clerics who 'lyke Rammis in to thair rage, / Unpissillit rynnis amang the yowis' (*The Monarche*, 4706–7). However, this behaviour – referred to in almost identical language in *Ane Satyre* – is not used merely to make the moral point but rather to support the principle of clerical marriage. Lindsay's advocacy of clerical marriage can be dated at least to 1530 and *The Testament of the Papyngo*. Believing sexual laxity to be consequent upon the imposition of clerical celibacy ('Wantyng of Wyffis bene cause of appetyte', 870) he calls for the marriage of prelates to be sanctioned under papal licence. (Elsewhere Lindsay also supports his argument by harking back to the practices of the apostolic church and the marriage of St Peter.) The advocacy of clerical marriage was a notable rallying point of continental reformers and there is evidence to suggest that it was an equally contentious issue in Scotland, one which often surfaced in early skirmishes between Protestant and Catholic. In 1539, a number of Protestant sympathisers – clerical and lay – said to have attended the marriage of Thomas Cocklaw, Vicar of Tullibody, were executed for heresy.[32] This was not the sole charge against the heretics, but the marriage ceremony does seem to have been the catalyst stimulating the church to action in the matter. Lindsay's poetry may indicate the existence of a more widespread sympathy for clerical marriage which eventually obliged the church to take up the offensive. It is interesting too that Lindsay's discussion of clerical celibacy is not entirely ethical in its nature. Denying that a moral effort on the part of the priesthood is an appropriate response to the problem, Lindsay proposes instead the abolition of clerical celibacy, a measure which, in *Ane Satyre of the Thrie Estatis*, is enacted by parliamentary legislation.

Brief and selective as this study necessarily is, it vividly demonstrates the ways in which literary texts can be used to assess how ideas were articulated and communicated within what were often very stylised generic forms. It is clear that many attacks on promiscuity, gluttony, and ambition were conditioned by long-established literary traditions. As such, they need not necessarily be regarded too seriously as specific criticism. It is, perhaps, striking that many of these stereotypes are applied to the regular clergy, a fact which may reflect the relative vitality of the monastic houses in pre-Reformation Scotland, helping to explain the later lack of vigorous action against them.[33] Equally significant are the differences between criticisms of the higher clergy and of those serving in the parishes. Again, those directed at the bishops depend to a much larger extent upon a very traditional literary anticlericalism. However, despite the highly coloured descriptions of gluttony and promiscuity in cloister and cathedral alike, it is clear that, for Lindsay, economic exploitation at a parish level represented a far more serious problem for the Church. His clever use of the *vox populi* tradition to articulate such grievances hints at how very gravely he felt the church ought to view the situation. Moreover, that this was appreciated by the authorities themselves is suggested by the Kirk's own legislation. The provision of preaching represents Lindsay's other principal quarrel with the pre-Reformation church and again, as we have seen, Lindsay's literary discussion echoes that being conducted elsewhere, not least at the church's own Provincial Councils.

Such examples demonstrate both how the conventions of a

traditional literary anticlericalism can be manipulated by an author to introduce his own ideas and how these can concur with historical reality. However, irrespective of any such overlap, the reality of literary anticlericalism has important implications for understanding how ideas concerning the clergy developed not only in the pre-Reformation period but thereafter. As we have seen, writing within the tradition of the complaint meant that Lindsay's discussion of the priesthood frequently relied upon questions of human ethics. In his early works, moral reformation was perceived as the key to rectifying what were often social or institutional problems. This type of approach proved long-lived. For example, *The Lamentation of Lady Scotland* written in 1572, viewed the post-Reformation Kirk in essentially very similar terms:

> . . . purgit . . . of Channoun, Monk and Freir
> Of Papist Priest, Papist, and Papistrie,
> Bot not allace, clene of Hypocrasie,
> Of auarice, pryde and ambitioun
>
> (150–3)[34]

This stress upon universal ethics and personal morality had important implications for the continuing discussion of the priesthood and the formation of Scottish expectations in the face of developing religious controversy. Writing in the middle of the sixteenth century, the Catholic author of *The Complaint of Scotland* insisted that the 'abusione and the sinister ministratione of [clerical] office is the special cause of the scisma and of divers sectts that trublis al cristianite'. Questions of doctrine are here ignored and, indeed, the extirpation of heretical opinion does less good than reforming clerical behaviour: 'Than for certan the gude exempil of ther gude conuersatione vald extinct and supercedeit mair haistyar al peruerst opinions & scismas nor al the punitione that al cristiantie can exsecut.'[35]

It is tempting to conclude that this stress on the need for moral reform above all other considerations, so clear in Lindsay's work, exercised a powerful influence upon attitudes towards the clergy. This is important because it is clear that with the sharpening of religious controversy, some of the subtleties of the pre-Reformation discourse became lost. Drawing up the confessional boundaries made for a more black and white discussion with stylised criticisms not necessarily perceived as such. It is interesting that in the post-Reformation period, Lindsay's work was more readily viewed as straightforward polemic:

> But as for the more particulare means whereby many in Scotland got some knowledge of God's trueth, in the time of great darkness, there were some books sett out, such as Sir David Lindesay, his poesie upon the Four Monarchies, wherein many other treatises are conteined, opening up the abuses among the clergie at that time.[36]

The difficulties experienced in reading literature as evidence of clerical behaviour and, indeed, of lay reaction to that behaviour, clearly set in early. Given that a more subtle interpretation was of little use to those Scots determined to ensure the sometimes uncertain future of the Reformed Kirk, this is hardly surprising. What is more surprising is the fact that such difficulties have proved so long-lived. However, the problems involved in using literature should not blind us to its value. As this study of some important Scottish pre-Reformation texts suggests, it is possible to formulate a meaningful framework within which historians can usefully assess how literature contributed to any discussion of the priesthood.

Notes

1 Sir David Lindsay, *Ane Satyre of the Thrie Estatis*, 2773. All Lindsay quotations are taken from Douglas Hamer (ed.), *The Works of Sir David Lindsay of the Mount, 1490–1555* (4 vols, STS, 1931–36). In cases where the poem is clear from the text, the exact line reference is given in brackets.

2 Christopher Haigh, 'Anticlericalism and the English Reformation', in his *The English Reformation Revised* (Cambridge, 1987), pp. 56–74 and A. G. Dickens, 'The Shape of Anticlericalism in the English Reformation', in E. I. Kouri and Tom Scott (eds), *Politics and Society in Reformation Europe* (Basingstoke, 1987), pp. 379–410.

3 Margaret H. B. Sanderson, 'Some Aspects of the Church in Scottish Society in the Era of the Reformation', *RSCHS*, 17 (1970), 81–98, 91.

4 In support of the existence of lost parent editions of Lindsay's poems, see Hamer, *Works*, IV, pp. 17–23.

5 Greg Walker, *Plays of Persuasion: Drama and Politics at the Court of Henry VIII* (Cambridge, 1991).

6 Carol Edington, 'Sir David Lindsay of the Mount: Political and Religious Culture in Renaissance Scotland' (St Andrews University unpublished Ph.D. thesis, 1991), pp. 92–110 & 329–35.

7 Greg Walker, 'Sir David Lindsay's *Satire of the Thrie Estatis* and the Politics of the Reformation', *Scottish Literary Journal*, 11 (1989), 5–17.

8 *State Papers of Henry VIII*, 11 vols (London, 1830–52), V, iv, 169–70.

9 Joanne Spencer Kantorwitz, *Dramatic Allegory: Lindsay's Ane Satyre of the Thrie Estatis* (Lincoln, Nebr., 1972), pp. 11–22.

10 Lindsay has provided rich pickings in this respect, e.g. W. Murison, *Sir David Lindsay of the Mount, Poet and Satirist of the Old Church in Scotland* (Cambridge, 1938). More recently Ian Cowan has cited Lindsay in a somewhat similar manner, *The Scottish Reformation: Church and Society in Sixteenth Century Scotland* (London, 1982), pp. 73–6.

11 John Peter's insistence that the two represent distinct literary genres, and, moreover, that satire was not really known in the Middle Ages, fails to convince, *Complaint and Satire in Early English Literature* (Oxford, 1956). For a more recent discussion of the problem with particular reference to Scottish texts, see R. Lyall, 'Complaint, Satire and Invective in Middle Scots Literature', in N. Macdougall (ed.), *Church, Politics and Society: Scotland 1408–1929* (Edinburgh, 1983), pp. 44–64. Lyall speaks not of different genres but of different 'rhetorical modes' (p. 46).

12 Ian B. Cowan, 'Some Aspects of the Appropriation of Parish Churches in Medieval Scotland', *RSCHS*, 13 (1959), 203–22, 203. See also Cowan's *Scottish Reformation*, where he points out that as these independent parishes were particularly coveted by pluralists they were not necessarily any better served (p. 65).

13 Simon Ollivant, *The Court of the Official in Pre-Reformation Scotland* (Stair Society, 1982), pp. 82–3, noted by R. Lyall (ed.), *Sir David Lindsay of the Mount: Ane Satyre of the Thrie Estatis* (Edinburgh, 1989), p. 191.

14 David Patrick (ed.), *Statutes of the Scottish Church, 1225–1559* (Scottish History Society, 1907), p. 281.

15 Ollivant, *The Court of the Official*, pp. 148 & 162. Lindsay himself pursued at least two actions for the recovery of teinds, p. 142.

16 George Chalmers, for example, suggested that *The Complaynt* (309–11) refers to the deprivation of Archbishop James Beaton in 1526 (*The Poetical Works of Sir David Lyndsay of the Mount*, 3 vols (London, 1806), I, p. 269).

17 *Ane Satyre*, 774–6, *The Tragedie of the Cardinal*, 313 and *Ane Satyre*, 750–2, *The Monarche*, 2589.

18 Penn R. Szittya, *The Antifraternal Tradition in Medieval Literature* (Princeton, 1986).

19 Cowan, *The Scottish Reformation*, pp. 44–8.

20 Dickens, 'Anticlericalism', p. 390.

21 James K. Cameron, 'Humanism and the Religious Life', in John MacQueen (ed.), *Humanism in Renaissance Scotland* (Edinburgh, 1990), pp. 161–77, esp. pp. 168–71.

22 Ibid., p. 171.

23 For a discussion of Lutheran influences on Lindsay's work, see: James K. Cameron, 'Aspects of the Lutheran Contribution to the Scottish Reformation', *RSCHS*, 22 (1984), 1–13.

24 *The Monarche*, 4438–47 & 4687–94, *Ane Satyre*, 2745–50.

25 Lack of preaching was one of the complaints made by the Lutheran

exile John Gau in his 'Epistle to the Noble Lords and Barons of Scotland', appended to his book, *The Richt Vay to the Kingdom of Heuine*, ed. A. F. Mitchell (STS, 1888) pp. 104–5.

26 Patrick, *Statutes*, 253.

27 Ibid., 274–5.

28 Some suggestions are put forward by Arthur B. Ferguson, *The Articulate Citizen and the English Renaissance* (Durham, NC, 1965), p.133. In Scotland, some of the principal catalysts seem to have been the social dislocation occasioned by the English invasions of the 1540s, the threat this – and French ambitions – posed to Scottish independence, and the highly charged religious situation. Dickens argues that taking the argument beyond questions of human frailty was distinctly Lutheran in character: criticism of a defective priesthood turned instead to criticism of a defective theology ('Anticlericalism', p. 399). However, as is illustrated by Lindsay (who was never a Lutheran), there was often more to it than this.

29 Jill Mann, *Chaucer and Medieval Estates Satire: The Literature of Social Classes and the General Prologue to the Canterbury Tales* (Cambridge, 1973), pp. 37–9.

30 Patrick, *Statutes*, 176.

31 Ibid., 180.

32 T. Thomson and D. Laing (ed.), *David Calderwood, History of the Kirk of Scotland* (8 vols, Edinburgh, 1842–49), I, pp. 124–5.

33 Cowan, *The Scottish Reformation*, pp. 38–9, p. 44.

34 J. Cranstoun (ed.), *Satirical Poems of the Time of the Reformation*, 2 vols, (STS, 1891–93), I, pp. 226–39.

35 A. M. Stewart (ed.), *The Complaint of Scotland (c.1550) by Robert Wedderburn* (STS, 1979) pp. 126 & 127.

36 D. Laing (ed.), *John Row, History of the Kirk of Scotland from the year 1558 to August 1637* (Edinburgh, 1842), p. 5.

3

Parish finance and the early Tudor clergy.

Beat Kümin

The delicate relationship between parishioners and their clergy has always been an important topic in the historiography of the English Reformation. Though they were once considered prerequisites for the changes of the sixteenth century, there is now a tendency to see tithe disputes, Lollard sympathies, and critical comments on the moral or intellectual qualities of priests as exceptional and motivated by particular circumstances rather than as an endemic feature of the later Middle Ages.[1] The current view on the state of the pre-Reformation clergy is perhaps still best represented by Peter Heath's statement that 'far from perfection though most of the parish clergy undoubtedly were, their ignorance, negligence, indiscipline and avarice have been crudely magnified by commentators'.[2] From a comparative reading of recent work, it seems that English clergymen were better organised and more conscientious than their Central European counterparts, and far less likely to provoke the sort of rampant anticlericalism found on the continent.[3]

The discussion of these issues has however tended to focus on certain quite restricted categories of evidence. Court cases and complaints literature are the mainstay of the debate, their frequency or intensity being regarded as indicative of the esteem or contempt in which the clergy were held by parishioners. But there are other types of records which may equally be adduced, sources furthermore which offer a more positive approach to the early Tudor parish. The most important example is the evidence for voluntary financial support of the clergy. Such payments were far from unusual and a logical consequence of a system which struggled to provide its servants with a decent living.

43

It is thought that around 1500, an income of £10 a year would have been a necessary minimum for any parochial incumbent. In practice though, very many English benefices were worth less than £7 and over a third had been appropriated to monasteries and other corporations, which reserved the greater part of the income for their own uses. For those unfortunate and more numerous clerics without a parochial living the economic situation was even worse.[4] No surprise, then, that many a priest was looking for further income-sources or a second job, and such opportunities were not too difficult to find in the pre-Reformation context. It is well known that religious guilds and chantries employed a great many clergymen, who were often involved in the parochial cure of souls and paid by lay people of sometimes quite humble social status.[5] Perhaps less of a commonplace though is the support provided by entire parochial communities for all sorts of clerics, in addition to tithes and customary dues, which in theory should have been sufficient to finance their spiritual needs. There has as yet been little discussion of the size and extent of this phenomenon. The pre-Reformation laity may now appear as 'devout' and ready to bestow money on the church, but the empirical evidence for this has been somewhat limited: Christopher Haigh concluded on the basis of a few isolated examples and the revised data on philanthropy in England that individual bequests 'peaked in the 1510s and fell rapidly only in the 1530s and after'.[6] The communal dimension of lay investment in pastoral provision, however, has escaped quantitative analysis altogether, even though over two hundred sets of pre-Reformation churchwardens' accounts are available for detailed scrutiny. Parishioners administered considerable resources, and exercised a degree of choice in how they were allocated.[7] Decisions to bestow some of their money on priests were certainly no less significant than those made by individual testators and provide at least an indirect index to the popularity of clerical services. Furthermore, most payments had some strings attached and created a new kind of parish employee with closely defined duties, who would be ill advised to scandalise his communal patrons and paymasters by negligence or immorality.[8] It could be argued therefore that the parishioners' investment served the dual purpose of increasing divine service and tackling one potential source of tensions within the parish by assuming control over their clergy's discipline.

This essay offers a preliminary assessment of the size and beneficiaries of contributions from general parish funds by discussing the evidence from ten case studies: two from London (Andrew Hubbard, Botolph Aldersgate), two from Bristol (All Saints St Ewen's), four from smaller market towns (Ashburton, Devon; Halesowen, Worcs.; Prescot, Lancashire, and Peterborough), and two from a rural background (Boxford, Suffolk and Yatton, Somerset).[9] They have been entered on a database covering all the information from the first surviving fifteenth-century accounts through to 1560. Owing to the vagaries of source-survival, it will always be difficult to construct a truly representative sample, but an attempt has been made to include a wide range of locations, populations (between 56 and 1,100 communicants in 1547), sizes (from a few houses in the case of St Ewen's, Bristol to the 50 square miles of Prescot) and social structures. In addition, parts of other parish accounts and information from secondary literature have been used to fill some of the many remaining gaps.[10] It is clear that the results will still reflect many local peculiarities, but any general trends derived from such heterogeneous material should be of wider significance. Due allowances have to be made for the particular characteristics of accounting in various places, the possibility of further now unavailable documentation and the idiosyncrasies of mediaeval arithmetic. Even so, there is no doubt that parish accounts can sustain careful quantitative analysis. They were on the whole regular, carefully compiled, and thoroughly audited records of the churchwardens' activities.[11]

The first striking result is the fact that the accounts reveal the accumulation and disbursement of much larger sums than the wills and life-time bequests which are conventionally used to assess the financial dimensions of lay piety. In W. K. Jordan's sample of ten counties and 2,685 parishes, a total of £12,918 5s. given for clergy maintenance can be traced between 1480 and 1560.[12] Expressed as an annual quota of 1s.2½d. per parish, this was much less than the average contribution made by the wardens of the ten parishes selected here, which amounted to £1 17s.11d. *per annum* in the same period. It is impossible to say whether individual gift-giving and support was indeed that much smaller in real life, but it is certainly worthwhile not to ignore this additional evidence. Even more so, when it reaches as far down the social ladder as churchwardens' accounts.

As expected, there is considerable variety in the size of resources allocated to priests in parochial budgets. Expressed in average percentages over the whole period, the spectrum ranges from practically zero in the cases of Salisbury, Prescot and Halesowen to 53 per cent of total spending at St Mary-at-Hill (or over £30) in the late fifteenth century. For most prosperous and bigger-city examples though, the figure seems to lie somewhere between 10 and 35 per cent, or about £1-£5.[13]

Whom was this money spent on? Undoubtedly the most common recipient was the parish or holy water clerk. Normally in lower orders, he occupied an intermediary position between laity and clergy. Generally, clerks carried the holy water on many occasions, lighted candles and assisted the incumbent at mass and other services, but – to name but a few other tasks encountered in the records – he could also be responsible for visiting the sick, keeping the clock or cleaning the church.[14] The formulation of the Statutes of Exeter (1287) suggests that election and payment had often been a source of conflict between parsons and parishioners.[15] The canonical view was quite clear: clerks were appointed by priests and supported by weekly and quarterly collections among the local laity. But in reality things were more complex: at Hawkhurst in Kent for example, the parson was told to contribute to the wages 'without prejudice to the right of the Parishioners to choose the Clerk'.[16] Other evidence also suggests that in many places he was already a communal officer, who received detailed regulations of his duties. At St Stephen Coleman Street in London, he was ordered to be obedient to the parish and to ask amiably for his quarterages and casuals.[17] In my sample, he is mentioned everywhere except at Halesowen, but the customs and methods of his payments varied considerably. The canonically required quarterly collections do appear in London and Bristol parishes, while in no fewer than seven out of twelve cases the financial dimension of the clerk's office remains predominantly outside the scope of the churchwardens' accounts. Even where contributions are mentioned, they vary from year to year (between 2s.5d. and a full annual salary of £4 at St Andrew Hubbard) and sometimes explicitly state that they are just meant 'to make up his wages', which clearly implies a separate but mostly unrecorded collection mechanism. The accounts of 1487–8 at St Botolph Aldersgate allow an unusual glimpse of this practice when the wardens record that no money was 'by theym recevyd for the clerke wage thys yere ffor asmoche as the clerke gadereth hyt hymsylf'.[18] In other years though, and without a recognisable pattern, the responsibility shifts back to the parish. In 1507–08, 4s.6d. was passed on by 'John Strode and William Hobson off the clerke wages more then they paid'.[19] Individual contributions, preserved predominantly in the form of outstanding debts, ranged from a few pence to something like 2s., and were hence graded according to social status and most probably raised from householders only.[20] At Andrew Hubbard references survive to the prykyng bill or 'quarter book', a list of parishioners' names and their contributions, ticked off four times a year.[21] Clearly, the absence of regular contributions to the holy water clerk from a set of churchwardens' accounts does not mean that the parish community did not pay him. Rather, it reminds us of the quite complex administrative structure of a late mediaeval parish, where the wardens' reckoning often represented just the tip of the iceberg. Some responsibilities were delegated to special officers, and accounted for in separate records which rarely survive.

It has to be kept in mind that the figures presented here, though considerable, are very probably underestimates of the true extent of communal investment. Further support for suspecting hidden collections is provided by places where the clerk's wages appear only temporarily, as at Boxford under Edward VI. Evidently paid out of the receipts of the waxsilver gatherings in the pre-Reformation period, additional parish collections and full yearly payments seem to have become necessary when old and possibly 'superstitious' ways of fundraising were disrupted by Reformation measures.[22]

Apart from the humbler levels of clerics, parishioners also supported the rectors and vicars themselves.[23] Parochial contributions in addition to the usual tithes and dues could take a very straightforward and explicit form. In some parishes in the archdeaconry of Leicester on the eve of the Reformation 'there was a custom, or probably a byelaw passed by the majority of the parishioners assembled in vestry, to supplement the stipend of the Vicar by parochial contributions'.[24] Elsewhere, religious fraternities were founded especially to complement the salary of their struggling rector: in 1365 the initiators of the Holy Trinity Guild in Stamford noticed 'the poverty of the Rector to be such that the Church in its feeble state scarcely provided for his maintenance',

and decided 'at their own charges to found a fraternity in augment-
ation of divine worship',[25] to which each member contributed as
he pleased. The evidence from the sample shows that additional
parochial payments were not unusual. At Yatton in 1462 the vicar
received 6s.8d. from the wardens, at Ashburton an equal reward
was paid to a neighbouring vicar in 1496, while at St Ewen's,
Bristol, payments to the parson were largely responsible for an
increase in the clergy's share of the parish's budget to over a third
under Edward VI. He received the substantial sum of £2 13s.4d.
in both 1551 and 1552, and these unprecedented payments were
probably the result of a change in the tithe system.[26] Still under
Edward VI and again in the first years of Elizabeth's reign, St
Andrew Hubbard went as far as a parish might possibly go, by
farming the whole benefice from its rector. The parish having
suffered from a series of quarrelsome clergymen, parochial provision deteriorated further with the appointment of a new incumbent, William Swift, in 1545. He proved to be a notorious absentee,
whose habits could not be changed even by excommunication, and
this probably convinced the parish to take matters into its own
hands.[27] After a few preliminary payments in the regular churchwardens' accounts of 1546–48, the wardens then went on to compile
a separate reckoning for the parsonage from 1549 to 1552. Over
these four years, the parson's duty amounted to over £71, the rent
revenues from the parsonage to £4 3s.4d., the regular offering days
brought almost £7 and the provision of the holy loaf £2 14s. Even
a marriage fee of 8d. was paid to the wardens. On the expenses
side, the parson received £30, the necessary curate almost £34 and
£1 10s. was spent on bread and wine for the communion. The
parish also commissioned two sermons, met the clergy's expenses
at episcopal visitations and even paid £10 16s.8d. to the king for
subsidies and tenths.[28] It needs to be mentioned only in passing
that this extraordinary effort raised the priests' share of parish
expenses to 53 per cent. If there ever was such a thing as complete
local control over religious affairs, St Andrew Hubbard must have
come very close indeed.

Between these two extremes, that is providing for a humble
clerk and farming the whole benefice, there was a great range of
opportunities for parochial investment in better religious services.
Popular objects were the various clergymen, be they called stipen-
diary, auxiliary or assistant priests, who helped or substituted for

incumbents in providing for the cure of souls. In Lancashire, notorious for its large parishes and the constant need of additional clergy, only 33 of these priests in 1541 were paid by the local parson, 70 however by individual gentleman and a considerable 26 by the local population at large.[29] But the situation in the south of England was not fundamentally different. At St Leonard Foster Lane, parishioners subscribed for an additional priest to help their rector out 'of devotion and good will at their own charge'.[30] In the diocese of Winchester at Christmas 1541, one in eight of a total of 300 auxiliary clerics derived their livelihoods not from any regular ecclesiastical fund, but from additional resources raised by the flock in the local community.[31] Also on the eve of the Reformation in the diocese of Ely, parishioners at Bassingbourne, Holy Trinity, Ely, St Andrew and St Peter in Cambridge are known to have employed chaplains or curates.[32] The frequency of this sort of investment is confirmed by the sources entered on the database: at Andrew Hubbard, there are payments to a Sir Richard in 1468, a Sir Roger in 1485, a Sir William in 1486 and a Sir John in 1506 (churchwardens normally use the title 'Sir' when referring to clergymen). The biggest single cash sum of £5 in 1454 and 1458 went to an anonymous priest to sing for a benefactor's soul. At Ashburton, the curates William Austyn and Nicholas Laneman received regular payments of between 3s.4d. and £1 4s. for specific supplementary services, while the first ever record of a similar expense at Prescot dates only from Mary's reign, when an item of 11d. reveals the hiring of Sir James Jackson.[33] This does not mean that nothing similar happened before, but rather that communal investment in Lancashire parishes was more likely to focus on the many scattered chapels of ease.

Characteristic for the whole period is the provision of supplementary and especially morrow masses, in order to accommodate travellers or other people unable to attend the regular services. At Wakefield, parishioners had introduced a morrow mass for all servants and labourers, while at Rotherham a stipend was founded around 1500 for an 8 o'clock mass celebrated every Saturday at the Lady altar and also a further service of St Katherine.[34] In the 1520s, Norwich parishioners supported masses in the churches of St Peter Mancroft, St Stephen's and St Gregory's. In this sample, morrow mass priests were paid at least partially by the wardens at Peterborough, All Saints, Bristol, and Andrew Hubbard,

London, while particular services devoted to Jesus, the Blessed Virgin Mary or St Katherine are recorded in the accounts of Ashburton, again All Saints, and Halesowen.[35]

But parochial support could still take further forms. The generally close relationship between parishes and their religious fraternities is expressed in the contributions made to guild chaplains, as in the case of Ashburton, where John Vyne was paid £3 for half a year each in 1519–20 and 1520–21. The need for additional clerical provision was officially endorsed by the chantry commissioners for the large extramural parish of Botolph Aldersgate with its 1,100 communicants. After the dissolution, the Crown paid the salary of an assistant, while on top of this the parishioners employed former fraternity priests at least temporarily.[36] In the rural context of Yatton, chapel priests like Sir Richard York in 1510 could count on regular contributions from the parish wardens and occasionally, the vicar or clerk got a few pence from reciting the bede-roll.[37] Payments to friars or monks though occur very rarely, the only example in the sample being the few pence spent at Andrew Hubbard in 1485, 1494, and 1535. Just as scarce (and late) is the evidence for the provision of sermons, with only 1s.10d. recorded at Botolph Aldersgate in 1557–58 and 3s.4d. at Boxford in 1560–61. This does not mean that there was no interest in religious instruction, but in theory at least late mediaeval incumbents were expected to preach themselves four times a year. Indirect evidence that the frequency was increasing comes from the ground plans of rebuilt churches, whose naves were extended partly to provide more room for larger audiences.[38] There is occasional late mediaeval evidence for the endowment of lectureships, but rather as a result of municipal or individual than parochial initiative.[39] More common especially in urban parishes are the yearly payments of a few pence or shillings to vicars, priests, clerks, and sextons at the occasion of obits or anniversaries for past parishioners: examples could be quoted from All Saints and St Ewen's, Bristol, Mary-at-Hill, Andrew Hubbard and Botolph Aldersgate in London as well as from Peterborough. Clearly and logically, the beneficiaries of the wardens' investment were those who did a useful job for the community, and not members of the hierarchy or the regular clergy.

A last but very important aspect to be discussed in this context is the churchwardens' share in the administration of parochial chantries. In his recent analysis of long-term developments in Bristol, Clive Burgess underlined 'the increasingly significant role the parish community played in founders' strategies'.[40] By 1500 the wardens were commonly the trustees of such institutions, and that meant that they also paid the priest.[41] The most explicit example can be found at Mary-at-Hill: the accounts for 1494 list the income and expenses of no fewer than seven chantry endowments.[42] One of these, the Causton chantry, produced an income of £18, of which only £12 had to be spent on services and maintenance; the difference profited the parish. The seven chantry priests, one specifically responsible for the morrow mass, could expect a yearly income of £6 13s.4d. each, paid by the wardens who also managed the landed endowments, collected the rents and – occasionally – started legal proceedings against reluctant tenants. While these arrangements are well documented through their inclusion in the parish accounts, chantry affairs at All Saints, Bristol, were dealt with in separate records. In order to avoid comparing different set of sources these figures have not been entered on the database, but they certainly deserve a closer look as another useful reminder of how seriously parish responsibilities could be underestimated by looking just at the main set of accounts: the churchwardens kept special accounts for the Halleway chantry and submitted them to the yearly parish assembly.[43] Over time however, this became a burden rather than an asset: while the average balance from chantry affairs in the first ten surviving accounts 1463–82 had amounted to £2 18s.4d., the parish found itself covering a deficit eight times in the last ten documented years (1527–40).[44] Usually, at the foot of the church-warden's account a simple note would add after the final parish balance: 'of the which sum the seid accomptante askith to be allowid vs. xd. which he hath payd more then he hath recevid of the emolimentes of the chantree as it apperith more playne in the booke of ye chantre this yeare'.[45] On the whole, the last ten years of chantry life cost the parish over £55. This was mainly due to extensive repair and maintenance work, while the priest's yearly emoluments remained relatively stable at around £6 6s.8d.

In a comparative perspective, the social milieu and relative wealth of a particular parish undoubtedly affected its investment in additional religious service: there is almost nothing on record for Halesowen, Prescot, and St Edmund, Salisbury. All were large in size, based in moderate market towns and the first two at a disadvantage because of the inclusion of respectively seven and fifteen heterogeneous townships. In such a context, one would expect local religious provision to take preference over investment in the distant parish church. As for St Edmund, 30 per cent of the parish budget was spent on a rich ornamental and ceremonial life. We know about the existence of guilds and at least ten altars,[46] but it seems that direct payments to the clergy were simply not recorded in the main parish accounts. The Jesus Fraternity, for instance, well integrated in communal parochial life, maintained a chaplain for daily mass at a cost of £5 6s.8d. and may have met the most pressing needs. If such evidence were incorporated, St Edmund would probably not look too different from a structurally similar place like Peterborough. As for Boxford and Yatton, they were both prosperous rural parishes and – at least temporarily – up to a quarter of their budget could support the local clergy. At Boxford in the immediate pre-Reformation period, this meant a considerable 5d. from each of the 101 male adults listed in the 1522 muster rolls, at a time when the disposable surplus income of large sections of the peasantry may have been as little as 7s.[47] In the big-city parishes, the evidence becomes positively plentiful and the sums involved even more impressive. In the late 1540s and 1550s, communal contributions could amount to no less than 10–16d. per inhabitant (in Bristol, Mary-at-Hill and Andrew Hubbard). For central London, these figures amount to as much as the per-capita revenue of their respective rectors in 1548.[48] Large peripheral parishes on the other hand were less likely to involve each of their members to a similar degree: the extramural St Botolph Aldersgate with its over 1,000 souls spent a maximum figure of only 2½d. per parishioner.[49]

Whatever the local circumstances, it is clear that testamentary bequests and tithes reveal only parts of the laity's financial engagement. Any attempt to discuss contemporary attitudes towards the clergy without due reference to churchwardens' accounts presents only a very partial picture, and one which may seriously understate the degree of involvement of many parishioners in providing for the local ministry. Whether in the form of occasional support, regular payments or the initiation of new services, the cumulative effect of the amounts spent by churchwardens all over the country must have been considerable. The organisation of this sustained fundraising effort was no mean feat, and its success testifies to the strength of late mediaeval parochial institutions.

What can be said about the development over time? It seems that on the basis of this evidence it would be difficult to argue for a fundamental dissatisfaction with the old religion on the eve of the Reformation: everywhere the clergy's share of parish resources is higher in the last years of the old regime than over the whole pre-Reformation period. The scarcity of references to preachers or sermons does not suggest that the parishioners opted for advanced religious opinions. However, in the absence of overall totals for all types of financial investment (given the uneven survival of sources most probably an unattainable goal), conclusions must be treated with a great deal of caution. Some increases might turn out to be mere shifts from one type of record to another, and sudden drops could have easily resulted from generous bequests of anonymous donors; there is simply no way of telling. Looking at the absolute figures in these accounts, two parishes invested most in the immediate pre-Reformation years,[50] but no fewer than five, including all the metropolitan examples, did so later. In the reign of Edward VI between 1547 and 1553, Boxford spent a record yearly average of £2 3s.4d., St Ewen's £2 15s.9d. and Andrew Hubbard £15 19s.4d. Having allocated an average of £8 14s.3d. to their clergy during the Edwardian years – about a third more than between 1538 and 1542 – All Saints, Bristol, further increased its expenditure to £10 17s.8d. under Mary. Similarly, Botolph Aldersgate raised its Edwardian average of £11 12s.8d., which was three times as much as the immediate pre-Reformation figure, to £14 2s.6d in the reign of Mary. Here, in contrast to overall parish expenditure and W. K. Jordan's revised data from wills, there is neither an all-time high in the early sixteenth century nor a collapse in the first Reformation years. The graphs in the accompanying figure reveal a different pattern. Two curves are shown for each parish: the absolute annual expenditure expressed as an eleven-years moving average in old pence (£1 = 240d.), and the inflation-adjusted figures underneath.[51] The graph at the top shows the development of the annual average of all eight parishes with significant expenses on priests and clerks: steadily increasing support for priests and clerks, more rapid growth after 1500, and – in real terms – a peak in 1546–47. It should not be assumed though that contemporary par-

THE REFORMATION OF THE PARISHES

Payments to priests and clerks, absolute and adjusted (eight parishes)

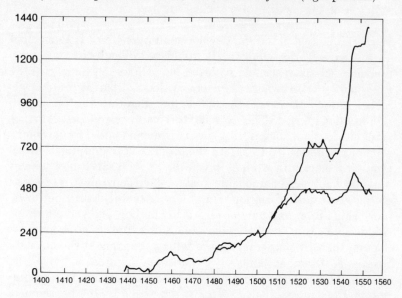

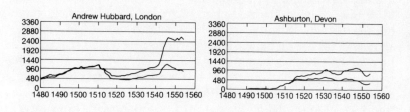

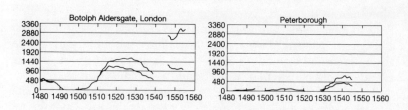

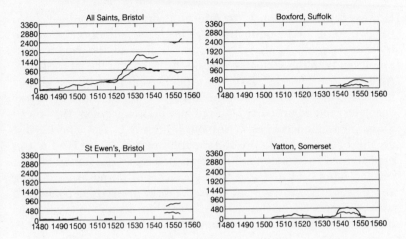

ishioners would have judged the level of their expenditure by this particular index, whose applicability is certainly questionable. Subjectively, their heaviest burden would have come under Edward and with the absolute peak of 1554–55.[52] There may be many different local reasons for this, but on the whole two factors would have played an important role: certainly the Marian return to the old religion but also (throughout these early Reformation years) the loss of sub-parochial and 'superstitious' institutions. The existing network of clerical provision supported by guilds and chantries had been disrupted, and parishioners seem to have picked up the bill.[53] Clearly, if part of the English reformers' motivation for changing the country's religious system derived from the impression that the church had too high a share of the nation's resources,[54] then their initiatives backfired, not for the Crown of course, but at least for parish communities. Rather than freeing resources for other purposes, most places ended up spending most on their clergy after the first Reformation impact. This happened at a time when total income and expenditure were in decline and it would have been quite unnecessary, had they severely disapproved of the clerical services that were on offer.

However, it is inadequate to interpret this process exclusively in religious or even denominational terms. First and foremost, all the indications point to the growing importance of the parish community in both the secular and ecclesiastical life of the later Middle Ages. Its revenues increased to a point well after 1520 and parishioners entrusted their wardens with ever-increasing powers over chantries, landed property, and public works long before the official Tudor legislation on parish responsibilities.[55] In fact, the biggest growth over the whole pre-Reformation period is observed not in expenditure for worship (which remained ralatively stable) but for secular, administrative, and local government purposes. Grouping all items into the three main areas of 'fabric' (everything connected with the upkeep of the church), 'worship' (ceremonial/religious life) and 'administration' (accounting, parish employees, property management, public works), 'worship' took up roughly 50 per cent both in the first-ever accounts and on the eve of the Reformation, while 'administration' grew from 11 per cent to 27 per cent.[56] Against this background, the growing expenditure on priests should not be seen as evidence for ever more enthusiastic support of traditional religious practices, but rather as one element in the general strengthening of communal institutions. Lay control over clerical provision became an increasingly natural phenomenon in all levels of society, and while few parishioners would have been in a position to employ priests individually, they all had a share in the supervision of collective foundations.[57] The endowment of benefices, the hiring of priests, and the administration of church goods all made the local church less susceptible to clerical or seigneurial interference, and reinforced the common people's power over their own affairs.[58] This was by no means just an English phenomenon. In late mediaeval central Europe, the aspirations of both peasants and townspeople concerning church organization 'boil down to the desire to communalize it'.[59] The self-governing local political communities assertively expanded their influence on to the ecclesiastical field, some achieving as much as communal control over advowsons and administration of tithes already in the fifteenth century, others using the Reformation as an opportunity to formulate such claims.[60] In England, where the parish lacked the backing of strong secular communal institutions, progress was less spectacular. Even so, its importance gradually increased: where the sources allow a comparative assessment, the sub-parochial level of chantries and fraternities seems to lose ground between the mid fifteenth century and the Reformation. At All Saints, the first account of the Halleway chantry (1463–64) recorded marginally higher revenues than the parish, but on the eve of the Reformation the churchwardens, who significantly looked after both, raised over £47 for the parish and just £10 15s. for the chantry.[61] After 1520, when deteriorating economic circumstances[62] and the Crown's religious policy combined to restrict the common people's investment in traditional religious practices, it looks as if parishioners had even more reasons to concentrate increasingly limited pastoral resources on their communal institutions.

Over a longer-term perspective, there seems to be a continuity of additional lay support for local religion from the earliest available evidence to the Puritans of the seventeenth century, but with the Reformation as an important turning-point. The pre-Reformation church with its emphasis on a rich sacramental and ceremonial life had required the financing of a wide variety of priests. Hence the general parish funds supported everything from rectors down to extra-confessors, while early modern wardens, in a time of reduced scope for clerical services, would rarely deal with anyone else than the local incumbent. With the disappearance of spiritual incentives for gift-giving, parish officers increasingly relied on compulsion: in this sample, there are post-Reformation rates at Halesowen and St Ewen's, and more entertainment-related fundraising methods like church ales were in decline.[63]

The Reformation then did not start or stop the phenomenon discussed in this paper, but changed its character in line with the increasing particularization of the religious landscape. The emphasis was no longer on attempts by the whole parish community to provide a greater variety of (doctrinally) more or less the same thing, but on individual or municipal support of services catering for a wide spectrum of often incompatible religious beliefs.

Notes

1 The traditional view in G. G. Coulton, *Ten Medieval Studies* (Cambridge, 1930), pp. 137f and A. G. Dickens, *The English Reformation* (London, 1964), pp. 90–102. C. Harper-Bill, *The Pre-Reformation*

Church in England 1400–1530 (London, 1989), pp. 75–9 summarises the current more positive view.

2 *The English Parish Clergy on the Eve of the Reformation* (London, 1969), p. 187.

3 C. Haigh, 'Anticlericalism and the English Reformation', in his *The English Reformation Revised* (Cambridge, 1987), pp. 56–74; R. W. Scribner, 'Anticlericalism and the German Reformation', in his *Popular Culture and Popular Movements in Reformation Germany* (London, 1987), pp. 243–56.

4 Harper-Bill, *The Pre-Reformation Church*, p. 46.

5 J. J. Scarisbrick, *The Reformation and the English People* (Oxford, 1984), pp. 19–39; C. M. Barron, 'The Parish Fraternities of Medieval London', in the collection of essays co-edited with C. Harper-Bill, *The Church in Pre-Reformation Society* (Woodbridge, 1985), pp. 13–37; K. L. Wood-Legh, *Perpetual Chantries in Britain* (Cambridge, 1965); C. Burgess, 'For the Increase of Divine Service: Chantries in the Parish in Late Medieval Bristol', *JEH*, 36 (1985), 46–65.

6 Haigh, 'Anticlericalism', p. 72.

7 At All Saints, Bristol for example the average annual income in the last four pre-Reformation accounts amounted to over £49: Bristol Record Office, Churchwardens' Accounts [hereafter CWA] of All Saints, P/AS/ChW/3, 1538/9–42/3.

8 At Ludlow, a dispute with the rector over the rebuilding of the church ended with the parish farming his benefice and employing him as a mere salaried official: R. Swanson, *Church and Society in Late Medieval England* (Oxford, 1989), p. 218.

9 Guildhall Library London, CWA of St Andrew Hubbard, MS 1279, vols 1 and 2, and ibid., CWA of St Botolph Aldersgate, MS 1454, rolls 1–65; Bristol Record Office, CWA of All Saints, P/AS/ChW/1+3; *The Church Book of St Ewen's, Bristol, 1454–1584*, ed. B. R. Masters and E. Ralph (Publications of the Bristol and Gloucestershire Archaeological Society, Records Section, 6, 1967); *The CWA of Ashburton 1479–1580*, ed. A. Hanham (Devon and Cornwall Record Society, new series, 15, 1970); *Halesowen CWA 1487–1582*, ed. F. Somers (Worcestershire Historical Society, 1952/3); *Peterborough Local Administration: Parochial Government before the Reformation: CWA 1467–1573, with supplementary documents 1107–1488*, ed. W. T. Mellows (Publications of the Northamptonshire Record Society, 9, 1939); *The CWA of Prescot, Lancs, 1523–1607*, ed. F. A. Bailey (The Record Society for the Publication of Original Documents Relating to Lancashire and Cheshire, 104, 1953); *Boxford CWA 1530–61*, ed. P. Northeast (Suffolk Record Society, 23, 1982); Somerset Record Office, CWA of Yatton, D/P/yat/ 4/1/1–3. Herafter all references to these sources: [parish] CWA, [year].

10 Particularly St Edmund, Salisbury: *The CWA of St Edmund and St Thomas, Sarum 1443–1702*, ed. H. J. Swayne (Wiltshire Record Society, 1896) and St Mary-at-Hill, London: *The Medieval Records of a London City Church*, ed. H. Littlehales (Early English Text Society, 125/128, 1904–5).

11 Many places had regulations concerning the time and compilation of the wardens' reckoning, as well as about the parishioners' duty to attend the audit: e.g. Botolph Aldersgate CWA, 1480/2 and 1485/6. 'The surviving pre-Reformation accounts may fairly be described as full and detailed': Masters and Ralph, *Church Book St Ewen's*, p. xxiii.

12 *Philanthropy in England 1480–1660* (London, 1959), pp. 24, 28, 375. There are of course considerable methodological problems for any such study, but they need not concern us for a rough comparison of the overall size of financial investment visible in surviving wills and CWA.

13 Mary-at-Hill CWA, 1477–95 (yearly average). Most places had at least one period of high spending on priests: e.g. St Ewen's 47.6 per cent under Queen Mary (6.6 per cent overall) or Yatton 22 per cent in the last pre-Reformation years (CWA 1541–5; 2.6 per cent overall).

14 Heath, *Parish Clergy*, p. 19.

15 *Councils and Synods with other Documents relating to the English Church*, eds F. M. Powicke and C. R. Cheney (Oxford, 1964), II, pp. 1026f (c. 29).

16 *Lambeth CWA 1504–1645 and Vestry Book*, ed. C. Drew (Surrey Record Society, 1941), p. lii.

17 E. Freshfield, 'Some remarks upon the Book of Records and History of the parish of St Stephen Coleman Street', *Archaeologia*, 50 (1887), 21. A detailed list of the clerk's duties was also drawn up by the parishioners of St Nicholas, Bristol, in 1481: J. R. Bramble (ed.), 'Howe the Clerke and the Suffrigan of Seynt Nicholas Church ought to do', *Proceedings of the Clifton Antiquarian Club*, 1 (1884–88), 143–50.

18 St Botolph Aldersgate CWA, 1487/8.

19 Ibid., 1508/9.

20 At St Ewen's, Bristol, John Mathew left 6s.8d. yearly in his will on condition that the poorest householders would be relieved of their contributions to the clerk's wages: Masters and Ralph, *Church Book St Ewen's*, p. xxiii. 'The Booke of the clarkes wages' in St Mary-at-Hill CWA, 1483/5 lists only a certain number of people and not every communicant.

21 St Andrew Hubbard CWA, fo. 14a.

22 Boxford CWA, e.g. 1551/2 (19s.3d.) and 1553/4 (£1 4s.8d.) on the income side; 1551/2 and 1552/3 £2 13s.4d. among the expenses.

23 For an analysis of parochial revenues from the rector's point of view, cf. R. Swanson, 'Standards of Livings: Parochial Revenues in Pre-Reformation England', in C. Harper-Bill (ed.), *Religious Belief and Ecclesiastical Careers in Late Medieval England* (Woodbridge, 1991), pp. 151–96. He stresses the scarcity of sources and the overall decline of rectors' incomes; an interesting contrast to the wealth and generally rising trends of CWA.

24 A. P. Moore (ed.), 'Proceedings of the Ecclesiastical Courts in the Archdeaconry of Leicester 1515–1535', *Associated Architectural Societies' Reports and Papers*, 28 (1905–6), 125.

25 H. F. Westlake, *The Parish Gilds of Medieval England* (London, 1919), p. 177.

26 Masters and Ralph, *Church Book St Ewen's*, p. xxxiii.
27 E. L. C. Mullins, 'The Effects of the Marian and Elizabethan Religious Settlements upon the Clergy of London 1553–64', (London University, unpublished M.A. thesis, 1948), p. 69.
28 Andrew Hubbard CWA (separate parsonage accounts: 1549/50 and 1550/52).
29 C. Haigh, *Reformation and Resistance in Tudor Lancashire* (Cambridge, 1975), p. 65. A search of *A List of the Clergy in eleven Deaneries of the Diocese of Chester 1541/2*, ed. W. F. Irvine (The Record Society for the Publication of Original Documents relating to Lancashire and Cheshire, 33, 1896) reveals that 21 of 315 assistant priests were financed 'ex stipendio parochianorum'.
30 Barron, 'Parish Fraternities', p. 36.
31 *Registra Stephani Gardiner et Johannis Poynet Episcoporum Wintoniensium*, ed. H. Chitty (Canterbury and York Series, 37, 1930), pp. 174–85.
32 Cambridge University Library, Bishop Goodrich's Register, EDR G/I/7, fols 162ff. I am grateful to Patrick Carter for these references.
33 E.g. Ashburton CWA, 1497/8, 1512/13 etc.; Prescot CWA, 1555/6.
34 E. L. Cutts, *Parish Priests and their People in the Middle Ages in England* (London, 1898), p. 481 (Wakefield) and *The Victoria History of the Counties of England: Yorkshire*, III, pp. 41f (Rotherham).
35 At Andrew Hubbard e.g. £5 for a morrow mass in 1465/6 and smaller sums in 1539/40 and 1541/2. At All Saints various priests were paid up to £1 10s. a quarter for the same purpose (e.g. 1527/8), while Sir Roger Channce and Sir John provided a St Katherine's mass at Halesowen (CWA, 1502/3, 1505/6ff).
36 *London and Middlesex Chantry Certificates 1548*, ed. C. Kitching (London Record Society, 1980), p. xxvii. The assistant received £7 from 1551 and Sir Olyver, former chaplain of the Holy Trinity Fraternity, £1 in 1548–9.
37 E.g. at All Saints the vicar got 8d. in 1450/1, or the parish priest at St Edmund, Salisbury 6s. in 1478/9.
38 Heath, *Parish Clergy*, pp. 4ff (preaching requirement); D. Owen, *Church and Society in Medieval Lincolnshire* (Lincoln, 1971), pp. 109f (larger naves at Croft and Ingoldmells, Lincs.).
39 E.g. the engagement of friars by the city authorities of York: D. M. Palliser, *Tudor York* (Oxford, 1979), p. 227, the preaching almshouse priest sponsored by the Coventry merchant Thomas Bond in 1507 (Scarisbrick, *Reformation*, p. 169), or the preaching duties of the cantarist at Havering: M. K. McIntosh, *Autonomy and Community: The Royal Manor of Havering 1200–1500* (Cambridge, 1986), p. 236.
40 'Strategies for Eternity: Perpetual Chantry Foundation in Late Medieval Bristol', in C. Harper-Bill (ed.), *Religious Belief*, p. 23.
41 Swanson, *Church and Society*, p. 218.
42 St Mary-at-Hill CWA, 1494/5. For the general importance of landed endowments bequeathed by former parishioners and the difference this made to parish management cf. C. Burgess and B. Kümin, 'Penitential Bequests and Parish Regimes in Late Medieval England' (forthcoming).

43 Bristol Record Office, Halleway Chantry Accounts, P/AS/C/1.

44 Not all annual reckonings survive.

45 All Saints CWA, 1521/2.

46 A. Brown, 'Lay Piety in Late Medieval Wiltshire' (Oxford University unpublished D.Phil. thesis, 1990), p. 86 (altars) and pp. 141ff (the Jesus guild).

47 Northeast, *Boxford*, p. xii (muster roll figure). That is 5d. on top of tithes, offerings, mortuaries, and other customary dues. Dyer 1989, p. 149 (disposable income of Robert Smyth, half-yardlander at Bishop's Cleeve, Glos. in the late fifteenth century).

48 The rector's per capita (i.e. communicants multiplied by 1.33 according to E. Wrigley and R. S. Schofield, *The Population History of England* (Cambridge, 1989), pp. 565–7) revenue was c. 1s. at Hubbard (Kitching, *Chantry Certificates*, p. 44) and 1s.6d. at Mary-at-Hill (ibid., p. 6). For St Mary it has to be remembered that the figures for priest support date from the late fifteenth century. No reliable figures for rectorial income survive for the Bristol parishes.

49 Kitching, *Chantry Certificates*, p. 30. The rectors' income was only £12, i.e. even less than 2d. per inhabitant.

50 Ashburton: £5 10s. (CWA 1541–6; 22 per cent of total expenditure); Yatton £3 14s.5d. (CWA 1541–5; 22 per cent).

51 For the deflated curve, the eleven-year moving average of the absolute expenditure has been divided by the eleven-year average of the price index of the composite unit of consumables chosen by E. H. Phelps-Brown and S. V. Hopkins, 'Seven Centuries of the Prices of Consumables, compared with Builders' Wage-rates', *Economica*, new series, 23 (1956), 312. The resulting figure has been multiplied by 100 to express it in the monetary value of the stable 1451–75 period, which forms the basis of the Phelps-Brown/Hopkins index.

52 In that year, the eleven-year average of the expenditure in all eight parishes was £5 16s.4d.

53 Cf. the payments to guild chaplains at Botolph Aldersgate, the sudden increase in payments to clerks at Boxford and the changes in the financial system at St Ewen's, Bristol mentioned above. One wonders, too, whether Andrew Hubbard's decision to farm the benefice under Edward VI was motivated by the fact that, with the disappearance of clergymen connected to 'superstitious' institutions, the non-residence of its rector became even more of a nuisance.

54 W. J. Sheils, *The English Reformation 1530–70* (London, 1989), pp. 6, 26.

55 For a detailed discussion of parish finances and government cf. my Cambridge thesis, 'The Late Medieval English Parish'.

56 This is an average for all parishes in the sample; in a place with large landed endowments like All Saints, Bristol, 'administration' jumped from virtually zero (1406–09) to 51 per cent (1538–42).

57 Swanson, *Church and Society*, p. 250.

58 Caroline Barron has identified the hiring and firing of priests as one of

61

the attractions of religious guilds ('Parish Fraternities', p. 33), but the same no doubt applied on the parish level, too.

59 P. Blickle, 'Communal Reformation and Peasant Piety: the Peasant Reformation and Its Late Medieval Origins', *Central European History*, 20 (1987), 221.

60 By the fifteenth century, communal control was fully developed in the cantons of central Switzerland: C. Pfaff, 'Pfarrei und Pfarreileben: ein Beitrag zur spätmittelalterlichen Kirchengeschichte', Historischer Verein der Fünf Orte (ed.), *Innerschweiz und frühe Eidgenossenschaft* (Olten, 1990), I, p. 230; the demands of local communities were a crucial feature of the early part of the German Reformation (up to 1525): P. Blickle, *Communal Reformation: The Quest for Salvation in sixteenth-century Germany* (1992; German original: Munich, 1987).

61 Bristol Record Office P/AS/C/1 and Bristol CWA, 1463/4 and 1539/40; at Botolph Aldersgate, the fraternity of the Holy Trinity and Sts Fabian and Sebastian accounted for £31 15s. in the early 1450s (*Parish Fraternity Register*, ed. P. Basing (London Record Society Publications, 18, 1982), pp. 18ff), the first surviving CWA of 1468–81 on average for just over £10. At the dissolution however, the guild was valued at £17 16s (Kitching, *Chantry Certificates*, p. 30), while the churchwardens raised over £30 per annum: CWA, 1533/9.

62 Both inflation and population picked up at around this time (R. B. Outhwaite, *Inflation in Tudor and early Stuart England* (London etc., 1969), pp. 9ff; J. Hatcher, *Plague, Population and the English Economy 1348–1530* (London, 1977), p. 66), and standards of living were falling for those lower down the social scale: Dyer 1989, p. 277.

63 Halesowen CWA, p. 3, Masters and Ralph, *Church Book St Ewen's*, p. xxxiv. For the tendency to replace ales with rates: J. M. Bennett, 'Conviviality and Charity in Medieval and Early Modern England', *P & P*, 134 (1992), 36.

4

Preaching and the reform of the clergy in the Swiss Reformation

Bruce Gordon

'By the way,' writes the Bernese Reformer Berchtold Haller to Heinrich Bullinger in 1535, 'our clergy are not really so despised, except those who make themselves despicable before honourable and pious people with their offensive living, drinking and persistent quarrels with farmers and overlords under the guise of the faith and religion, or through their outrageous customs which give the common people reason to abuse or laugh at them.'[1] This guarded assessment, based on a recent visitation of the rural parishes in Berne, draws our attention to a crucial fact of the Swiss Reformation: it was not *that* the priests became ministers, but how the clergy performed their duties in the parishes which concerned most laity. The reformation of the clergy proved remarkably uncontroversial; the success of this reformation, however, as Haller intimates, depended upon the relationships between ministers and parishioners. In each of the villages, the local minister was the public face of the Reformed faith; his teaching and conduct, for better or worse, had more influence on the laity than the endless flow of mandates from the city. The Reformation in Zurich began with Zwingli's petition in 1522 to the bishop of Constance decrying the moral turpitude of the clergy; it was the degenerate state of the clergy and their laxity, rather than an explicit rejection of the old faith, which stoked the fires of anticlericalism and prepared the ground for the introduction of sweeping changes. Zwingli's call for the spiritual renewal of the community proved extraordinarily attractive to a laity starved of pastoral care, but the basis of this renewal, the preaching of the Word of God, was fraught with difficulties of its own.[2]

Huldrych Zwingli's understanding of reformation was essentially anticlerical and local. Under these two tags lay a profound theological and historical vision pregnant with implications for the daily life of the church. Zwingli's break with the mediaeval cycle of penance was precipitated by his reading of Augustine's *Commentary on John* and the *City of God*, both of which were published by Frobin in Basle in 1506.[3] Zwingli tells Oswald Myconius how he profited from Augustine's exegesis of Matthew 13: 24–30, 36–43, the parable of the weeds and tares: the earthly church is a mixed body consisting of the elect and the damned, who will be separated only at the last day.[4] Neither the local church nor individuals should concern themselves with salvation, for God has effected that in Christ; their obligation is the fulfilment of the divine will, a continual reforming of the self after the likeness of Christ (*imago dei*). Christ is the author and the end of reformation and human participation is limited to obedience to the Spirit. Spirit and Word are one, and it is only through the Spirit that the Word, as it is fully revealed in Scripture, can be understood.[5] Scripture contains all that is necessary for salvation, but through the mediation of human language. The Spirit which inspired the writers of Scripture is naturally the same spirit which dwells in the believer (or community), providing the inner illumination required for a correct understanding of Scripture. Preaching in the church, the proclamation of the Word, is the image of Christ's preaching; it is the activity of reformation.[6]

Zwingli is careful to stress that neither preaching nor Scripture is itself the Word of God; they are the 'verbum externum', or tools, and do not themselves bring faith. Faith is an unmerited gift of God which is received by the elect through inner illumination. The external forms of the Word stimulate, educate, and admonish, but they are secondary to the presence of God in the Christian and the community in the Holy Spirit. The point of reformation is the ordering of the external world to the service of the spiritual. Zwingli's message was radical: institutions, laws, traditions, and all societal relationships possess no forensic value, they must be measured against the standard of the Word of God, or Scripture, and where they are found wanting, abolished or reformed.

All this may seem a long way from parishes and ministers, but the connection made by Zwingli between theology and reform is direct. Reformation occurs where the people encounter the Word of God; it is a local event, occurring in the parish churches. Zwingli rarely speaks of the priesthood of all believers, but its centrality to his theology, as for Luther, is unquestionable.[7] Zwingli prefers to speak in terms of the community (*Gemeinde*), by which he means the local church, within which the primary relationship is between the preacher and the congregation. What distinguishes the minister from the people is not an indelible mark conferred at ordination, but rather his ability and authority to expound the Word of God. The minister stands apart from the people and employs his training in biblical exegesis to rouse through preaching the inner Word present in the community. He is to teach and admonish the flock; but the relationship is mutual, for the Spirit which enables the minister to preach dwells in the congregation, allowing the faithful to discern whether or not the truth is being proclaimed. Zwingli replaced the sacrificial priesthood with the preaching office, but he provided the ministers with a critical audience. This remained the foundation of the Reformed ministry in the Swiss Reformation.

It was Zwingli's preaching which forced the breakthrough of the Reformation in Zurich. The effects of his sermons in the city were immediate and dramatic: spontaneous acts of iconoclasm broke out and services were interrupted. Zwingli's sermons decrying the swindle of the old church nourished the latent resentment among the laity towards the clergy.[8] Anticlericalism was rife both within and without the clerical estate, and Zwingli deftly played upon an assortment of grievances to build a broad base of support. Beginning with his petition of 1522, Zwingli established a strong constituency among the lower clergy, who objected to the restrictions imposed by higher ecclesiastical officials.[9] Further, Zwingli appealed to the dissatisfaction of the laity with the decrepit state of pastoral care and moral depravity of the priests, monks, and bishops. This calculated incitement of clerics and laity was intended to pressurise the cautious magistrates into taking action.

The tumults unleashed by the sermons in the Grossmünster frightened many politicians in Zurich.[10] The city council, by no means persuaded to adopt the Reformation, moved to establish peace by summoning the clergy in January 1523 to the Rathaus to debate the charges of heresy against the preachers.[11] The story is well known and need not be repeated here other than to note that the occasion convinced the magistrates that Zwingli's preaching was not to be stopped. The magistrates sanctioned the new preaching, which was somehow to take its place alongside the old rites of the church, i.e. the mass. The proviso, however, was that the clergy were to restrict themselves to preaching on matters of the faith and not address other (i.e. political) questions. This was the first step towards the adoption of the Reformation, but the way forward was far from clear. During the course of the January Disputation Zwingli formulated his understanding of the local church. The gathering of the faithful in the Rathaus in Zurich was, through the presence of the Holy Spirit, an assembly of the true church, and thus able to make decisions on spiritual matters. Zwingli gave to a reluctant magistracy the authority to act as arbiters in matters of faith and doctrine. At the same time, Zwingli continued to affirm the ability of the laity to judge critically the sermons of their preachers. The problem of how Gospel preaching and authority were to be reconciled emerged early and forced Zwingli to define the office of the minister.

In the sixty-second article of his Sixty-Seven Theses written for the January Disputation, Zwingli rejects the idea of the sacrificial priesthood, arguing that a true minister is one who preaches the Word of God.[12] The first extended treatment of the subject is found in Zwingli's sermon before the ministers and magistrates at the second Disputation of October 1523. The work is entitled *The Shepherd*, and is devoted to outlining the two central features of the office of minister: preaching from the Bible and purity of living. The connection between the two is crucial for Zwingli, for ministers witness before the community to the truth of Christ's words through right preaching and moral rectitude. The imperative of godliness is binding for the laity as well, but what distinguishes the minister from the layman is his training in interpreting and expounding Scripture and his authority to preach. Two years later, in a work entitled *The Ministry* (1525), Zwingli states unequivocally that the teaching of Scripture is not entrusted to the congregation but to the trained ministers.[13] The revelation of the Word of God is to all, and the laity can discern true preaching from false, but this, for Zwingli, does not preclude the mediating role of the ministry. Zwingli argues that the laity may speak only after those learned in the Scriptures have spoken and interpreted the text. Zwingli uses various biblical names (bishop, presbyter etc.) for the minister, but he prefers above all the title of 'prophet'.[14] Looking to the Old Testament for his models, Zwingli understood the prophet as one possessing authority to interpret Scripture and teach the people.[15]

Zwingli's sacramental theology broke the old bond between the priest and the laity in which grace was transferred automatically in the celebration of the mass.[16] His doctrine of the Eucharist, as it took shape during the 1520s, abandoned the binding of grace to the sacraments which made it, in his words, dependent upon where and when they are celebrated.[17] As B. A. Gerrish has written, 'The clergy would then have infallible power to grant or withhold salvation. Indeed, they would have the fearful power to sell God at a higher price than Judas asked. Zwingli is therefore speaking as a reformer and pastor in his protest against the abuses in sacramental theology and practice.'[18] The celebration of the Eucharist became a memorial, or thanksgiving, of the redemption received from the one sacrifice of Christ. In participating in the sacrament of the Lord's Supper the parish church acknowledges the free gift of salvation from God. Because there is no repetition of the sacrifice of Christ in the Eucharist, the parishioners themselves become the subject of the celebration; it is for their benefit, an outward act to strengthen the inner faith.[19] Nevertheless, the sacramental system in the parish remained a relationship between the minister and the people. Against the charges of the Anabaptists, the Reformed churches retained the mediaeval connection between the sacraments and the priesthood.

In contrast to the dramatic progress of the Reformation within the walls of the Zurich, the impact of Zwingli's message on the rural parishes is much more difficult to measure. It is impossible for us to know how much of Zwingli's theology was understood by the ministers and laity in the countryside.[20] The sacking of the monastery at Ittingen, an act of iconoclasm which shocked both the magistrates in Zurich and the Catholic states alike, argues for the depth of the feeling against the clergy.[21] Also, the trend towards autonomous parishes evident in the later Middle Ages, where the community took over control of the benefice, often, though not always, prepared a receptive audience for the Reformation message.[22] A survey of the rural territories taken by the Zurich council in 1524 to determine whether the rural officials approved of the magistrates' handling of the religious question yielded interesting results. The rural officials expressed their support for the Reformed faith and their readiness to defend it in the event of an attack, but they had little taste for coercing Catholic lands to adopt the faith.[23] The Peasants' War of 1525 likewise provides ambiguous evidence for Swiss territories. In Zurich, Basle, and Schaffhausen the peasants framed their demands in terms of an appeal to the Gospel as normative for Christian living and political order, and there was a clear intertwining of the resistance to tithes and Anabaptism.[24] In Berne, however, as Peter Bierbrauer has shown, there was no connection between the peasant revolt and the acceptance of the new faith.[25] All these aspects provide tantalising insights into the reception of the Gospel preaching, but the fact remains that we do not yet have a clear picture.

With the abolition of the mass in Zurich at Easter 1525, the clergy were relieved of their priestly status and became preachers.[26] The drama of this break was less than might have been expected. The council had lagged well behind the demands of the clergy and laity, and by 1525 many of the clergy had married and long abandoned the mass. Further, the direction of events in Zurich had been clear for some time, and those clergy who opposed the changes had left the city for other Catholic lands. The religious houses were dissolved and those monks who opposed the Reformation were removed to a monastery to live out their retirement.[27] The turning-point of 1525 was really a pouring of new wine into old sacks. First of all, the mediaeval parish structures were confirmed: the parish boundaries, the rites of patronage and the payment of tithes were all retained. There was no extensive examination of the clergy to determine their theological orientation; if the incumbent ministers were prepared to swear an oath of obedience to the council they were permitted to remain in situ. An overview of the parish clergy in Zurich during Zwingli's period illustrates the conservative nature of reform. There were approximately 167 clergy serving in the rural parishes between 1523 and 1531.[28] Of these 125 (75 per cent) had served in some capacity as clerics before the Reformation. Among those who had been Catholic clergy, the majority had been priests, deacons and lower clergy who held stipends to celebrate particular masses – though the last abbot of the monastery at Kappel was a notable convert. Ten are known to have been conventuals and two were former mendicants. Clearly many of the clergy in the city who opposed the changes left of their own volition, but it is remarkable how little resistance to the Reformation came from the rural clergy. A mere dozen parish ministers are known to have voiced opposition to the introduction of the Reformation, and of these only four were removed from their parishes. The others either decided to join the Reformed camp or died.

The small number of ministers removed from their parishes during the period indicates that the council proceeded only against those who openly opposed the reforms. Johannes Jestetter, who had been the priest in Eglisau from 1507, was dismissed on account of his preaching against the Reformation in 1523. This dismissal was in fact more of a retirement than a punishment as he was permitted to retain the parish living until his death in 1531.[29] Konrad Häfeli, a Swabian, was similarly removed from his parish in 1524 for opposing the reforms. As both men were dismissed before the abolition of the mass in 1525, it can be surmised that they had expressed opposition to the preaching of the Gospel. Daniel Baumgartner in Rorbas, however, doggedly rejected the Reformation. He preached against Zwingli at the 1523 Disputation and continued to celebrate the mass after its abolition. It was for his adherence to the mass that he was dismissed, though he too remained in the parish and lived off the income of the benefice until his death in 1533.[30] Simon Mägeli in Winterthur was suspected in 1523 of continuing to receive pensions from foreign officials, an offence punishable by execution, and forced to resign. As a native of St Gall, he was ordered to leave Zurich territory and promise never to return.[31] The expulsion of parish clergy from Zurich's territory was used against two other ministers who expressed Anabaptist sympathies, Johannes Brötli and Wilhelm Röubli. On 21 January 1525, the council demanded that Brötli, who was from St Gall, and Röubli, from Rothenburg am Necker, should leave Zurich within eight days.[32] The pattern which emerges is clear; those clergy from Zurich who resisted the changes were dismissed, while foreigners were expelled. It was not a question of ministers being suitable or not, for few had much notion of the implications of the Reformation. The first phase in reforming the ministers involved the rooting out of recalcitrant elements. Importantly, this general retention of incumbent clergy, a process replicated in Berne, Basle, and Schaffhausen, involved an implicit acknowledgement of the validity of their pre-Reformation priestly status.

Working from the patchy prosopographical evidence available, it is clear that the clerical body in Zurich at the Reformation

was far from homogeneous. From the figure of 167 clergy mentioned above, it is known that at least 41 (25 per cent) of these
men were not natives of Zurich territory. Although some were
from neighbouring Swiss lands such as Berne, Schaffhausen, Thur-
gau, and St Gall, several of the foreign clergy came from Swabia
and Bavaria. An example is Johannes Mantel, who was born in
Miltenberg am Main. From 1500 he was a prior in the Augustinian
monastery in Nuremberg. He studied at the universities of Tübingen and Wittenberg before becoming a priest in Stuttgart. It was
while he was in Stuttgart that Mantel joined the Reformation, for
which he was placed in prison for two years. Through Zwingli's
intervention Mantel came to Zurich where he became the minister
in Elgg.[33] Zwingli's reputation brought many of the foreign ministers to Zurich, but so too did the prospect of protection against
persecution. Hans Oechsli was born in Einsiedeln in Schwyz but
served as priest in Stein-am-Rhein, near Schaffhausen, from 1503
until 1524 when he was arrested by the Landvogt for promoting
the Reformed faith. He was charged with inciting the iconoclasm
which led to the storming of the monastery at Ittingen. Oechsli
was taken to Lucerne where he was tortured before being released,
whereupon he was made the minister in Elgg in the Zurich
countryside. Waldshut, a centre of the Peasants' War, likewise
provided Zurich with a flow of ministers who streamed into the
area following the capture of the town by Austrian forces in 1525.[34]

The absence of any purge of the rural clergy at the Reformation in Zurich and Berne reflected events in Germany where,
as Scribner has shown, the reform of the clergy was 'a revolt led
from within'.[35] The building of the new church was undertaken
with the same men who had previously served as Catholic clerics.
Yet despite these elements of continuity, the effects of the reforms
in the parishes were profound. Zwingli's preaching and the communication of the Reformation ideas, whether in their unadulter-
ated form or not, ignited an explosion of reform activity. Zwingli
had won over the magistrates by convincing them that the preaching of the Word would unify the people, that it would provide the
basis for the urgently required communal renewal. For Zwingli,
there was a natural connection between the response in faith to
the Word and obedience to ruling authorities; this was the key to
his teaching on the unity of the political and religious community.
What happened, however, was that the 'freedom of the Gospel'

was variously interpreted and the pulpit became the centre of a storm. Preachers trawled through the Bible to find texts to support their grievances against public officials or to administer a tongue-lashing to their parishioners. The combination of the Reformation teachings with the idiosyncratic manner in which they were preached produced, in Scribner's words, a 'shock and great scandal to those hearing it for the first time'.[36] The preaching of the Gospel was clearly accepted by the laity, and it was understood as central to the office of the minster, but the content of these sermons proved highly combustible. A few examples will illustrate the point.

In 1525, Adam Schmid, minister in Neftenbach, demonstrated the mixed nature of his views by preaching against the tithes and pronouncing from the pulpit that 'the pope is better than my lords'.[37] It was made clear to Schmid that the punishment for such seditious language was execution, but the council contented itself with putting him in prison and fining him 50 pounds. The local bailiff (Vogt) reported that Schmid had preached that tithes belong not to the wealthy but are, as the Bible teaches, for the improve-ment of the church and the care of the poor.[38] Further, the Vogt reports, he twice from the pulpit told his parishioners that the 'pope is more pious than my lords in Zurich' and he entreated the people to spread this message.

The role played by the Zurich magistrates in reforming the church brought them much criticism from the pulpit. In 1527, one preacher in Stein, Jakob Grotsch, emulated his hero Zwingli when he fulminated against the Zurich council for their mishandling of the Reformation. The background to his preaching was the dispute between Stein and Zurich over the use of the goods from the secularised monastery at Stein am Rhein.[39] In the course of a sermon on Jesus and the miraculous catch of fish (John 21), Grotsch distinguished between the true sheep and the wolves among the flock. The parallel drawn was between Christ's appearance to the Apostles while they were fishing and his blessing of those engaged in honest labours. This necessarily precludes the clergy, for the prelates and monks have superficially accepted the Word of God, but, in truth, are interested only in preserving their wealth.[40] Then, in reference to the disputed church goods, Grotsch remarks pointedly that King Hezekiah had also reformed but he had not stolen the goods, and asked what good was it for Zurich to ban mercenary service but continue to take the goods of the widows and orphans.[41]

A week later the minister presented to the council a written defence of his sermon. He began by confirming that he had preached on John 21: 'Simon, son of John, do you truly love me more than these? (John 21: 15).[42] The first point concerned God's graciousness in sending his son into the world, as seen in chapter 20. In the same chapter, he states, it is clear that not only Peter but all the Apostles are called to feed the sheep. The minister, following Zwingli's teaching, stated that to feed the sheep, to bind and loose, to teach the people and to proclaim the Gospel to all creation are the same thing. In interpreting the question put by the Lord to Peter as to whether he loves him, the minister says that the first quality which a minister must possess is love, for only when he loves the Lord will he be able to feed his sheep. His critical remarks here, the minister admits, were directed against the false shepherds who feed themselves and poison the souls of the faithful. Following the example of John the Baptist, the ministers must lead the people away from sin; repentance and the turning away from sin is what should be preached. When a sinner is brought to see the depravity of his character then he will comprehend the graciousness of God in Christ. The shepherd must also lead the faithful away from false forms of divine worship, just as Christ led the first people away from the religion of the pharisees. The minister must make every effort to lead the people away from the worship of the antichrist (the mass).[43]

To this point the sermon can be read as a faithful expression of Zwinglian teaching on the nature of the ministry and preaching. The sting followed when the minister came to the most sensitive core of Zwingli's message: the role of the minister as prophet in the community. Not only the prelates, priests, and monks are evil, the minister continues, but the rulers now emulate their evil ways. The rulers possess no fear of God and no love of neighbour; rather, they abuse and scrape (*schinden und schaben*) the poor people. They drink the blood of the poor in their gluttony, whoredom and licentiousness, and against this outrage the minister must raise his voice. For the prophets of the Old Testament rebuked not only the clergy but also the king, and the minister refers to the story of Elijah and King Ahab of Israel (I Kings 17–22).[44] Grotsch remarks that throughout the sermon he illustrated his points with numerous

references to Scripture. He concludes the sermon with the provo-
cation that should he be punished by the magistrates he has no
fear, for had he not rebuked them then he would not be a true
minister. He would rather pay homage to God than the council,
for as the Lord has said, one must fear not those who can kill the
body but those who can kill the soul. It is for this, he concludes
defiantly, that he is held to have offended the council.

In a second sermon, which was preached before the Bürger-
meister of Zurich, the minister picks up on many of the same
themes, particularly the abuse of power and the maltreatment of
the poor by the avaricious rich. He turns the language of anticlericalism on those officials who previously had spoken against the
abuses of the clergy but were now indulging themselves in the
same things. These former farmers have become bailiffs (*Vögte*)
and have been corrupted by power. Grotsch draws the parallel
between these men and the young Saul, a pious youth but a corrupt
king. He says that he rebuked the officials in Stein for not doing
enough for the poor and widows in the community. Grotsch enumerates in his defence a list of grievances proving how the poor
had either been denied moneys owed them or were forced to pay
a burdensome amount of taxes. Grotsch concludes his petition to
the council with a plea that they look after the poor. He was,
however, arrested for his preaching and imprisoned in the Wellen-
berg. Zwingli himself commented that Grotsch had preached in an
unruly manner, charging that the magistrates no longer took pensions but stole church goods.[45] Eventually Grotsch was expelled
from Zurich, leaving the territory for Bohemia.[46]

The minister in Stein clearly believed that his authority extended
beyond the boundaries of his community to encompass a right to
admonish the rulers in Zurich. This apprehension of Zwingli's
prophetic office was wide-spread. In 1528, Johannes Schlegel,
assistant in Höngg, preached that just as Pontius Pilate had falsely
judged, so do many judges in Zurich.[47] Schlegel's questioning of
the authorities may well have been prompted by an earlier encounter with the Anabaptists in his parish, which illustrates the centrality of preaching in the communities. The previous year Schlegel
had preached on the parable of the ten minas (Luke 19: 11–26),
and he used the text to attack those self-appointed preachers who
instruct in secret (*Winkelprediger*).[48] In the course of the sermon

Schlegel was interrupted by a journeyman (taglöner) who asked: 'who ordained you?' Schlegel replied that he, in contrast to the 'secret' preachers, sectarians and bands, had been properly summoned and ordained. The man, named Curradin, retorted: 'They [the other preachers] are of the opinion that they have been called and not you.' Schleger: 'it is not about opinions, but about what has actually happened.' Curradin: 'Christ went to the people in their houses and preached to them.' Schleger: 'Christ answered Annas, who asked him about his teaching, that he had not taught in secret, but had spoken openly to the world, in temples and synagogues, where all the Jews come together. John 18.' Curradin demanded that Schleger should go to the people outside the church and make peace with them. Schleger refused, arguing that those who met in secret did not belong to the flock; if they believed that he was in error, then they should prove it openly before the church.[49] Curradin was not easily put off, and charged: 'They believe that you are a false prophet.' Schlegel: 'So far as I have understood them, Christ, whose word I have preached here in truth and love, is false. Curradin: 'You have long worked in the field, however it will bear no fruit.' With that he left the church and joined a number of sympathisers outside. Schlegel continued with his sermon.

The Anabaptists, and not the Catholics, provided the most coherent opposition to the established ministry in Zurich.[50] They refused to come to church and they did not acknowledge the authority of the ministers, whom they derided as 'false prophets', who 'rage and scream from the pulpits' but 'do not follow their words with deeds'.[51] The despair of the ministers is reflected in the complaint of Ulrich Rollenbutz, minister in Bülach.[52] The Anabaptists, he reports, maintain that they alone preach the proper Gospel and that the ministers speak only lies. The disruption caused by these people in the community (Gemeinde) is so great that he is worried about a rebellion if these gatherings are not stopped. No one is present at the Lord's Supper, for all have run out of the church. Last year, Rollenbutz remarks, he had to introduce the new Lord's Supper, but this year the people say that whoever comes to the table belongs to the Devil.[53]

The dynamics of sermon-reception were endlessly variable. In the records of the Berne Chorgericht there is an example of a minister admonishing several parishioners for being drunk and climbing trees. One particularly literal-minded parishioner looked through the Bible, and having found nothing about trees charged the minister with false preaching.[54] Marti Weber in Zurich, when asked why he did not attend sermons, replied that he was not missing much because all the sermons are the same.[55] Besides, he adds, when he goes home his wife will preach to him. Weber had a rather functional view of preaching, remarking that as he already does what the preachers tell him to do, he does not need more sermons. Johannes Ammann, minister in Rifferswil, is an example of how the pulpit could be used to create conflict between the clergy and laity. During a sermon he accused his parishioners of being thieves and murderers.[56] The enraged parishioners demanded that he should either prove these accusations or be punished for slander. Ammann replied that it was simply his duty to admonish the parishioners from the pulpit; but his argument was not accepted by the Vogt, who fined Ammann for a misuse of authority.[57]

While Zwingli lived, preaching remained at various levels the focal point of Reformation activity. In the city, Zwingli and his colleagues preached the forceful expansion of the Reformation, supported Reformed preachers in Catholic lands, and argued for the use of military force to coerce the recalcitrant Catholic confederates into the fold. In the rural areas the ministers were instructed to use the pulpit against the Anabaptists and the adherents to the old faith. The aggressive promotion of the Reformed faith in the city was not, however, mirrored in the countryside. In the rural countryside, especially in areas bordering on Catholic lands, there was much less antagonism towards Catholics, and certainly little desire to wage war on old neighbours.[58] The rural communities resented having to fall into line behind the dictates of the urban churches who paid scant attention to their needs. These tensions, however, were temporarily masked by the remarkable success of the Reformation in Zurich.[59] The defeat of the Reformed states at Kappel in October 1531 changed everything and unleashed a tremendous backlash against the Reformation. This precipitated what is known as the 'crisis of the Swiss Reformation'.[60]

The defeat at Kappel exposed deep divisions between the city and the rural parishes in both Zurich and Berne. The rural communities had long expressed their opposition to any religious war, but Zwingli had taken little notice of their objections. The situations in Zurich and Berne make for an instructive comparison on account of the divergent roles played by the two cities in the war. Zurich bore the brunt of the defeat militarily and politically; the suddenness of the calamity and the subsequent collapse of political authority in the state underscored the precarious state of the Reformation. Berne, however, had not involved herself, and thus escaped the chaos, but the city was spared neither the wrath of the victorious Catholic Confederates nor the dissatisfaction of the rural communities. In both states representatives of the rural communities came to the city demanding a restraining of the clergy, whose incendiary preaching was believed to be culpable for the disaster.[61] While in neither case was there any suggestion of abandoning the Reformed ministry, both petitions express an understanding of the priestly office distinct from the Zwinglian line. On 28 November, the representatives of the rural communities gathered in Meilen to draw up a petition to the Zurich council.[62] In their petition the representatives demanded that those clergy who disturbed the peace with their inflammatory preaching should be removed from the parishes and that ministers should be prohibited from preaching anything other than what is in Scripture; in other words, they were to avoid speaking on political matters. In Berne the petitions of the rural communities was presented on 5 and 6 December 1531, and the principal points relevant to the clergy had a similar tone: the Reformed religion was to be re-affirmed, the rural areas were to be fully consulted on political and religious matters, the clergy were to be removed from their positions on the Chorgericht, or morals tribunals, and the magistrates were to appoint ministers from Berne to the parish churches and not foreigners, whose language was difficult to understand.[63]

The petitions of 1531 articulated the worries of the rural communities concerning the progress of the Reformation, and the demands which they made, although by no means fully accepted, set the agenda for the second phase of the Swiss Reformation. The demand that the rural communities should be more adequately consulted was an old debate in Swiss history, but the Reformations in Zurich, Berne, and Basle gave this question a new urgency. None of the urban magistracies was prepared to surrender authority to rural communities, but the failure of the Zwinglian Reformation, which had been concentrated in the city, brought home the need for a more flexible relationship between town and country. Both of the petitions readily acknowledged the authority of the councils and accepted the principles of the Reformed faith. Preaching was affirmed as the central function of the ministry, but the idea of preaching expressed in the petitions was not Zwingli's but that of the preaching ordinance of 1523; the minister ought to preach from the Gospel alone and not speak on political matters. This was a circumscription of the role of the minister as prophet, and reflected the dissatisfaction of the rural laity with what was being said from the pulpits. The brief for the second-generation reformers involved a clearer delineation of the office of minister, an elucidation of the term Gospel preaching, and a stronger integration of preaching into the life of the church. The Reformation was clearly leading to a concentration of authority in the city over the church, but, as events had proved, this could be achieved only through a more sensitive relationship between the city and the rural parishes.

In both Berne and Zurich the response to the need for consolidation was the convening of synods. Two sermons catalysed the debates in the two cities: Caspar Megander's denunciation of the Bernese magistrates in October 1531, and Leo Jud's castigation of the enemies of the Reformation in Zurich in June 1532.[64] These two preachers, who can rightly be called true Zwinglians, brought into sharp relief the danger of overtly political preaching and the unacceptable consequences for political authorities and laity of granting wide-ranging freedoms to the clergy, as Zwingli had wanted. The preaching, which was supposed to bring about a renewal of the church, had in fact turned the Reformation on its head: the Reformed ministers found themselves besieged by the very anticlericalism which had made the Reformation possible.

Essentially, the two authors of the Bernese and Zuricher synodal ordinances, Wolfgang Capito and Heinrich Bullinger, were in agreement on the nature of the ministerial office.[65] Above all, as Zwingli had argued, the minister is a preacher of the Word of God, and the distinction between the minister and his parishioners is expressed in the ritual of ordination. Bullinger enumerates the four stages of ordination as examination, selection, installation, and the swearing of the oath in the synod.[66] The candidates were to be examined on their life and doctrine and selected for a particular community on the basis of their suitability for that parish. The installation involved the presentation of the candidate before the community by the church and state together, represented by the rural dean and the local bailiff (Vogt). If the parish expressed its approval, the candidate was installed with the laying on of hands, which made him the minister of that parish. At the next session of the synod he was to swear an oath of obedience to the Zurich magistrates. This highly symbolic act of installation represented the bonds between the minister and that particular parish and between the minister and council in the city. His authority came from the synod but was to be exercised within the boundaries of the parish into which he had been installed. The Reformed ministry was thus theologically and spacially circumscribed: the minister possessed his authority only in so far as he preached the Gospel, and this authority was confined to the boundaries of the parish in which he had been ordained. Should he neglect his duties or leave the parish he forfeited his ministerial status.

This relationship was further developed in the treatment of the duties and life of the minister. He was to preach, and regularly, even if no one came to the church. The services of the parish church are the outward expression of the piety and obedience of the community, and if the people refuse to comply then the minister must uphold the order and worship in their name.[67] This idea of the minister representing the community was a refinement of Zwingli's thought, and reflected the high view of the ministry held by the second-generation reformers. Although externally the minister's authority came from the state, or synod, and the community, the power of that authority was effected in the act of preaching. The pronouncement and expounding of the Word of God is a unifying force; it unites the believers with Christ, with one another, and elevates the parochial church to a union with the universal church. The believers are not only led to Christ, but made aware of their obligations in this world: worship, purity of life, and obedience to the state. As Capito writes:

> The sermon ought to be held with great warmth and fervent love for the listeners, for their improvement and edification in God as takes place among the pious. Thus the sheep of Christ hear the voice of their Lord, the true shepherd. They follow it because they recognize it. Through coarse onslaughts the gentle hearts will only become embittered and ravaged. Then our sermons only give rise to irritable, hostile, rebellious and harmful people.[68]

As Pamela Biel has argued, the Reformed ministers did not possess powers over the laity derived from their sacramental role, but they retained their role as mediators or 'conduits' of God's Word.[69] The minister was, in Capito's paraphrase of I Corinthians 4: 1, 'a guardian of the secrets of Christ and servant of the Spirit'.[70] As 'shepherds' the ministers stand before the community as representatives of the one Shepherd, Christ. This analogy is developed further to make the minister responsible, to a certain extent, for the sins of his parishioners, though the Swiss reformers did not want to deny the primacy of the relationship between the believer and God. Capito writes that it is the duty of ministers to face the pious commons and open the way to salvation through Christ; and when this is not done, and a parishioner remains ignorant of the truth, then 'his blood will be demanded from the hands of the minister, who as a false shepherd has not tended the injured animal'.[71]

This language of a priestly relationship of the clergy to the laity goes well beyond Zwingli's description of the preacher, and it reflects Bullinger's tendency to think of the parish ministry in mediaeval terms. The minister assumes responsibility for the parish in three important ways: liturgically, pastorally, and morally. The work of the minister is dramatically presented in the liturgy of divine worship.[72] As the representative of Christ the minister has two audiences: in preaching he is the voice of the Spirit to the people, and in leading the faithful in common prayer he articulates the needs of the community before God. This relationship is perhaps most vividly expressed in the liturgy for the Lord's Supper; the laity were neither dependent upon the minister for release from sin nor for the reception of grace, for that is a private matter between God and the individual, but in presenting the bread and wine together with the Word of God, the minister reveals the truth behind the symbols.[73]

The pastoral role of the minister comprehended numerous elements. In preaching the minister was to address the particular needs of his community without being personal. In his pastoral work he was to live with his family in the community and cultivate personal contacts with each member of the parish, as Capito writes: 'For personal contact goes more directly to the heart than that which is publicly spoken to someone.'[74] The minister's own life, and that of his wife and family, was to be the model for the parishioners, for the purity of his own conduct gave the minister the authority to admonish others.[75] The centre of each parish was to be the church and the minister's house, and throughout the sixteenth century there were repeated efforts to control gathering points which competed with these: taverns, dances, Catholic chapels.[76] The work of each minister went beyond worship; he was to care for the poor, elderly, widowed, and orphaned, and was particularly enjoined to visit the sick. In sixteenth-century Zurich, the rural minister was responsible for the administration of social welfare in the parish and for the education of youth.[77]

Finally, the minister was responsible for discipline in the community. This had two sides: he was both the moral overseer of the parishioners and was himself subject to the discipline of his brethren. Officially, the social norms of parish behaviour were based on the morals mandates issued by the councils, and the minister was responsible for reading these mandates from the pulpit and for ensuring popular compliance. Preaching and worship not only taught the laity to be good Christians but also obedient members of the state, and to this end the minister worked together with the local officials to police every aspect of the parishioners' lives.[78] Ministers themselves were not immune from supervision and were required to submit to the rigorous discipline of the synod in Zurich, or the Chorgericht in Berne, where they were answerable for their parish.

Returning to Haller's letter to Bullinger, the study of the disciplinary cases in the Zurich synod during Bullinger's tenure supports the verity of the Bernese reformer's contention that the laity were prepared to accept the clergy as long as they performed their duties. The structure of the synod permitted the parish communities to petition the church in the city when they were unsatisfied with their minister, thus preserving in institutional form Zwingli's high view of congregational authority.[79] The evidence overwhelmingly shows that the neglect of the parish, poor preaching, drunkenness, and adultery were the most common complaints. Above all it was preaching which proved most troublesome.[80] That the ministers should preach was generally accepted, but the inability or disinclination of many ministers to preach or, worse, the misuse of the pulpit remained an enduring problem.

The building of a professional clergy in the Swiss Reformed states was a complex and slow process. It was in many ways a circular movement, for where Zwingli broke the old bond between laity and the clergy, Bullinger, in the light of events, sought to knit them together again. Bullinger wanted to anchor preaching in a more clearly defined role for the minister, and this required the development of strong parochial structures and clerical education. Bullinger's distinctive mark in reforming the ministry was the emphasis he placed on the role of the minister as representative of the parishioners he served. This proved extremely difficult; the minister was answerable before the synod for the lives of his parishioners, he was to teach, admonish, and care for them, but never enter too far into their lives. He was to preach against and avoid all social activities and events (marriage feasts, carnivals etc.) thought by the church to be improper for the Christian community. But the boundaries were far from clear. The minister was obliged to live in the community with his family, though from the points of view of the church and the laity he could not properly belong. The clergy served in the villages where the church placed them, they were outsiders, and this was reinforced by the entrenchment of the distinction between priest and laity in the Reformed states. It was the inability of many ministers to balance the often conflicting demands placed on them by the ruling authorities and the communities which accounts for the continuation of disciplinary problems. The Reformed ministry reaffirmed the dependence of the laity on the clergy, and in so doing retained many mediaeval structures to bolster this relationship. What it also inherited, and had to face, was the anticlericalism which quickly rose to the surface when the laity did not get what they wanted.

Notes

1 StAZ E II 343/77. 26 July 1535.

2 On literacy and the Word in Zurich, see Arnold Schnyder, 'Word and Power in Reformation Zurich' *ARG*, 81 (1990), 263–85.

3 There is a debate on the role of Augustine's commentaries in Zwingli's conversion, see A. Schindler, *Zwingli und die Kirchenväter* (Zurich, 1984), pp. 34–41, and U. Gäbler, 'Huldrych Zwinglis "reformatorische Wende"', *Zeitschrift für Kirchengeschichte*, 89 (1978), 120–35.

4 Zwingli to Oswald Myconius, 24 July 1520. *Huldreich Zwinglis Sämtliche Werke*, ed. E. Egli et al., (Corpus Reformatorum, 88- , 1905-), VII, pp. 341–5. Gäbler, 'Zwinglis "reformatorische Wende"', 123–4.

5 G. W. Locher, 'Huldrych Zwingli's Concept of History', in *Zwingli's Thought. New Perspectives* (Leiden, 1981), pp. 101–2.

6 Locher, 'Zwingli's Concept of History', p. 102.

7 See Klaus Peter Voß, *Der Gedanke des allgemeinen Priester- und Prophetentums. Seine gemeindetheologische Aktualisierung in der Reformationszeit* (Wuppertal and Zurich, 1990), pp. 142–3.

8 On Zwingli's preaching in Zurich, see Hans-Jürgen Goertz, *Pfaffenhaß und groß Geschrei* (Munich, 1987), pp. 134–47; also Hans-Christoph Rublack, 'Zwingli und Zürich', *Zwingliana*, 16 (1985), 395–426; M. Haas, *Huldrych Zwingli* (Zurich, 1969), pp. 86–93.

9 G. Potter, *Zwingli* (Cambridge, 1976), pp. 78–83.

10 On the political leadership in Zurich, see W. Jacob, *Politische Führungsschicht und Reformation. Untersuchungen zur Reformation in Zürich 1519–1528* (Zurich, 1970).

11 Above all, see H. Oberman, *Masters of the Reformation. The Emergence of a New Intellectual Climate in Europe* (Cambridge, 1981), pp. 210–39.

12 *An Exposition of the Articles, Zwinglis Werke*, I, p. 465. On Zwingli and the ministry, see W. P. Stephens, *The Theology of Huldrych Zwingli* (Oxford, 1986), pp. 260–281.

13 Ibid., p. 277.

14 Ibid., pp. 279–80; also, F. Büsser, 'De Prophetae Officio. Eine Gedankerede Bullingers auf Zwingli', in his *Wurzeln der Reformation in Zürich* (Leiden, 1985), pp. 199–216.

15 F. Büsser, 'Der Prophet – Gedanken zu Zwinglis Theologie', in his *Wurzeln der Reformation in Zürich*, pp. 48–59.

16 On Zwingli's doctrine of the Eucharist, see Stephens, *Theology of Huldrych Zwingli*, pp. 219–59.

17 See B. A Gerrish, *Old Protestantism and the New* (Edinburgh, 1982), p. 129.

18 Ibid.

19 F. Schmidt-Clausing, *Zwingli als Liturgiker* (Göttingen, 1952).

20 On communication of Zwingli's ideas, see above all the seminal P. Blickle, *Gemeindereformation. Die Menschen des 16. Jahrhunderts auf dem Weg zum Heil* (Munich, 1987).

21 Potter, *Zwingli*, pp. 144–9.

22 Three case studies revealing the connection between communalisation in the rural areas and the acceptance of a Reformed minister are found in Peter Blickle (ed.), *Zugänge zur bäuerlichen Reformation* (Zurich, 1987). Peter Bierbrauer, 'Die Reformation in den Schaffhauser Gemeinden Hallau und Thayngen', pp. 21–53; Hans von Rütte, 'Bäuerliche Reformation am Beispiel der Pfarrei Marbach im sanktgallischen Rheintal', pp. 55–84, and Peter Kamber, 'Die Reformation auf der Zürcher Landshaft am Beispiel des Dorfes Marthalen. Fallstudie zur Struktur bäuerlicher Reformation', pp. 85–125.

23 C. Dietrich, *Die Stadt Zürich und ihre Landgemeinden während der Bauernunruhen von 1489 bis 1525* (Frankfurt, 1985), pp. 209–11.

24 On the debate concerning the connection between the Peasants' War and Anabaptism in Swiss lands, see Hans-Jürgen Goertz, 'Aufständische Bauern und Täufer in der Schweiz', in Blickle, *Zugänge*, pp. 267–89.

25 In Berne the rural communities, on account of their highly developed freedom from the city, resisted the introduction of the new preaching

ordinances and later of the Reformation. See P. Bierbrauer, *Freiheit und Gemeinde im Berner Oberland 1300–1700* (Berne, 1991), pp. 250–5.

26 Haas, *Huldrych Zwingli*, pp. 140–4.
27 U. Gäbler, *Huldrych Zwingli. Eine Einführung in sein Leben und sein Werk* (Berlin, 1985), p. 91.
28 The basis of this calculation is E. Dejung and W. Wuhrmann (eds), *Zürcher Pfarrerbuch 1519–1552* (Zurich, 1953), hereafter referred to as ZPB.
29 *ZPB* p. 367.
30 *ZPB* p. 191.
31 *ZPB* p. 416.
32 *Actensammlung zur Geschichte der Zürcher Reformation in den Jahren 1519–1533*, ed. E. Egli (1879 rpt. Aalen, 1973), 624, p. 278. Hereafter referred to as Egli, *Actensammlung*.
33 *ZPB*, p. 418.
34 T. Scott, 'Reformation and Peasants' War in Waldshut and Environs: A Structural Analysis', *ARG*, 69 (1978), 82–102, 70 (1979), 140–69.
35 R. Scribner, 'Preachers and People in the German Towns', in his *Popular Culture and Popular Movements in Reformation Germany* (London, 1987), pp. 123–43.
36 R. Scribner, 'Oral Culture and the Diffusion of Reformation Ideas', *Popular Culture and Popular Movements*, p. 52.
37 23 August 1525. Egli, *Actensammlung*, 808 pp. 385–6.
38 Ibid., p. 386.
39 Ibid., 1312 pp. 569–71. F. Vetter, 'Die Reformation von Stadt und Kloster Stein am Rhein', *Jahrbuch für Schweizerische Geschichte*, 9 (1884), 213–357.
40 Egli, *Actensammlung*, 1312 p. 569.
41 Vetter, 'Stein am Rhein', 332.
42 Egli, *Actensammlung*, 1317 p. 572.
43 Ibid.
44 Ibid, p. 573.
45 Vetter, 'Stein am Rhein', 340.
46 Ibid.
47 Egli, *Actensammlung*, 1391 p. 607.
48 Ibid., 1337 Dec. 1527 pp. 581–2.
49 Schleger refers to John 3: 21. 'But whoever lives by the truth comes into the light, so that it may be seen plainly that what he has done has been done through God.'
50 On Anabaptism in Zurich, see W. Packull, 'The Origins of Swiss Anabaptism in the Context of the Reformation of the Common Man', *Journal of Mennonite Studies*, 3 (1985), 35–59; J. Stayer, 'Die Anfänge des schweizerischen Täufertums im reformierten Kongregationalismus', in Hans-Jürgen Goertz (ed.), *Umstrittenes Täufertum, 1525–1975* (Göttingen, 1977), pp. 19–49.
51 Egli, *Actensammlung*, 1360, 27 January 1528 p. 589.
52 Egli, *Actensammlung*, 1358, January 1528 pp. 587–8.
53 Ibid.

THE REFORMATION OF THE PARISHES

54 T. de Quervain, *Kirchliche und Soziale Zustände in Bern unmittelbar nach der Reformation (1528–1532)* (Berne, 1906), p. 50.
55 Egli, *Actensammlung*, 1868 pp. 809–10, July 1532.
56 Ibid., 1538 pp. 654–5, 20 January 1529.
57 Ibid., p. 655.
58 H. Meyer, *Der Zweite Kappeler Krieg* (Zurich, 1976), pp. 20–21.
59 K. Maeder, 'Die Bedeutung der Landschaft für den Verlauf des reformatorischen Prozesses in Zürich (1522–1532)', in B. Moeller (ed.), *Stadt und Kirche im 16. Jahrhundert* (Gütersloh, 1979), pp. 91–8.
60 J. W. Baker, 'Church, State and Dissent: The Crisis of the Swiss Reformation, 1531–1536', *CH*, 57 (1988), 135–52.
61 On Kappel, see B. Gordon, 'Switzerland', in Andrew Pettegree (ed.), *The Early Reformation in Europe* (Cambridge, 1992), pp. 84–9. The best full length study is H. Meyer, *Der Zweite Kappeler Krieg* (Zurich, 1976).
62 Egli, *Actensammlung*, 1797 28 November 1531 pp. 768–70.
63 The text of the petition is printed in de Quervain, *Kirchliche und Soziale Zustände*, pp. 231–5.
64 On Megander's sermon see my forthcoming article in Zwingliana. On Jud, see Pamela Biel, *Doorkeepers at the House of Righteousness. Heinrich Bullinger and the Zurich Clergy 1535–1575* (Zürcher Beiträge zur Reformationsgeschichte, 15, 1991), pp. 93–8.
65 *Der Berner Synodus von 1532*, ed. G. Locher (Neukirchen-Vluyn, 1984). Bullinger's synodal ordinances are printed in Egli, *Actensammlung*, 1899 pp. 825–37; See Hans Ulrich Bächtold, *Heinrich Bullinger vor dem Rat* (Berne, 1982), pp. 29–35. The most comprehensive study of Bullinger's teaching on the ministry is Biel, *Doorkeepers*.
66 Egli, *Actensammlung*, 1899 pp. 827–9.
67 *Der Berner Synodus*, p. 155.
68 Ibid., p. 152.
69 Biel, *Doorkeepers*, p. 132.
70 Ibid.
71 Ibid., p. 156. Capito is refering to Ezekiel 3: 18 and 34: 4.
72 See Biel's treatment of the liturgical role of the ministry in Zurich, *Doorkeepers*, pp. 107–36.
73 See Bruce Gordon, *Clerical Discipline and the Rural Reformation. The Synod in Zürich* (Zürcher Beiträge zur Reformationsgeschichte, 16, 1992), pp. 136–43.
74 Biel, *Doorkeepers*, pp. 107–36.
75 On the pastoral duties of the ministers in Zurich, see Gordon, *Clerical Discipline*, esp. 169–209.
76 Ibid., pp. 124–36.
77 Gordon, *Clerical Discipline*, pp. 161–76; Bächtold, *Bullinger vor dem Rat*, pp. 266–9.
78 Gordon, loc. cit.
79 Ibid., pp. 84–90.
80 Ibid., pp. 210–14.

5

Rural resistance, the Lutheran pastor, and the Territorial church in Brandenburg Ansbach-Kulmbach, 1528–1603

C. Scott Dixon

Modern Reformation historiography tends to survey religious change from a structural perspective. The Reformation has been perceived as an 'urban event', ordered by a civic magistracy to gratify the needs of the cities and towns; it has been labelled a 'communal Reformation' (*Gemeindereformation*), a programme of reform adopted by the rural commune to appease God and answer the call to local autonomy; it has been viewed as a 'princes' 'Reformation' (*Fürstenreformation*), the imposition of religious change from above by mandate.[1] These are not analogous models of reform, but they share a common premise: that the Reformation movement was a contextual event. Luther's assault upon the mediaeval Catholic church was conditioned by the society into which it was broadcast.[2] In the case of the third model, the princes' Reformation, this often meant putting Lutheran doctrine into the service of the prince. Ultimately, it has been claimed, religion served to bring the average subject into line; the process of religious reform, Protestant or Catholic, the formation of dogma, propaganda, and rules of discipline ran parallel with the centralisation of power and the emergence of the absolute state. This 'formation of confessions' or 'confessionalisation' has been seen as a fundamental process of the sixteenth and seventeenth centuries.[3]

Central to this enterprise was the agent of reform, the clergyman. If the concept of confessionalisation has any validity it must be assessed at the meeting point between injunction and practice: the parish. And if the historian wants to reconstruct the process then he or she must examine the experience of its main participants: the pastor pre-eminent among them. The following investigation will examine one aspect of the interface between the Lutheran clergy and the rural parish in the former German principality of Brandenburg Ansbach-Kulmbach during the first century of reform. In particular, this work will investigate the status of the pastor once he was in the parish; that is, the security of his office, the scale of his maintenance, and the scope of his ability to command local resources. What was the quality of the average Lutheran clergyman in Ansbach and Kulmbach? What was the status of his livings? How was the pastor received by the parishioners? What was the nature of the resistance to payment? What were the reasons for resistance? How were these problems overcome? This is an analysis of a presumption fundamental to the vitality of a broad abstraction such as confessionalisation: that the Lutheran authorities were able to staff the rural parishes with a working clerical estate.

The Reformation was introduced into the lands of Ansbach and Kulmbach by fiat. Mandates had been issued by Margrave Casimir during the first decade of the movement (in 1524, 1525, and 1527) calling for the preaching of the Word, 'clear and pure'; but it was not until his brother George the Pious came to power in 1528 that Luther's teachings were adopted and applied as a programme of religious change. In 1528 a provisional church ordinance was drafted; that same year a visitation was mounted (a joint effort with the Imperial city of Nuremberg). This visitation, based upon its predecessor in Saxony, provided the margrave and his councillors with a window on to the parishes; they were able to take stock of the steps needed to consolidate reform.[4]

It was necessary, in the absence of a centralised bishopric, that the margrave should exercise control over the appointment of the clergy. This was not only an inevitable consequence of his usurpation of ecclesiastical power, but an ultimate eventuality of the margrave's practising philosophy: that the prince had a God-given right to exercise control over the visible church. A 1526 resolution had stipulated that no pastor or chaplain should be invested into a parish without first consulting the margrave or a district official. George the Pious repeated this injunction in 1528.[5] At this stage it was feared that the bishops would fill vacant posts with Catholic clergymen. As a consequence, the secular authorities kept a watch over vacant parishes and waited for the council to dispatch instructions. In 1528 the district official of Gunzenhausen confiscated the keys to the church and the sacristy in Aha following the death of George Sorg. In 1532 the property of a deceased clergyman in Alfershausen was confiscated by a local official to deter the bishop of Eichstätt. The benefice was held in suspension until the Ansbach council issued further orders.[6] And again in 1541 the officials safeguarded the parish of Rohr: 'so that the clergy of Eichstätt [*die Eystetischen*] do not appoint a pastor according to their pleasure, we have locked the church and ordered that no one without authorisation [*on bevelch*] be allowed access'.[7]

This battle for patronage was enmeshed within the wider struggle for religious supremacy, and it seeped down to the level of the parish. The secular authorities and parishioners near Meinheim, for example, came to the support of Johann Fröschlein in 1525 when his evangelical sympathies got him into trouble with the bishop of Eichstätt. Fröschlein refused to appear in Eichstätt: 'for I feared the use of force, and worried that I would not be allowed a hearing but rather immediately placed under arrest'.[8] A correspondence between Eichstätt and Ansbach worked out a compromise: the absent clergyman Leonhard Bart would let Fröschlein retain office for three years. But when the contract came to an end a Catholic man was empowered to exercise the office (4 February 1528). He made his way to Meinheim, where he was greeted by the parishioners (Fröschlein's relatives prominent among them): 'Pfaff, take yourself and your letter out of this village or we'll chop off your hands and feet. The Eichstätt clerics are no longer the patrons of our church; we know of other patrons.' Fröschlein remained in Meinheim until 1558.[9]

In most instances, neither the local parish commune nor the local patron exercised liberties of appointment. When Peter Hochmuther, pastor of Döhlau, protested in 1590 that the Rabenstein nobles had taken the church key from his daughter in an effort to bar him from the church (ultimately dismissing him altogether by 1596), the Kulmbach council made clear in the subsequent investigation that the power to dismiss or to appoint a clergyman, whatever the cause, was not within the purview of the nobility.[10] Rather, to paraphrase the regional official of Birkenfels, the margrave had exclusive right to present and invest the clergy, in keeping with his power to exercise high jurisdiction over his subjects.[11] As for election through the parish commune (*Gemeinde*), although it may have figured large in peasant demands during the

1525 uprising in other parts of Germany,[12] it found limited application in Brandenburg Ansbach-Kulmbach. The archival materials yielded eight occasions when the villagers forwarded or suggested a candidate, and, of these, five were met with a final rejection or discountenanced altogether. If the commune's proposal was approved, some sort of provision or justification accompanied the examiners' draft.[13] The Margrave and his councillors exercised conclusive control over the installation of the clergymen.

The question is thus raised: what was the quality of the clerical estate in the principality of Brandenburg Ansbach-Kulmbach in the sixteenth century? Bernard Vogler's study, *Le clergé protestant Rhénan au siècle de la Réforme (1555–1619)*, makes a number of observations about the Rhineland clergy which appear to hold true for much of Protestant Germany. First, concerning social origins: the majority of the first and second generation Protestant clergy were themselves the sons of clergymen. Vogler suggests in fact that this was encouraged by the authorities.[14] Aside from this 'clerical caste', a large proportion stemmed from modest 'bourgeois' households, covering a spectrum of stations, from mechants to artisans. On the other hand, both the nobility and the peasantry were poorly represented. Martin Brecht's study of Württemberg supports these findings.[15]

Another observation Vogler makes is that the vast majority of these clergymen had been educated at a university. In the Electoral Palatinate, by 1605, up to 90 per cent of the clergy spent some time at a university.[16] Compared with some areas of Germany this is comparatively high; nevertheless a university education was common. In Württemberg, of 2,700 clergymen of the sixteenth century, 1,779 (65 per cent) attended a university.[17] Of course such statistics must be weighed against the historical situation. It is unlikely that the standard of the clergy at the beginning of the century, when there was a dearth of candidates, was as high as the standard fifty years later. In Ernestine Saxony only 20–31 per cent of the first-generation clergy in the Altenburg district had attended a university.[18] As late as 1548 the pastor in Frauenthal (Kulmbach) was reported to have said: 'At the present time tailors, cobblers, and the like come forward and preach as priests and preachers, without understanding the Word of God.'[19] But generally by the end of the century, in line with the increase in the number of students attending university, the majority of Protestant clergy were university-educated.

Hermann Jordan's investigation of the clergy in Ansbach and Kulmbach yields the following figures: in 1540, 28 per cent of the clergy had attended a university; in 1560, the number rose to 32 per cent.[20] On the whole, using Matthias Simon's compilation of Ansbach clergymen (*Ansbachisches Pfarrerbuch*) as the source book, the trend in Ansbach would seem to reflect the picture described above. Over the course of the century, as the new faith became more secure, the educational quality of the clergy improved. A survey, categorised according to twenty-year periods, bears this out. There was a 25–30 per cent increase in the proportion of university-educated clergy from the decades 1520–40 to 1580–1600.[21] For the final decades, the number of parish clergymen that had matriculated at a university may have been as high as 80 per cent. The visitation returns (1580–91) from the Neustadt superintendency also reveal that at least 80 per cent of the parishes in this region had a university-educated pastor during that period.[22] The clergy of sixteenth-century Ansbach and Kulmbach, it would seem, had the educational qualifications to perform the tasks expected of them.

In order to measure the quality of the clergy once they were in office the researcher is left with the judgement of two sections of the populace: the higher clergy and the villagers. Even if the expectations of the former group were kept within reasonable bounds, they were unlikely to mention a local pastor unless he had fallen foul of the faith or the synodal ordinances. In the 1520s and 1530s many of the clergy were still Catholics; and if not Catholic, then half-hearted Protestants. The 1528 visitation counted (out of a total of 52) 21 as good, 13 as mediocre, 13 as bad, and 5 as very bad.[23] General appraisals do not surface again until the visitations had been established (from 1565 onward). As such it is not possible to trace the development of the clergy through the mid-section of the century; but it is clear that by the end of the century complaints from the higher clergy about the local pastors were rare. Although there were of course a few exceptions, the lack of citations in the visitation reports would suggest that the vast majority of the clergy had an adequate knowledge of the faith and were considered suitable incumbents.[24] As Justus Bloch, the Bayreuth superintendent, concluded in his 1572 report:[25]

For although they did not respond in the manner which the office and strict necessity demands, all of them, however (God be praised), have been found to be of good mind and understanding in the principal articles of our Christian religion and our faith as defined by Holy Writ and the Augsburg Confession.

Twenty years later the review was the same. The superintendents were generally satisfied with the level of learning and the theological make-up of the parish clergy.

The parishioners were also expected to evaluate their local pastors at least once a year. The visitations encouraged the officials of the village, or any number of parishioners (depending on the visitation process), to evaluate the life and learning of their pastor and forward the grievances they might have. In the larger towns, such as Bayreuth, this was done in the presence of a secular official. With the clergy absent from the room, he would take each person in hand and collate the results.[26] Again, on the whole, complaints about the pastor's performance of his religious duties were infrequent. The entire visitation progress of the 1576 Neustadt superintendency unearthed a single grievance – and this concerning his personal nature (*seltzamen und strittigen Kopffs halben*), nothing about the pastor in his office. This holds true for the other visitations in this region through to the end of the century. By far the most regular comment is 'no complaint at all about the pastor'. In 1579, of 23 parishes visited in the superintendency of Neustadt, two alone found fault.[27] The visitation protocol from Gunzenhausen tells the same story: 'It is very seldom that the representatives of the parish forward a complaint about their pastor. . . .'[28] In Kulmbach the vast majority of parishes were 'well satisfied with the life and teaching of the pastor'.[29] The results of a Bayreuth visitation (1592) might be taken as paradigmatic: eighteen of the clergymen received 'a good appraisal', 'a really good appraisal', or 'a very good appraisal', two 'a reasonable appraisal', while the pastor of Pegntiz alone was considered to be inadequate.[30]

Given the infrequency of complaints about a pastor's competence in office, it would seem that most parishioners thought that the Lutheran clergyman could perform the tasks they desired of him. Anticlericalism, perceived as a range of action directed against a pastor's theological or sacerdotal competence, was rare to non-existent in the rural parishes of Ansbach and Kulmbach in the sixteenth century. If a catalogue of ecclesiological misdeeds preceded, or followed upon, a set of grievances drafted against a clergyman, it was usually the derivative of a more pedestrian village quarrel or a legal disagreement.[31] Anticlericalism existed, but it was not an assault upon the church. Rural resistance to the Lutheran clergy in Ansbach and Kulmbach was roused in response to a perceived violation of standard village relations. This is most readily illustrated by examining a main point of contact between the new Lutheran church and the traditional filiation of parish affairs: the collection of dues, fees, and labour.

For the 1572 visitor of Kulmbach the equation was straightforward: 'For when there is not enough wealth to support the pastors (*pfahrgüter*), then preachers cannot be maintained; and when there are no sermons, then there is also no Word of God; and where there is no Word of God, there is no chance of salvation.'[32] The preaching of the Word required a trained clergy, and a trained clergyman required an income and a home. This was a fact of life whose sensibility had been compounded by the Reformation. Sources of income had been eliminated outright or atrophied with time – masses for the dead, foundations, cloisters, clerical offices. Adam Weiss, pastor of Crailsheim, wrote to Ansbach in 1528 describing the ill-effects religious change was having on his income. Since the introduction of the Lutheran faith into the principality, the income of the Crailsheim incumbent had declined by up to 130 Gulden, as previous sources of wealth such as mass offerings and foundation endowments were no longer available.[33] In another letter Weiss added in conclusion that he therefore found himself preaching the Gospel to the people at his own expense.[34] Clerical poverty was not new; but Weiss was certainly correct to point out that many of the foundation masses, *accidentia*, and feast days (previously a valuable source of income) had disappeared. Nor was this situation quick to improve. The Ansbach folklorist Karl-Sigismund Kramer's conclusion holds true for the entire sixteenth century: the poor pastor was the rule.[35] Reliant as he was upon the co-operation of the parishioners, the village clergyman was never in a position of financial security.

Attempts have been made to chart the rise and fall of clerical incomes in sixteenth-century Lutheran principalities.[36] Susan Karant-Nunn has surveyed the fortunes of the clergy in the Ernestine countryside; and it seems that, by degrees, their lot did in fact improve. But tallying a cross-section of salaries (as she notes) ignores the wider context. Incomes varied greatly: from cash to kind to labour service. The average cash salary in Ansbach and Kulmbach (taken from a composite of sixty-eight mid-century incomes) equalled roughly 50 Gulden – with figures ranging between 23 Gulden and 225.[37] No doubt the higher salary denotes a more lucrative post, but a cash income was only one part of the yearly intake. Moreover, even if the historian were granted full listings, there is no guarantee that this would represent the income of the pastor in real terms. Salaries varied from year to year, as the inspector in Gunzenhausen (1573/4) found to his dismay: 'It is impossible for me to know exactly the pastors' yearly income, and how much each has brought in from year to year.' The clergy were unhelpful, since they thought that an investigation worked to their disadvantage.[38] And of course the parishioners were likely to be very unhelpful, both in the drafting of the annual tally and in the actual distribution of the tithes. In Gunzenhausen, the residents harvested the crops – including the pastor's share – and meted out the ration according to their pleasure.[39]

Notwithstanding the uncertainty a quantification of the materials would present, however, there is no doubt that the first few generations of Lutheran pastors suffered financial hardship. The visitation returns are full of petitions for an increase or an addition to a salary. To cite select examples (amongst many): the Seibelsdorf incumbent was hard hit by the removal of the *opfergeld* (1583); the parishioners saw it as a continuation of Catholicism (*Babstisch grifflein*) and refused to pay.[40] The clergyman of Kurzen-altheim could not maintain his wife and four children on his salary without an increase.[41] The upkeep of the pastor of Joditz (1572) was so meagre that he was forced to catch fish and birds to sup-plement his diet.[42] Another pastor was forced to go door to door and beg.[43] Gerson Reis of Meinheim looked to the Jews for a loan in his need.[44] Mainstockheim's Erhard Döberlein suggested in a sermon that while costs continued to rise, the desire amongst the parishioners to pay had declined:[45]

> The preachers these days must have more income than before, since everything is nearly three times more expensive now than it was ten years (or less) ago; and, moreover, the people are no longer as charitable as those people were when the Gospel was first broadcast.

For almost nothing, or very little, is being given to the preachers these days.

Döberlein's lament on the expensive times was a common one. Many supplications begin with 'in these dear years' or 'during these bleak, expensive times'. And indeed it was not just rhetoric. During the course of the sixteenth century the population in Franconia rose, food demand increased, prices doubled and trebled, while the salaries of the middling professions (especially one so precarious as that of a clergyman) remained fixed.[46] This mirrored a general trend in the German-speaking lands, where the onset of inflation influenced the price of basic foodstuffs, such as rye and grain, to the detriment of many rural inhabitants.[47] A tight budget, or 'bad economy', could affect the pastor in office. 'The economy hinders him [the pastor of Mistelgau] and other pastors in the countryside in their studies' was the conclusion of a Kulmbach visitor.[48]

With the visitation of 1528 the margrave instructed the regional officials to inspect the parishes and the clergymen within their jurisdiction.[49] In the visitation which followed (1536) the directives were more explicit: the financial state of the parish and the condition of the church became objects of inquiry.[50] Two years later a large-scale investigation took place in Kulmbach. In that year George the Pious wrote to the mayors and councillors of Hof, Bayreuth, Kulmbach, and Wunsiedel instructing them to aid the efforts of Heinrich Blechschmidt, who had been ordered 'to establish a register [Salbuch] and make a record of the foundations [die Spitall] and churches which have special rents and assets, and also of their old conventions and privileges'.[51] This seems to have followed a general effort in 1538 to inventory the wealth of church property in both principalities.[52] With the advent of visitations (1565) it was then possible to inspect the financial condition of the parishes (underhaltung, gepeu) on a yearly basis.[53] To add to this, administrators of local cloisters were instructed to visit dependent parishes and inspect the church buildings. It seems that the first few years after 1565 was the period in which a serious programme of inspection began. A letter (1569) to the administrator of Feuchtwangen indicates that a widespread effort was being made to keep track of the condition of the residences.[54]

In order to supplement an income or buttress a crumbling

residence the margrave had recourse to two basic sources of wealth: the parish itself – the church fund, the tithes, the defunct votive masses – or an external source, such as a neighbouring cloister or foundation. The confiscation of local masses and endowments was treated with some circumspection at first. Since the church ordinances do not go into detail about the fate of endowments, it seems that each was incorporated according to local conditions or needs. 'In time they were probably incorporated into the *Grosse Almosen* or elsewhere into the common chest. Otherwise, the state treasury incorporated them when there was no longer an interested party.'[55] By 1536 it was expected that the towns would have a common chest; most endowments merged with this central fund. Both this fund and the church buildings were managed at the local level by laymen – the churchwardens – as they were before the Reformation. These men went under the title of *Heiligenpfleger* or *Gotteshausmeister* and were called to answer to the visitation commission. In general the Reformation did not uproot the existing system of endowments, but rather integrated the funds and benefices into the new ecclesiastical system.[56]

On a grander scale the Reformation brought with it the secularisation of the cloisters and the confiscation of their wealth. The Benedictine cloister of Wülzburg, already in a state of moral and administrative disarray, fell under the sway of Casimir as early as 1523. Using the Peasants' War as justification for his intervention, Casimir ordered a similar inventory of all of the cloisters in Ansbach. He promised that the wealth would be returned after the war, as it was just a precautionary measure. George the Pious was uncertain about this matter when he entered rule in 1528. George wrote to Luther for suggestions. Luther advised that the cloisters be left in relative peace until the last of the Catholic clergy died out (reception of novices was correspondingly forbidden). Luther agreed that the wealth might be used for religious ends (scholarships, schools), but the foundations should not be rent to the ground. In 1529 the margrave ordered an inventory. Through this strategy the cloisters were gradually emptied and the wealth put to use. Evangelical preachers lectured to the remaining members and the 1533 church ordinance was introduced. Administration (in most instances) was managed by a margravial official, though an abbot or prior might stay on if he worked in the same capacity. These men were often consulted when it was necessary to repair a neighbouring residence or supplement a pastor's income.[57]

Thus the margraves did have a stock of ecclesiastical funds at their disposal; some of it was the inheritance of the mediaeval system of dues and endowments, some of it was appropriated after the introduction of the evangelical faith. All of it, however, was reliant upon the participation of the parishioners if it were to be raised or implemented effectively at the local level. It remains to be seen whether the reform of clerical maintenance was helped or hindered by the rural inhabitants; and whether these problems, if they existed, could be overcome.

A dispute which surfaced in 1568 may serve to shape the context of the following discussion. On 15 September of that year a group of neighbouring parishes drafted a note of complaint. Emphasising their poverty, they claimed that some clergymen had incomes to equal those of the nobility; and one pastor in particular, whose parish (they insisted) would maintain three or four incumbents, wanted to build a house to match his wealth: 'for he proposes to have a castle and not a pastor's house'. To add to this, he continued to use their wood for his alchemy, insulted them from the pulpit, denied them the sacrament, and wished an infamous illness upon them (*frantzossen kranckheijdt*). At the conclusion of the draft, they asked for a new pastor.[58]

The superintendent of Kulmbach ordered a resident official (*Forstmeister*) to investigate the matter, and an inquiry soon followed. It was then revealed that the complaint stemmed from the parish of Neudrossenfeld, directed against the clergyman Kaspar Günther. But most of the accusations against Günther were waved aside. To the charge that Günther should be the object of discontent, the official's initial reaction was one of suspicion. He put it down to the machinations of 'a number of fiendish people, of whom one is not certain what belief they are'.[59] Another official (*Kastner*) Desiderius Hedler of Wunsiedel also cleared Günther of all blame. And with regard to the issue of the house and the income: the parish was far from lucrative, as Günther was expected to support a chaplain on a salary that did not extend beyond 130 Gulden. Hedler suggested an investigation, to bring the 'Authors of this conspiracy' to justice as an example for the rest. The nobleman German von Wirsberg also expressed his concern over the 'poisoned' letter and gave Günther a very good reference.[60] The super-intendent absolved Günther of all blame.

If he was a suitable pastor, or at least innocent of the faults placed before the authorities, what then was the motivation behind the accusations ranged at Günther? In an earlier deposition (23 July 1568) Günther pointed his finger at a small clique of outlying villagers who refused to help in the construction of the parsonage. This defiance continued, despite the previous margravial orders to the contrary, and the fact that they had been punished for an earlier refusal. In the words of a participant, they stood fast as sworn brothers (*geschworne Brüder*) against the pastor.[61] This union of inhabitants believed that the construction of the house – more specifically the aid they were to supply – was detrimental to, or at least in contravention of, their traditional rights. An earlier copy of the complaint (9 December 1567) illustrates the problem:[62]

> Each village community complains strongly that such a condition should be introduced by this pastor; which, to the best of their knowledge, has never been done by any pastor before; and (more especially) nor have the parishioners in the past ever been burdened or troubled with the construction of the pastor's residence.

In the past each minister, so claimed this league of 'conspirators', had set aside a small store of money for construction as a type of fabric fund. The parishioners feared that Günther's novel demands would take permanent root, thus entering the cycle of annual dues and labour services extended to the church, many of which had been opposed during the Peasants' War of 1525. Resistance built up to the plan, until some parishioners were meeting in the local inn discussing alternative possibilities. An inquisition confirmed the picture painted by Günther.[63] Two or three neighbouring communities had set themselves against the pastor; the other parishioners could do nothing. Once these men had committed themselves to resisting Günther's demands, they then won over other members of the parish, and not without resorting to threats.[64] The authorities responded to this knowledge by promising to punish the ringleaders and re-imposing the former demands. Associated documentation ends in the year 1568.

A series of related issues emerges from this dispute. There is no doubt that a few parishioners of Neudrossenfeld opposed the impositions simply because they did not want to pay. But two observations of more general application can be adduced from this quarrel that are worth making. First, the Lutheran authorities were often forced to impose material change on to a community of inhabitants still in thrall to the immutability of nature. Raw materials were available in limited quantity; the regeneration of wood and farm land occurred at a slow, uncertain rate in accord with seasonal rhythms. Labour, at the same time, its yields and its demands, was fixed. The dynamics of distribution, that is the degree of yearly fluctuation experienced in a regular lifetime, was largely serene: 'a faithful execution of traditional ways in this sphere helped to create a moral atmosphere within the more practical dimensions of tradition which could maintain their force.'[65] That Günther should make unprecedented demands was not only an inconvenience, and a violation of custom and right,[66] but an infraction against the moral order. His status as a Lutheran pastor did not grant him the right to demand more from the parish without offering something in return. The parishioners thought as Desiderius Hedler suspected: 'I believe however that the godless peasants focussed their attack to this end: that this or any other pastor should be paid according to the sermon, like the artisans according to the piece or the daily wage, and no more.'[67]

Secondly, while a demand for income or labour may have precipitated a quarrel, there were often underlying tensions and unresolved disputes that flamed into being as a result. Such was the case in Neudrossenfeld. Günther claimed that the very same people who first rallied against him were those who had been punished five years earlier because of their recourse to a wise woman. Günther had then refused them confession, and an extended quarrel followed.[68] Like some of the clergy who suffered attacks of anticlericalism for their devotion to office, Günther may have experienced a similar fate. (One witness testified that he was too diligent.) The attempt to rebuild Günther's house, and the unprecedented demands it evinced, gave rise to a dispute which was soon subsumed under the logic of long-term local discontent. The Lutheran authorities may have mounted large-scale efforts to reform clerical maintenance, but each parish, with its distinct concerns, was the context in which they would take hold.

In order for the authorities to effect reconstruction or add to a pastor's salary it was thus often necessary – as the example of Neudrossenfeld illustrates – to overcome deeply embedded animosities and an innate aversion to change, all shaped by local subtraditions of regulation and concession. But what was the nature of this resistance? Was the opposition directed at the church or the state? How were the practical problems of construction and income additions overcome? And is it possible to assess the effort to reform clerical maintenance in general terms?

Despite the opposition to tithes during the 1525 Peasants' War (on the basis that tithes could not be justified by Scripture and were thus human invention), this line of defence did not play a role in the tithe disputes later in the century. True, in 1524 opposition to tithes in Nuremberg's territorial lands had become a source of concern for the council, who were ultimately forced to abolish the collection of tithes during the revolt (1525). But this was a period of violence spurred, in no small part, by clerical preaching against tithes.[69] The lands of Ansbach and Kulmbach were affected in the same manner. But again this should come as no surprise, given the overtly anti-tithe stance of the pamphlet literature and the peasant manifestos like the Twelve Articles.[70] This sentiment appears to have ended with the war itself. The visitation of 1528 revealed tithe disputes, but on each occasion the peasants withheld the tithe only when the pastor did not resume or acknowledge traditional services.[71] This remained the form of justification throughout the sixteenth century. There is no evidence to suggest that the evangelical faith, with its emphasis on Holy Writ, engendered a new attitude towards the payment of the tithe, or its non-payment, amongst the peasantry in Brandenburg Ansbach-Kulmbach.

An analysis of extant tithe disputes bears this out. In Oberferrieden (1491) the parishioners were unwilling to pay a tithe on lambs, since it 'is not a convention from the past' (*von alter nit als herkommen sei*). In 1575, when a quarrel over clerical income resurfaced, it was settled by reference to the 1491 contract. All forms of payment remained constant 'aside from the Papal superstitions and mass'; there was no attempt to diminish the pastor's income with reference to a law outside of the original agreement.[72] Repeatedly, tithe disagreements were contested with recourse to an original (often pre-Reformation) contract. The parishioners would justify their refusal, as at Frommetsfelden in 1571, on the basis of a written agreement, an 'old sealed letter established one hundred years before'.[73] Parishioners of Hechlingen (1575) went so far as to refuse certain tithes when their original (1448) sealed contract was at hand; whenever it was thought to be lost, however, they would render up dues without resistance.[74] In general, when the tithe in Ansbach and Kulmbach was refused or contested – and these occasions were few – it was not the object of a theological or specifically evangelical discourse. Both the parishioners and the clergymen sought the justifying presence of custom, tradition, or the more powerful endorsement of a margravial contract. For all parties involved, a tithe dispute was a local concern; it had specific legal and temporal reference, and nothing to do (in the first instance) with God's Word.[75]

In the majority of cases, conflict between the pastor and the parish – including antagonism that was strongly 'anticlerical' in tone – stemmed from a disagreement over custom or the payment of fees. The issue of maintenance worked as a catalyst; it was the root cause of peasant resistance and the seed of further (often unrelated) discord. Events in Hechlingen demonstrate how a desire to defend parish rights (against the encroaching demands of the Lutheran church) might be disguised beneath an ulterior logic. When the clergyman Michael Von Castell first brought a tithe dispute in Hechlingen to the attention of the authorities in 1525, the contest revolved round a plot of common land. Apparently some members of the parish would not pay tithes on it, seeking refuge in the alleged immunity granted them by the 'contents and writ of an old letter'.[76] In fact the very reason that the dispute arose in 1525 at all was the rediscovery of this letter. The matter was momentarily put to rest; but in 1532 the new incumbent complained, and then again in 1556. As before, it was the rediscovery of the letter that gave rise to a conflict. Before the unearthing of this document the tithe appears to have been paid; but 'when the letter was once again uncovered they gave no more tithes'.[77] More to the point: the dispute dealt exclusively with the right of the clergyman in relation to a margravial contract.

In 1574, when the conflict resurfaced, a new language of defence was at work. On 29 July 1574 a deposition was presented against the pastor Christoph Planck. Although the central issue was still the tithes, other themes now entered the dialogue. A tithe dispute dealt with the quality of the pastor in office and his suitability in relation to the expectations of the faith.[78] Most damaging of all, it was claimed that the principal task of the clergyman – to preach the Word – was abused in his hands. His alleged habit of using the Gospel for dishonourable ends worried the parishioners. The deposition ended with the lament that the parishioners feared that the honour of God and the ministry would be discredited if the quarrel persisted.[79] At the latter end of the century, it was not unusual for parish complaints against the clergymen to deploy this strategy: irrespective of the real issue under dispute the pastor was measured against the backdrop of the Lutheran faith and the expectations of his office.[80] This is, in a backhanded way, testimony to the impact of the Reformation. But beneath many such disputes, especially those involving the parish commune, the essential concern remained the same (as they did for Hechlingen): tithes, fees, and dues rendered to maintain the clergy. The point to be made is this: that the reform of clerical maintenance was not peripheral to the process of confessionalisation, but fundamental in relation to its aims.

James C. Scott, in his work on peasant resistance, has identified a strategem behind this reluctance to pay fees. Scott entitles it 'resistance without protest', or 'everyday acts of peasant resistance' which he views, over the long term, as more deleterious to the appropriating classes than explosions of discontent, like rebellions or mass movements. The most damaging type of tithe resistance occurred in the forms of flight, evasion, misreporting, false declaration, fraud, concealment, and noncompliance. And more significantly, often this violation of a tax, rent, or property became a custom or tradition, acquiring an authority of its own.[81] This gradual transmutation of resistance into custom hardened the parish mind to reform or correction. In Ansbach and Kulmbach, the consequence was complex discord between the pastor and the parish. Such a mentality, in concert with the increase in population, denuded woodlands and clearings (plus the restrictions placed upon them by the nobility), the general economic malaise, and the complex of underlying social relations suggested above, made the effort to improve clerical maintenance difficult.[82] How then did the authorities overcome these problems?

The margave could approach the reform of maintenance from two angles. He could effect improvement from within, keeping a check on the management of funds within the parish; and he could impose order from above, at the expense of local traditions of rule.

In order to secure an addition, the clergyman would either

submit an application to a higher official (secular or spiritual) or he would send his request directly to Ansbach. Upon reception, an inquiry was made by the regional official to determine whether the increase could be shouldered through parish funds, or whether it had to be raised from an external source. If the latter, the money from a local foundation might be used and integrated into the wealth of the church fund. These small foundations, sometimes in the form of a chapel, were generally used *ad pias causas* in accordance with the Peace of Augsburg (1555). They were not ravaged and destroyed for secular ends; but with the original purpose lost, they fell prey to the erosion of time and neglect, either disappearing altogether or assimilated into the church. In other instances, if the request was approved, a neighbouring cloister might be expected to raise the money. It was not unusual at the end of the century for the cloister administrators to plead poverty to the demands stemming from the chancellery.[83] But whatever method was used, the addition was joined with the parish funds, and together these were managed by the wardens of the church.

The visitation returns are littered with complaints about the management of parish funds. The fund itself might be very meagre, composed of what was collected during services.[84] Equally the church fund (*Gotteshaus*) might be in debt; or indeed parishioners themselves might owe the church large sums of money.[85] Patrons interfered with the audit, thinking that the wealth was under their care. In the chapter of Gunzenhausen parish funds fell to the management of men ranging from the officials of Gunzenhausen, the superintendent, Eichstätt officials, the regional official of Hohentrüdingen, the administrators of Heidenheim and Ansbach, or, in the case of Windsfeld (a *freidorff*), the parishioners alone.[86] It was quite common for the pastor to be excluded from the yearly audit altogether, despite the margravial warnings to the contrary.[87] A very common complaint was that the caretakers of the church fund were using the money for their own ends. A report from Langenzenn (1584), to cite an example, made it clear to the margrave: '[that] we must assume from this that they [the wardens] would fain want to have, as has happened up to now, a free hand with provisions and other things – which, however, is in no way to be permitted to them.'[88]

To counter such licence, the margrave specified that yearly audits should take place. Although the 1536 visitation ordered inspection of the common chests, it was not until the visitations of 1565 that an annual inspection threatened the churchwardens to any real degree.[89] In 1578 the Chapter Ordinance commissioned the superintendents to investigate whether the churchwardens handled the church funds with honesty, and whether they made the requisite repairs to ailing parish buildings (which would include the church, the pastor's residence, and the school).[90] By 1594 the margrave expected that the elected representatives in charge of the parish fund would keep an orderly register of all income and expenses, which they would then present before the visitors every year.[91] Abuses continued despite this crusade; but it is one measure of the effort made to reform the management of parish funds that the complaints brought forward in the visitations rarely repeat themselves from year to year. Of the available examples of such abuse after 1565 (from the visitation returns), in each instance the local official was ordered to correct the situation. Parish liberties were severely curtailed.

But it was not always feasible to regulate matters from within the parish. In the case of a reconstruction, or a sizeable increase in a clerical salary, the margrave and his officials were forced to intervene directly. In this situation, reform was imposed on the parish, not coerced from the parish officials. Three cases that emerged in the year 1562 illustrate the nature and extent of this intervention.

In July 1562, upon the conclusion of the visitation, the secular officials of Uffenheim had been commissioned to inspect the condition of the residences in Langensteinach and Adelhofen. The officials inspected the church funds (*heijligen*) of both villages, and found that neither could support the proposed reconstruction. Ansbach acknowledged this state of affairs; and it was then suggested that the cloister of Heilsbronn (which exercised patronage) should supply the needed support for Langensteinach. The abbot was ordered to render up the appropriate building materials and expense from the cloister's stores. This money was to be given to the warden who was also to ensure that expenses were kept to a minimum. In response to the directives, the administrator of Heilsbronn protested that the cloister had no available funds. Instead, he suggested that the cloister's woodlands be used to supply the materials, which could be had for minimal expense and fuss.[92] Ansbach followed this advice, and the council delegated a member of the parish to oversee the construction and to keep a listing of all expenses.[93] In Adelhofen the wealth was gathered from local foundations. The official was to keep a record of all transactions; in addition, he was to inspect the buildings on a yearly basis, and indeed all parish buildings within the compass of his district.

One year later in another parish, pastor Andreas Trebel of Münchenaurach wrote to Ansbach requesting repairs to his 'very small and meagre' quarters. A cloister official inspected the building, in the company of a group of men versed in the construction trade, and recommended repairs which would run to 40 Gulden.[94] Negotiations continued for the next few years over the construction of a cellar, but it was not until 1587 that the possibility of reconstruction was once again countenanced. As before, the cloister official assessed the house as in need of repair; it should be built from scratch, he added, and the expense must be supplied from margravial coffers, since the parish in question had no independent income.[95] Blueprints were drawn up by the cloister administrator, along with estimates. According to the report, this residence had been visited in the past by the regional official of Cadolzburg, an authority from Ansbach, and the chief engineer (*Bawmeister*) himself.[96] Ansbach gave the orders to rebuild in June 1588. The construction was to take place in line with the proposals drafted at court; the parishioners were to help with shipment and repairs.[97] As the parish was home to subjects of Eichstätt and Ernst von Crailsheim, some of the outlying hamlets (*eingepfarte*) resisted, pleading poverty; later the parishioners of Münchenaurach themselves protested that such service was not possible, that it would force them into beggary. Indeed, the regional official of Cadolzburg supported their objections, suggesting that neighbouring subjects of the cloister be inducted for the task.[98] But Ansbach was unmoved; the parishioners were forced to assist. In 1589 the house was largely completed, and the following year a detailed inventory was taken, exposing to the glare of the authorities the use, and misuse, of funds in Münchenaurach.[99]

Also in the year 1562, as Johannes Schmidt of Offenbau hoped for an increase in his salary, measures were taken to rebuild his house. Explicit instructions from the chancellery outlined the progress: all of the parishioners were to help with transport and construction; 45 Gulden was provided from an ecclesiastical source.

But the villagers themselves had to effect reconstruction.[100] The sources fall silent about the rebuilding. However, in 1576 the parish of Offenbau wrote a letter of complaint about Schmidt.[101] They claimed that he was involved in a dispute with an Italian merchant (*ein welscher mit einer Khram*). They asked for peace between the two men. Another supplication, also directed against Schmidt, later accused him of letting the residence fall into disrepair. It seems that this second accusation was in part the dénouement of a latent power struggle within the parish.[102] The parishioners had refused to help the pastor from at least 1574 onwards. By 1585 another supplication from the pastor spoke of a crumbling residence; he said in 1587 that a new stable had been necessary for fourteen years.[103] Ansbach mounted an investigation. Difficulties were multiplied as some of the parishioners answered to foreign authorities. All of the neighbouring subjects were listed (of five different lords); the church fund was assessed. In 1592 the directives went out to rebuild. In order to overcome the poverty of the church fund, and to ensure that the village quarrel would not preclude reconstruction, a local tax was introduced (*paw steür*) and the responsibility of repair was placed directly upon the parish.

In each of the cases cited above, the margrave was able to facilitate reform of clerical maintenance by shifting the locus of control from the parish to the chancellery or to one of its district appendages. The very process of investigation and correction defused the impediments that hampered reform. If a pastor needed an addition to his income an official was sent to the parish, tithes were catalogued, church funds were assessed, village rights, prerogatives, customs, and claims were established – and all of this was done by a margravial official, who then inherited the annual job of scrutinizing the parish audit. If a church building had to be repaired or rebuilt, the church was inspected, supplies were sought, first from within the parish, and then from a neighbouring foundation; once the construction began, it was supervised by a cloister official, a district authority, or a parish resident. But the direction of the process was in the hands of the margrave. The parishioners were given specific duties; if they resisted, their legal status was investigated; if a village quarrel hindered progress, an investigation was mounted or a solution was proposed (like the above building tax) which could, by its very nature, circumnavigate local disputes. This, as the authorities observed in 1570, was not a legacy of the past, but a recent innovation.[104] The process was slow, often punctuated with years of inactivity or resistance; but a start had been made and a policy was in motion. The Reformation in Ansbach and Kulmbach brought with it a greater degree of supervision and control over the parish church and the maintenance of its servants.

These observations lend some credence to the notion of confessionalisation. The territorial church in this principality did have a suitable clerical estate; the authorities did take concrete steps to improve income and housing; the margravial officials did intervene into local affairs and defuse resistance to fees and dues. In this sense, the Reformation imposed itself upon the parishioners in Ansbach and Kulmbach in the sixteenth century. But this was only one aspect of the movement; and the regulation of parish wealth was only one step (if fundamental) in the process of religious change. In many ways, an analysis of the reform of clerical maintenance obscures as much as it reveals. The Lutheran authorities were able to staff the rural parishes with a working clerical estate; but their efforts often unleashed considerable resistance. More to the point, it was resistance with its own logic, its own frames of perception and transformation. This type of dynamic makes it difficult to accept a static intellectualisation like confessionalisation without first qualifying the limits of its claims. For it is one thing to reform a parish economy; it is quite another thing to reform a human being.

Notes

1 See the summary and cited literature in Euan Cameron, *The European Reformation* (Oxford, 1991), pp. 208–72; 474–88.

2 This of course applies to the 'Reformation' (or Counter-Reformation) implemented by other confessions as well. See Walter Ziegler, 'Territorium und Reformation. Überlegungen und Fragen', *Historisches Jahrbuch*, 110 (1990), 52–75.

3 H. Schilling, 'Die Konfessionalisierung im Reich. Religiöser und gesellschaftlicher Wandel in Deutschland zwischen 1555 und 1620', *Historische Zeitschrift*, 246 (1988), 1–45; Ernst Walter Zeeden, *Konfessionsbildung: Studien zur Reformation, Gegenreformation und katholischen Reform* (Spätmittelalter & Frühe Neuzeit), 15 (Stuttgart, 1985), pp. 647–91. For a research report on *Konfessionsbildung* see Peter Thaddäus Lang, 'Konfessionsbildung als Forschungsfeld', *Historisches Jahrbuch*, 100 (1980), 479–93; Richard van Dülmen, 'Reformation und

Neuzeit. Ein Versuch', *Zeitschrift für Historische Forschung*, 14, 1 (1987), 1–25. See the similar theme developed by Gerhard Oestreich, 'Strukturprobleme des europäischen Absolutismus', in *Geist und Gestalt des frühmodernen Staates* (Berlin, 1969), pp. 179–197; R. Po-Chai Hsia, *Social Discipline in the Reformation. Central Europe 1550–1750* (London, 1989).

4 The two most detailed works on the early years of reform are still Karl Schornbaum, *Die Stellung des Markgrafen Kasimir von Brandenburg zur reformatorischen Bewegung in den Jahren 1524–1527* (Nuremberg, 1900); Karl Schornbaum, *Zur Politik des Markgrafen Georg von Brandenburg vom Beginne seiner selbständigen Regierung bis zum Nürnberger Anstand 1528–1532* (Munich, 1906). On the growth of the visitation and the church ordinances see Gerhard Müller and Gottfried Seebass, *Andreas Osiander d. Ä. Gesamtausgabe* (Gütersloh, 1979), III, pp. 123–79, IV, pp. 219ff., V, pp. 37ff. A final church ordinance was drafted in 1533.

5 Emil Sehling (ed.), *Die evangelischen Kirchenordnungen des XVI Jahrhunderts* (Tübingen, 1961), 2, I, (Bayern: Franken), pp. 90, 105.

6 Landeskirkliches Archiv Nürnberg (hereafter LKAN), Markgräfliches Konsistorium Ansbach (hereafter MKA), Spez. 14, fol. 19. 'wollest du auch dieser pfründt nutzung hinfuro hinderlegen bis uff fernern bescheid, und nymand nichts davon folgen lassen.'

7 LKAN, MKA, Spez. 720, fol. 19.

8 LKAN, MKA, Spez. 572, fol. 6. 'Ist nit zu verwundern, noch (als ich hoff) mir zuverweysen dann ich gewalt forchtet, und besorgt man würd mich nit zu verhor lassen kumen, sonder als bald in kessel gefangen liegen.'

9 LKAN, MKA, Spez. 572, fol. 23. 'pfaff, heb dich mit den brieffen aüss dem dorff, oder wir wollen dir hendt und füss abhawen, dan die pfaffen zü Eÿstett sein unser pfarkÿrchen nit mer lehenherren, sonder wir wissen ander lehenherren.' See Karl Schornbaum, 'Der Beginn der Reformation in Altmühltale', *Beiträge zur bayerischen Kirchengeschichte*, 16 (1910), 1–27.

10 LKAN, Markgräfliches Dekanat Hof, XX, 3, fol. 7. Letter from Kulmbach council 7 May 1596. Also fols 1–7.

11 LKAN, MKA, Spez. 655, 28 March 1560. 'Die presentation, aber, one mittel: desgleichüng aüch die Investirüng, wie Ich gedencke, gebürt E. f. g. von wegen der gaistlichen Jurisdiction, die E. f. g. in Iren herrschafften, Landen, und gebietten, von wegen der hohen obrigkeit, dits orts, *Ex decreto senatus Imperij*, haben.'

12 Peter Blickle, *Gemeindereformation. Die Menschen des 16. Jahrhunderts auf dem Weg zum Heil* (Munich, 1987), pp. 50ff.

13 LKAN, MKA, Spez. 1010, fols 40–2. Weiboldshausen 1574; LKAN, MKA, Spez. 443, fols. 23–5. Holtzhausen 1559; LKAN, MKA, Spez. 724, fols 82; 86–7. Rosstal 1546; LKAN, Markgräfliches Dekanat Langenzenn, 703, fol. 22. Cadolzburg 1581 and LKAN, MKA, Spez. 169, fols 90–101; LKAN, MKA, Spez. 813, 10 August 1556. As for the successful candidates: the examiners approved the choice of the parish Johann Reuter

('des lateins ungeübt') for the chaplaincy of Geilsheim since he was a 'dorffkind' and his functions would be limited – 'Aber wo es ein pfar were wolten wir nit bewilligen'. LKAN, MKA, Spez 346, fol. 23. 1551; equally Konrad Langer was approved in 1537 by Johann Rurer for the parish of Buch am Wald (despite his youth) because of the paucity of available clergyman ('sonderlich in solchem mangel der kirchendiener, so zu diesen zeiten wirt gespürt'). LKAN, MKA, Spez 135, fol. 12.

14 Bernard Vogler, *Le Clergé protestant Rhénan au siècle de la Réforme (1555–1619)* (Association des Publications pres les Universités Strasbourg, Paris, 1976), pp. 21; 18–21.

15 Martin Brecht, 'Herkunft und Ausbildung der protestantischen Geistlichen des Herzogtums Württemberg im 16. Jahrhundert', *Zeitschrift für Kirchengeschichte*, 80 (1969), 172–3; Cameron, *The European Reformation*, pp. 390–6.

16 Vogler, *Le Clergé protestant*, p. 57.

17 Brecht, 'Herkunft und Ausbildung', 170.

18 Susan C. Karant-Nunn, *Luther's Pastors: The Reformation in the Ernestine Countryside* (Transactions of the American Philosophical Society, 69, 1979), p. 19.

19 Cited in Hermann Jordan, *Reformation und gelehrte Bildung in der Markgrafschaft Ansbach-Bayreuth* (Quellen und Forschungen zur bayerischen Kirchengeschichte, 1, 1917), p. 299.

20 Cited in Bernard Klaus, 'Soziale Herkunft und theologische Bildung lutherischer Pfarrer der reformatorischen Frühzeit', *Zeitschrift für Kirchengeschichte*, 80 (1969), 45.

21 Calculated from a survey of 330 clergy, based upon the date when they took the clerical oath or entered office in the principality. Matthias Simon, *Ansbachisches Pfarrerbuch* (Einzelarbeiten aus der Kirchengeschichte Bayerns, Neustadt/Aisch, 1957). Simon's collection, though by his own acknowledgement far from comprehensive, would seem to increase Jordan's figures by some 20 per cent.

22 D. H. Clauß, 'Kirchenvisitation des 16. Jahrhunderts im Dekanat Neustadt a. A.', *Zeitschrift für bayerische Kirchengeschichte*, 9 (1934), 155–8.

23 Sehling, *Evangelischen Kirchenordnungen*, p.115.

24 Clauß, 'Kirchenvisitation des 16. Jahrhunderts', 158. 'Die Pfarreien sind alle besetzt, und die Geistlichen erhalten im Allgemeinen das Lob einer treuen und tüchtigen Amtsführung.'

25 LKAN, Superintendentur Kulmbach (Hereafter MSK) 157, *Bericht der Spetial Visitation, In der Süperintendentz Beÿrreüth Ao 1572*. fol. 3. 'Dan obwoln bej allen, nicht der gestaldt Respondiret, wie es woll das ampt, und hohe Nottürft erfordern, sind sie doch alle, beÿ rechtem Sinne, und verstandt, der fürnembsten Artikel unserer Christlichen Religion, und glaübens, Nach Inhaldt der haÿligen schrift, und Aügspürgischen Confession Gott lob erfunden.'

26 Staatsarchiv Bamberg (hereafter StaB), C2 1823, fol. 31. The clergy reported how, once back in the room following their exit, 'ist uns angezeigt worden, das der herr amptman von person zü personen die vota,

unser lehr und lebens halben, colligiert: und seÿ aller seites . . . weder lehr noch lebens halben kein mangel noch beschwer fürkommen . . .'.

27 Staatsarchiv Nürnberg (Hereafter StaN), *Ansbacher Neues Generalrepertorium*, Nr 49, rep. nr 103e. fol 14; 1576–94 passim.

28 Lic. Clauss, 'Aus Gunzenhäuser Visitationsakten des 16. Jahrhunderts', *Beiträge zur bayerischen Kirchengeschichte*, 3 (1925), 102.

29 LKAN, MSK, 157, passim.

30 StaB, C2 1823 1592 Bayreuth Visitation, passim.

31 Anticlericalism of this nature is discussed in further detail in C. Scott Dixon, 'The Reformation in the Parishes: Attempts to Implement Religious Change in Brandenburg Ansbach-Kulmbach 1528–1603' (Cambridge University Ph.D. Diss., 1992), pp. 93ff.

32 LKAN, MSK 157, fol. 12. (my pagination).

33 StaN, Ansbacher Religionsakten III, Tom. XI, Fols. 39–41. 'Es ist gn. f. und h. abgangen ierlichs einkümens (an opfer, todten gelt, sambt anderm, welchs nün durch verkundigung gottlichs worts gefallen) aller jar mer dann hundert und dreissig gulden, die ain pfarrher zu Crailßhaim weniger hat itzo dann vor, und aber ietz gelerter Capellan vil mehr zu teglichem predigen dan bey vorigem geringem meßhalten mir zu haben von note ist.' Weiss had to maintain two chaplains.

34 StaN, *Ansbacher Religionsakten* III, Tom. III, fols 297–8: 'In sümma Ich hab noch bißher denen von Crailßheim das Evangelion vergebens und schier uff mein Kosten gepredigt.'

35 Karl-Sigismund Kramer, *Volksleben im Fürstentum Ansbach und seinen Nachbargebeiten 1500–1800* (Veröffentlichungen der Gesellschaft für Frankische Geschichte, 15, 1961), p. 166. 'Das Bewußtein, den Pfarrer am Gängelband führen zu können, weil man seinen Gehalt aufbringt, überdauerte noch manches Jahrzehnt.'

36 Vogler, *Le Clergé protestant*, pp. 149–89; Karant-Nunn, *Luther's Pastors*, pp. 39–53; Susan K. Boles, 'The Economic Position of Lutheran Pastors in Ernestine Thuringia 1521–1555,' *ARG*, 63 (1972), 94–125.

37 StaB, C3 1229, passim.

38 LKAN, Markgräfliches Dekanat Gunzenhausen (Hereafter MDG) 71, fols 54–6. The clergy believed 'das Inen solche nachforschüng mehr züm nachthail, dan zw Iren nütz geschehe'.

39 LKAN, MDG 71, fol. 20. 'Auch haben die Bürger alhie ein braüch, oder wie sie sagen, ein gerechtigkeit aüff der pfarr, das so dem pfarrer sein zehendt getreidt gefelt, sie also balde mit den secken sich versammeln, das korn, aüch wider den willen eines pastorn, hinweg nemen, machen ein aufschlag wie sie wollen, den bezaln sie aüff ein ernante zeÿt bößlich, und mußsich ein pfarrer vil mit Inen mieten: kan ein pfarrer sich seines einkommens nit vil bessern.'

40 LKAN, MSK, 133, *Antwort uff des Herren Decani schreiben. pfarhers zu Seijwolßdorff den 11. Decemb.* [1583] fol. 8 (my pagination).

41 LKAN, MDG 71, fol. 8.

42 LKAN, MDH, V 1a, fol. 64.

43 LKAN, MSK, 157, Lehenthal 1573.

44 LKAN, MDG 71, fol. 81.

45 LKAN, MKA, Spez. 564, Fol. 96. 'Es müssen zwar die p[re]diger itziger zeit mehr und grösser besoldung haben, den züvor, seitemal alles fast 3 mal so theüer ist, als vor 10 oder wenig jaren gewesen: und sind die zühorer nicht mehr so wolthetig, als die ienigen waren, do das [Evangelium] züerst anging. den fast nichts oder gar wenig den p[re]digen [sic] zu dieser zeit gegeben wirt.'

46 Rudolf Endres, 'Zur wirtschaftlichen und sozialen Lage in Franken vor dem Dreißigjährigen Krieg', *Jahrbuch für Fränkische Landesforschung*, 28 (1968), 5–52; Herms Bahl, Wilhelm Otto Keller, and Karl-Ludwig Löffler, 'Ansbachs wirtschaftliche Situation in der zweiten Hälfte des 16. Jahrhunderts und die Almosenordnung von 1581', in *Ansbach – 750 Jahre Stadt* (Ansbach, 1971), pp. 65–83.

47 Compare Thomas Robisheaux, *Rural Society and the Search for Order in early Modern Germany* (Cambridge, 1989), pp. 148–9. See Wilhelm Abel, *Agrarkrisen und Agrarkonjunktur*(Hamburg, 1966), pp. 113ff.

48 LKAN, MSK, 157, Mistelgau 1578/9.

49 Karl Schornbaum, *Aktenstücke zur ersten Brandenburgischen Kirchenvisitation 1528* (Einzelarbeiten aus der Kirchengeschichte Bayerns, 10, 1928), p. 41.

50 Sehling, *EvangelischenKirchenordnungen*, p. 318.

51 StaB, C3 1223, fol. 20 'Mittwoch nach Michaelis 1538'.

52 StaB, C3 1223, fol. 18.

53 Sehling, *Evangelischen Kirchenordnungen*, p. 351.

54 LKAN, Markgräfliches Dekanat Feuchtwangen (hereafter MDF), 1, no. 15, 10 January 1569. 'Obwohl von dem dürchleüchtigen hochgebornen fürsten unserm gnedigen herrn, Marggraf Geörg Friderichen züerbaüüng und besserung der pfarr und pfründtheüser die verschinen Jhar uber, grosser uncost ufgewendet, und aüch daraüf von Iren f. g. allenthalben in die Embter bevelch gethün worden, das solch pfarr und pfründtheüser Jhärlich besichtigt werden, und solch einsehen geschehen soll, damit dieselben von den kirchendienern in Beülichen wesen erhalten werden das wir doch täglich erfharen, wann gleich an etlichen ortten die pfarrheüser oder andere gebew, aintweder von Neüem gebaüet, oder sünsten nach aller nottürfft widerümb zügerichtet worden sein.'

55 Hans Liermann, 'Protestant Endowment Law in the Franconian Church Ordinances', in L. P. Buck and J. W. Zophy (eds), *The Social History of the Reformation* (Columbus, OH, 1972), pp. 345–6.

56 Liermann, 'Protestant Endowment Law in the Franconian Church Ordinances', p. 351.

57 Karl Schornbaum, 'Die Säkularisation des Klosters Wülzburg', *Sammelblatt des Historischen Vereins Eichstätt*, 24 (1909), 1–18; Karl Schornbaum, *Die Stellung des Markgrafen Kasimir von Brandenburg zur Reformation Bewegung in den Jahren 1524–1527*, pp. 8–10; Karl Schornbaum, 'Zur Klostersäkularisation des Markgrafen Kasimir', *Beiträge zur bayerischen Kirchengeschichte*, 10 (1904), 129–140; Johann Baptist Götz, *Die Glaubensspaltung im Gebiete der Markgrafschaft Ansbach-Kulmbach in den Jahren 1520–1535* (Erläuterungen und Ergänzungen zu Janssens Geschichte des Deutschen Volkes, vol. 5, 3/4, 1907),

pp. 185–202; Hans Westermayer, *Die Brandenburgisch-Nürnbergische Kirchenvisitation und Kirchenordnung 1528–1533* (Erlangen, 1894), pp. 61ff.; Georg Muck, *Beiträge zur Geschichte von Kloster Heilsbronn* (Ansbach, 1859), pp. 131–139; R. G. Stillfried, *Kloster Heilsbronn* (Berlin, 1877), pp. 25–30.

58 StaB, C3 1223, *Süpplication Etlicher gemainden im Ambt Culmbach und Bayreuth von wegen allerley beschwerüng wider Ihren (doch unbenanten) pfarrern* fols. 90–3.

59 StaB, C3 1223, fols 94–7. 19 October 1568. He later spoke in a more limited sense of 'redleinpfarer', but the premise remained the same: 'das er [Günther] von seinen Rebellischen pfarkindern des ungründs beschüdigt wirdet'.

60 StaB, C3 1223, fols 94–9. 25 October 1568; 100–1. 13 October 1568.

61 StaB, C3 1223, fols 107–8.

62 StaB, C3 1223, fols 123–6.

63 StaB, C3 1223, *Aüssage Ettlicher Personen in genümener Inqüisition den Pferrherr zü Drosenfeldt und seine Pfarrkhinder betreffent*, fols 143–154.

64 As a Heinz of Waldau testified: 'Er thüe nicht gern wieder den Pfarrer, habe sich aber nicht dürffen von der gemeinde sondern, dan sie sich gegen ettlichen vernomen laßen, so sich von Ihnen in diesen bösen handel absondern wollen, Ihnen die gemeinde züverbieten, und Ihre heüser zu vermachen, oder züverschlagen'. StaB, C3 1223, Fol. 148.

65 Michael R. Mauss, 'Folklore as an Ethnographic Source: A "Mise au Point"', in Jacques Beauroy, Marc Bertrand, Edward T. Gargan (eds), *The Wolf and the Lamb: Popular Culture in France* (Stanford French and Italian Studies, 3, 1977), p. 118.

66 This was clearly a concern. For example the fear that 'es möchte ihnen iherlich zw einer gerechtigkeit aüfferben'. StaB, C3 1223, fol. 117.

67 StaB, C3 1223, fol. 98. 'Ich glaübe aber das di [sic] hailosen paüern Iren anschlag daraüf gerichtet, das der oder ein ander pfarrherr sein besoldüng nach den predigen, wie die werckleüt, nach den stücken oder taglohne haben soll, und mehr nit.'

68 StaB, C3 1223, fols 120; 129–42. *Des pfarrers zu drosenfeltt einfeltig und warhafftig Antwortt uf seyner pfar kinder gifftiges und unwarhafftiger furbringen.*

69 Lawrence P. Buck, 'Opposition to Tithes in the Peasants' Revolt: A Case Study of Nuremberg in 1524', *SCJ*, 4 (1973), 11–22; 15.

70 'Everywhere in Franconia rebels' grievances are directed against small tithes with no biblical justification'. Rudolf Endres, 'The Peasant War in Franconia', in Gerhard Benecke and Bob Scribner (eds), *The German Peasant War of 1525 – New Viewpoints* (London, 1979), p. 68; Otto Merx (ed.), *Akten zur Geschichte des Bauernkriegs in Mitteldeutschland* (Darmstadt, 1964), I, p. 11; Klaus Arnold, 'Die Stadt Kitzingen im Bauernkrieg', *Mainfränkisches Jahrbuch*, 27 (1975), 20; Tom Scott and Bob Scribner, *The Peasants' War: A History in Documents* (London, 1991), p. 181; Lorenz Fries, *Die Geschichte des Bauernkriegs in Ostfran-*

ken (Würzburg, 1883), I, p. 7; For the Twelve Articles see Blickle, *Die Revolution von 1525* (2nd ed., Munich, 1983), pp. 289–95.

71 Schornbaum, *Aktenstücke zur ersten Brandenburgischen Kirchenvisitation 1528*, pp. 57; 78; 81; 92.

72 LKAN, Markgräfliches Dekanat Schwabach (Hereafter MDS), 122 T.1. Sunday before St Veit's Day 1491; 8 August 1575.

73 LKAN, MKA, Spez. 135. 8 May 1571.

74 LKAN, MKA, Spez. 394. For example the testimony of a participant in the affair (fol. 218): '. . . er habe auch die gemaine Espen genossen davon er den zehenden einen pfarrer geben, und anderst nit gewüst dan er den selbig schuldig bis daher und erst als der gemain Brieff herfür kommen. Seÿ Er im erfarung kommen das man nit schuldig sei.'

75 Source materials for the above paragraph: LKAN, MDL, 51 Geslau 1588; LKAN, MDG 71, fols 20; 44 and 63 (Aha – with further reference to no. 29 above); 138; LKAN, MKA, Spez. 394, fols 1–282. Hechlingen tithe dispute 1525–76; LKAN, MKA, 135, 3 May 1574 – 26 May 1574.; StaB, C2 1858, 28 October 1581 – 29 April 1583; StaB, C2 986, 1592; LKAN, MKH, XX 3, fol. 5. A refusal to pay tithes had always been rare. See Giles Constable, 'Resistance to the Tithes in the Middle Ages', *JEH*, 13 (1962), 172–85.

76 LKAN, MKA, Spez. 394, fol. 1.

77 LKAN, MKA, Spez. 394, fols 68–9. (Three copies of the contract are extant: LKAN, MKA, Spez. 394, fols 50; 51; 94.)

78 LKAN, MKA, Spez. 394, fols 208–12.

79 LKAN, MKA, Spez. 394, fol. 248. 'Wie nun zwischen einem sollchen pfarrer, und Gemaindt, die Ehre Gottes, und sein hailig gotlich wort, das Ministerium wachsin und zu nemen, und die armen schäfflein wolfart befürtet.'

80 For further examples see Dixon, 'The Reformation in the Parishes', pp. 172ff.

81 James C. Scott, 'Resistance without Protest and without Organization: Peasant Opposition to the Islamic *Zakat* and the Christian Tithe', *Comparative Studies in Society and History*, 29, 3 (1987), 417–52; James C. Scott, *Weapons of the Weak. Everyday Forms of Peasant Resistance* (London, 1985).

82 On the scarcity of natural resources and the difficulties this caused see Karl Hasel, 'Die Entwicklung von Waldeigentum und Waldnutzung im späten Mittelalter als Ursache für die Entstehung des Bauernkriegs', *Allgemeine Forst- und Jagdzeitung*, 138 (1967), 141–50.

83 LKAN, MKA, Spez. 537, fol. 7. The administrator of Heilsbronn claimed that 'kein gellt bei dem Closter ist'; Muck, *Beiträge*, p. 191.

84 LKAN, MSK, 157, 22 October 1572. 'Das Gottshaüßist arm, und hat nichts mehr, den was die Sontag ins Secklein gefellet'.

85 StaN, *Ansbacher Neues Generalrepertorium*, Nr 49, rep. nr 103e, fol. 161; LKAN, MKA, Spez. 625, fols 25–7. The indebted parishioners of Oberferrieden asked the margrave 'noch ein kurtze Zeit gedült tragen'. Some parishioners were up to 23 Gulden in debt.

86 LKAN, MDG, 71, fol. 72 (1578).

87 StaN, *Ansbacher Neues Generalrepertorium*, Nr 49, rep. nr 103e, fol. 13; LKAN, MKl, 51, *Acta Specialis Visitationis Capitüli Leütershüsain 1584*; StaB, C2 1831, fol. 1, *Visitation Acta der Superinte[n]dents Wunsiedel Anno 92*. Against the charge from the pastor that the local authorities were using the money without his foreknowledge: 'daraüf der Rath die antwort geben. Es were nichts unnützlich angewendet, vermeineten nicht das sie schlüldig weren hierinnen mit deßpfarrers vor wißen zü handlen'; LKAN, MSK, 157, Stammbach 6 November 1589: 'Seid vor der zeit züm gemeinen Casten 3 schlussel gewesen deren pfarrer einen gehabt Wollen dem pfarrer itzt keinen züstellen. Redet der gemeine man ser ubel davon.'

88 LKAN, MDLz, 676 T.1, 22 June 1584.

89 Sehling, *Evangelischen Kirchenordnungen*, p. 320 (1536); pp. 352–3.

90 *Corpus Constitutionum Brandenburgico-Culmbacensium* (Bayreuth, 1746), p. 365.

91 *Corpus Constitutionum Brandenburgico*, pp. 280–2.

92 LKAN, MKA, Spez. 537, fols 2–9. 23 July 1562, 30 July 1562; 26 August 1562.

93 LKAN, MKA, Spez. 537, 9 September, 1562, fol. 11. '. . . und furter ÿemandt aüßder Gemeinde des orts uber solchen Baw verordndne und gebürliche Rechnüng von Inen nemen.'

94 LKAN, MDB, 324, 6 May 1564.

95 LKAN, MDB, 324, 16 May 1587.

96 LKAN, MDB, 324, 13 April 1588.

97 LKAN, MDB, 324, 21 June 1588 and 21 August 1588.

98 LKAN, MDB, 324, 24 September 1588. 'andern benachtbartten Ämptischen und Clösterischen Unterthonen'.

99 LKAN, MDB, 324, 28 August 1590.

100 LKAN, MKA, Spez. 640, 16 September 1562. The official was to ensure 'das von den eingepfardten zü solchem Baw mit füeren und aüch anderer handt raichüng zür nottürfft hülff gethon'.

101 LKAN, MKA, Spez. 640, 30 June 1576.

102 LKAN, MKA, Spez. 640. Letter from Schmidt, 1576.

103 LKAN, MKA, Spez. 640, 2 March 1587.

104 LKAN, MDLz, 666, Nr 213, 16 March 1570. A correspondence dealing with the supervision of the construction and maintenance of the church buildings near Langenzenn by the court. It contains the observation: 'solches beÿ der herrschaft mit alters nit herkommen gewest'.

6

The renovation of the ministry in Calvin's Geneva

William G. Naphy

The Reformation in Geneva under Calvin had a dramatic and permanent impact upon Geneva's parishes. Both in quality and quantity, Calvin's work in the city wrought a complete change in Geneva's local ministry. Geneva's pre-Reformation history as a Savoyard dependency and cathedral town, ruled by a Prince-Bishop, meant that politics and religion had always been inexorably entwined in the city. Moreover, because of the city's location beyond French control, yet on France's border, the religious situation there had a direct impact upon Geneva. This unique combination of factors provided the framework within which Geneva's reform would take shape; Calvin's presence in the city, however, would shape its character.

The unique nature of Geneva's Reformation must be stressed at the outset. Attempts to make comparisons between the ecclesiastical structure as it developed in Geneva and other Reformed areas are fraught with difficulties. Geneva's small size, its compact and unified Company of Pastors, the close identification between Protestantism and patriotism, and the presence of a substantial body of prominent foreigners made Geneva unique among Reformed states and churches. Comparisons serve only to highlight the practical impossibilities of transplanting the Genevan pattern into other areas. In this respect it is essential to study the Genevan Reformation and ministry for their own sake rather than reducing them to a mere model for other Reformations or treating them as simple addenda to Calvin's life.

Geneva's Reformation was, at its beginnings, the result of the city's attempts to free itself from Savoyard control. Initially, there were no moves against the old faith in the city but, when the

Bishop sided with Savoy, patriotic sentiments began to turn against the Catholic hierarchy. The constant unwillingness of Geneva's Catholic clergy, Savoyard dominated, to support the revolution associated the church with Savoy's oppression, alienating many leading Genevans. Already in 1527, that is prior to the beginning of any evangelical agitation, the ecclesiastical leadership began to abandon Geneva.[1] The later lack of any apparent support for the old faith in Geneva can be traced to the close identification of Genevan nationalism and Protestantism; Catholicism was seen as nearly identical with Savoyard domination. To win their freedom from Savoy the Genevans found it expedient to expel their Bishop, necessarily forcing themselves into the Protestant camp.[2] This move was wholeheartedly supported by the greater of Geneva's two military allies, Berne; the other, Fribourg, now abandoned its alliance with the city.

To understand the extent of the changes introduced with the Reformation, it is necessary to examine the situation in Geneva's diocese of 110 parishes prior to the removal of the Bishop and the Catholic structure.[3] Numerous religious orders were grouped in over 53 monasteries; in 1493 over 500 monks attended a diocesan synod.[4] The temporal power of the ecclesiastical structure was also extensive; the Bishop received two-thirds of the tariffs from Geneva's public markets and the revenues from the criminal justice system.[5] However, the principal source of the Bishop's wealth was his landed possessions; he ruled three rural mandements and shared control of Geneva with its citizens.[6] Some idea of the wealth of the church can be gathered from the sale of church goods between September 1536 and February 1537, after the evangelical coup; the 47,000 florins raised was nearly three times Geneva's normal annual revenues.[7]

The exact nature of the diocesan structure on the eve of the Reformation cannot be ascertained but records survive from the middle of the previous century which give some idea of the substantial number of clerics in Genevan territory. In the areas of the diocese roughly corresponding to the Republic's territory, 206 new clerics were tonsured in 1443.[8] A year later the diocese was examined to see what percentage of priests were actually resident. Pays de Gex had the best ratio with only 38 per cent (12 of 32) non-resident. Basse-Arve was the worst; 65 per cent (17 of 26) of its parish priests were missing. The other three areas which would fall within the Republic's control had rates of non-residency similar to Gex: 41 per cent were absent from both Côte and Bas-Chablais and 42 per cent from Bas-Genevois.[9]

The city itself, which had a population somewhat in excess of ten thousand in the 1530s, had at least 32 canons, six convents and five monasteries; the rural territories were of less significance. They had slightly over two thousand inhabitants and were easily dominated by Geneva; other Swiss cities, notably Berne, found their substantial rural possessions difficult to control.[10] There were over fifty confraternities in Geneva and perhaps another dozen in the surrounding territory, for the most part organised by various professions.[11] While undoubtedly exaggerated, some sense of the size of Geneva's clerical body can be gathered from the accounts of a riot led by monks in the early 1530s; contemporary accounts put the number of religious involved at about six hundred.[12] Any latent desire by lay officials to control Geneva's church would have been heightened by the extent of ecclesiastical influence in the city. The size, wealth, and power of the church completely frustrated any attempt by local Genevans to govern their own destinies.

Under pressure from the revolutionary party and faced with the exodus of many clerics, the Bishop agreed in 1528 to appoint only Genevans as canons.[13] In the end this proved unimportant as all of the canons departed in April 1535. They were followed, in August, by 24 of the 25 Poor Claires who were escorted, along with their possessions, to the Pont d'Arve by magistrates.[14] In December, the Dominicans and Franciscans were expelled. The Dominicans had resisted every attempt at reform but 13 of the 20 Franciscans remained in the city; four of them would follow the lead of their gardien, Jaques Bernard, and take wives.[15] The goodwill shown to the nuns of Ste Claire was the result of the high opinion held of them in Geneva for their exemplary morality.[16]

Not only was the ecclesiastical structure damaged by its association with Savoy and the magistrates' desire to enrich Geneva, but also by complaints about the clerics' morals. Even the nun Jeanne de Jussie, an ardent opponent of the Reform, was forced to admit that the 'prélats et gens de l'église' were notable for their debauchery.[17] In the decades before the Reformation spectacular cases had become public knowledge. A number of Dominicans had been charged with sodomy in 1513. Priests at the church of Madeleine had been arrested, and some expelled, in

1522, for sexual immorality; apparently, they were operating a brothel from the church.[18] In 1530, many Genevans had refused to pay their tithes because 'les chanoines menoient vie si dissolue'.[19] In the end, most of Geneva's monastic community simply abandoned the city.[20]

In 1534, the process which would destroy the remnants of the old faith accelerated. On 24 May 1534, there was an outbreak of iconoclasm when the Fransiscan convent at Rive was ransacked.[21] This was followed three months later by the Bishop's excommunication of the city's entire ruling elite.[22] The subsequent destruction of the city's suburbs for defensive reasons included the Cluniac, Dominican, and Benedictine monasteries.[23] In May 1535, the Augustinians made a last attempt to rally support when they claimed that they had been able to resuscitate a dead infant; the magistracy ruled this to have been a false miracle.[24] In August, there was another outbreak of iconoclasm, the mass was suspended and the church's goods were inventoried.[25] In September, the lands and possessions of the church were seized by Geneva and set aside for the new Hospital which was created to replace the numerous, small monastic charities.[26] The mass was finally abolished on 15 October 1535. In December, relics were removed from the churches; they were exposed to the public, examined, declared false, and destroyed.[27] By the end of 1535, therefore, the mediaeval Catholic church in Geneva, with its monasteries, relics, and hierarchy, had been destroyed.

However, the church's parish structure remained; it was essential for religious and political reasons that Geneva should assert its authority in these parishes and initiate the process of educating its subjects in the new faith. Obviously, the city could not dispense with the old parish priests immediately. Some priests were pensioned but many rural parishes had to rely on their old priests until 1544.[28] The lack of trained, qualified replacements and the turmoil surrounding the political crisis of 1538–41, during which Calvin and Farel were expelled from the city, meant that Geneva had no option but to avail itself of the services of these priests.

The rural parishes most important to the city, financially and politically, were quickly given new ministers. Thus, Henri de la Mare was assigned to the large parish of Jussy in 1537 and also given responsibility for Vandoeuvres. Clearly, Geneva attached great significance to Jussy's rapid reformation; the parish's five former priests, all of whom embraced the reform, were nevertheless replaced.[29] The large parish at Satigny was served by a preacher at St Germain until 1538 when a Protestant minister was supplied.[30] Armoy and Draillians remained vacant as they were the subject of a territorial dispute with Berne that was not resolved until 1543–44, while Moëns was abandoned by its priest, who refused to accept the new faith.[31] The seven smaller parishes controlled by the city were left with their old priests until 1544 when they were replaced by new ministers. At times this meant that several parishes were grouped under only one minister. Louis Cugniez, for example, served Russin, Dardagny, and Malval.[32]

These halfway measures produced a situation that was far from ideal; problems continued until all territorial disputes could be resolved and the parishes given new ministers. Disputes with France could not be settled as France refused to return Thiez, which it had seized, until the former monks were compensated.[33] The old priest of Armoy, caught between the competing ambitions of Berne and Geneva, pleaded for financial assistance.[34] Nor were the changes to the habits and beliefs of the old priests always successful. Jaques Baud had the misfortune to marry a woman who later committed adultery; the scandal and her banishment effectively forced Baud out of his parish as he was judged 'n'est capable de anuncer le st evangele'.[35] Pierre Noël, a former monk at Cluse, went too far in reforming his opinions; he was forced to beg mercy because of his strange religious beliefs.[36]

But Geneva was not without pity on the men who found themselves unable to find their way in the new religious order. Claude Veyron, former priest at Bossey, was provided with financial assistance.[37] After an examination of his morals and beliefs the city also agreed to aid Jaques Vuarouz, formerly a monk at Satigny.[38] Similar help was given to Anthoine Bochu, former monk at Pallex.[39] Finally, Pierre Molyon, a practising monk passing through Genevan lands, was even given some money to help him on his way.[40] The city was somewhat less forgiving when it was faced with avowedly Protestant ministers who had fallen foul of the magistrates. When Morand had abandoned his post in 1540 his goods had been seized.[41] A similar fate may have befallen Antoine Marcourt's possessions when he left his post without permission and then subsequently applied to visit the city in 1543. In a blatantly noncommital response the city assured him that 'toutes gens de bien peultre venyr en geneve'.[42]

Yet it would be wrong to assume from these latter examples that Geneva's magistrates endorsed wholeheartedly the programme of reform urged on them by their ministers. Indeed, throughout the years of rapid change the magistrates evidenced a less than enthusiastic desire to install the sort of uncompromisingly Protestant church envisioned by Calvin. The magistrates showed the greatest concern for the political problems associated with the revolution and a desire to prevent any increase in ministerial power. Indeed, it was the refusal by Calvin and Farel to obey the magistrates and refrain from meddling in politics that led to their expulsion from the city in 1538.[43] Afterwards, the city moved to bring its preachers under direct control. The previous system of paying 'gratifications occasionelles' was replaced with regular salaries, which were to remain constant until 1556; at the same time the 'prédicants' began to be referred to as 'ministres evangeliques'.[44] The greatest problem facing the city was its need for a settled ministry. Yet paradoxically, the city's haste in appointing new ministers, as shown below, resulted in pastors memorable only for the swiftness of their passage through Geneva. Not until 1546 was the city to collect a truly qualified and permanent Company of Pastors.

When Calvin returned to Geneva in September 1541, the Senate, Geneva's supreme magisterial body, immediately constituted a committee to meet with him to draft the Ecclesiastical Ordonnances which would form the cornerstone and blueprint of Geneva's religious settlement.[45] Calvin found the church seriously understaffed and unsettled as a result of the previous years of controversy. He was also in the position of having to work with ministers who had served the Articulants, the party which had exiled him and Farel in 1538. One would not be surprised, under the circumstances, if Calvin found his colleagues troublesome. The situation in Geneva in 1541, however, gave Calvin an excellent opportunity to rectify this situation. The Guillermins, who had ousted the Articulants in 1540, wanted order in the church and in Geneva. The city was short of ministers and Calvin was naturally given a great deal of latitude in hiring new men.[46]

The first task facing Calvin then upon his return was the quick establishment of a sound and ordered structure for the church. This however, raised a number of problems. First, Calvin required a substantial group of suitable colleagues. The drastic decrease in clergy after the Reformation had left Geneva's church seriously understaffed. These problems were now rendered more acute by the extensive programme of sermons, lectures, and catechisms designed to meet the spritual needs of Protestant Geneva. The mandatory nature of religious observance in Geneva only served to magnify the importance of the sermon and catechism in shaping Genevan society.[47]

What follows will show how, by 1546, Calvin had been successful in gathering a competent, powerful Company of Pastors as well as collecting a united body of lay elders in the Consistory, the second major component of the new ecclesiastical polity. As a result of these changes Geneva would finally acquire a settled ecclesiastical structure and the work of reformation, at the popular level, could be carried through effectively.

Serious obstacles faced Calvin upon his return, not the least of which was the ministerial body itself. To Calvin, his colleagues were truly deplorable, impediments, 'rude and self-conceited', having 'no zeal, and less learning'. Calvin's most damning comment about them is that he could not trust them.[48] To Calvin's annoyance, initial opposition to his proposed changes to Geneva's church structure, in this case the establishment of an independent Consistory, was articulated by these men. Worse yet, they put their case secretly after publicly agreeing with Calvin. These ministers said that the Senate should beware lest it give away to the predominantly foreign ministers a power which the magistrates should reserve for themselves; in the Genevan context this socio-political argument only served to highlight the different goals of Calvin and the magistrates.

It is not surprising then that Calvin moved swiftly to remove the ministers whom he found unsatisfactory, and to replace them with reliable supporters. The effect of this on the Genevan ministry was striking: in the eight years from Calvin's expulsion in 1538 until the end of 1546, no fewer than 31 ministers were employed by Geneva. Remarkably, only one minister, Jaques Bernard, served throughout this period. Nine ministers were deposed, five resigned and another two died. The result was that the church's leadership was wracked by instability; by 1545, the average tenure of ministers at Geneva was somewhat less than three years. The shifting of ministers from city to country parishes in an apparent attempt to find the best ministers for Geneva would have added to the perception that Geneva had nothing more than temporary ministers. This conclusion was reinforced by the fact that the ministerial body was composed, except for Bernard, entirely of foreigners.

In the earlier period many of these resignations represent the working out of the consequences of the 1538 crisis which had seen Calvin and Farel temporarily expelled from the city. Calvin and the Guillermins clearly resented those men who had worked in Geneva during the Articulants' supremacy. The string of resignations which accompanied the Articulant defeat in 1541 effectively left Geneva, at this point, with only three ministers: Bernard, De la Mare, and Calvin. Geneva's ministry was woefully understaffed.[49] However, by 1546 a new situation was beginning to develop. The new ministers hired in 1546 were a different sort. The Company of Pastors became marked by stability and an ever increasing pool of experience. Only three were deposed in the next eight years, another resigned, and one died. In this second period, 13 ministers remained throughout; both rural and city parishes finally experienced stability and continuity. Indeed by 1554, the members of the Company of Pastors had averaged ten years apiece in Geneva's ministry.

An effective programme of recruitment would eventually provide Geneva with the ministers necessary to fulfil the pastoral duties required of a state church. Unfortunately, the men hired in the four years after 1541 were not, as a group, of the best calibre or character. Of the 19 men hired in the five years 1541–45, 12 would be gone by 1554, of whom eight were deposed or resigned. Vandert was deposed for not visiting the sick and not performing 'aultres choses necesseres'.[50] The greatest loss of ministers occured between April 1545 and February 1546; four ministers were deposed in this period to the discomfort of the church. Two, Moreau and Delecluse, were sacked for misconduct. Moreau was removed after being arrested for fornicating with two women in the Plague Hospital.[51] Delecluse was sacked after embezzling 40 florins and abandoning his family for whom provision was made at the Hospital.[52] Ferron, who was hired in this period, would be deposed later for fornication as well.[53] Clearly, upon his return, Calvin and Geneva were so desperate to fill the ministerial vacancies that men of lesser ability were accepted only to be replaced as better ministers became available.

The city's consistent lack of concern for its ministers did not aid the search. The Senate's unwillingness to increase salaries kept the ministers in a precarious situation. All of the ministers, except Calvin, were in constant financial need because of their low salaries. The Senate, however, was notoriously unresponsive; once, the litany of complaints brought the response that the Senate had 'resolu de leur [the ministers] fere bonnes Remonstrances des grandes charges que la ville supporter & quil ayen ung peu de patience'.[54] The state had a valid point; it had hired an additional four ministers in 1542.[55] This meant that the total salary bill for ministers had climbed from around 1,800 florins a year to 2,700 florins.[56] Nevertheless, while an increase in personnel might have lessened the individual workload of the ministers it did not benefit them financially. By August 1544, Calvin was forced to complain that the ministers were all 'in a state of abject poverty'.[57] De la Mare complained, in December, that Jussy's church building even lacked doors and windows, a state which had existed since his arrival in May 1542.[58]

The magistrates were also keen to break the French control on the ministry. In 1545, they advocated the appointment as a minister of a citizen, Trolliet; he had been a monk in Burgundy and had returned to Geneva after embracing Protestantism. Calvin remained implacably opposed to him and was reprimanded for refusing to give any explanation for his rejection of Trolliet. Local connections could be a powerful protection against even Calvin's ill-will; one of the few ministers to survive throughout the period, Jaques Bernard, was probably able to remain because of his unique position as a member of a powerful local family. Trolliet eventually accepted Calvin's stubborn stance and became a notary, while remaining one of Calvin's fiercest opponents.[59] This xenophobic distrust of the minsters was largely an urban phenomenon. Unlike other areas in France and Switzerland it did not arise from linguistic problems; there are no recorded complaints about ministerial problems with the local dialect.

With the appointment of Nicholas des Gallars in 1544, one begins to see the first of a new sort of Genevan minister. He was of noble birth and would later serve in many prominent positions, for example as minister to the Queen of Navarre.[60] The other ministers called in 1545, Chauvet, Bourgoing, and Cop, show that Des Gallars was not a unique choice but a harbinger of things to come. Chauvet was already known as a dedicated French Protestant and had been imprisoned for his faith in France; later, he would be detained by the Bernese authorities for a sermon they found especially offensive.[61] Cop was even better known; his father was Guillaume Cop, doctor to Louis XII and Francis I and his brother was the famous rector of the University of Paris, Nicolas Cop. He was also a fiery preacher who was nearly deposed for one of his sermons less than a year after his arrival in Geneva.[62] Finally, Bourgoing, like Des Gallars, was of aristocratic birth. The advanced level of learning which these new men possessed is apparent in the fact all of them published respected religious works.[63] It is also worth noting that the one rural minister from this period to be moved to Geneva before 1554, St André, was, like Chauvet, detained by Protestant Berne for an uncompromising sermon which attacked Bernese religious practices; he was promoted that very same year.[64]

What one sees then is a process by which the Company of Pastors was remade during the years before 1546. The changes were substantial in many ways but in one significant area the ministers remained the same; except for Bernard, they were all French. The hallmark of those men who left by 1546 was their relative obscurity and apparent lack of education or expertise. Ironically, only Morand and Marcourt, the men enlisted to replace Calvin and Farel in 1538, were educated and relatively well known. The rest came and went leaving few traces to mark their stay in Geneva. The other striking feature of the Company of Pastors prior to 1546 was the degree of dissension and instability in the group as well as the shockingly high level of scandalous behaviour. Clearly, what Geneva needed and Calvin wanted was a stable, unified group of colleagues of good character and exceptional quality. By 1546 just such a body of ministers had been gathered.

It is essential to grasp the unique nature of this new Company of Pastors and the high level of learning, expertise, and quality united in them. Not only was such a group able to provide a good-quality ministry for Geneva but it would prove to be a formidable force in the later struggles with some of the magistrates. The respect such qualified men must have commanded among the Genevans helps explain the apparent unwillingness or inability of their magisterial opponents to move against them in later disputes. Ministerial solidarity deprived the magistrates of any opportunity to control their pastors by setting one group against another.

This change in the quality of the ministers was also reflected in their enhanced economic status. Prior to 1546, the ministers had always had to struggle to survive and were entirely dependent on the periodic donations from the magistrates which supplemented their insufficient salaries.[65] But, just as the ministers who arrived in 1546 were often of a higher social standing, they were also in a more secure financial position. In addition to Calvin, three ministers, Bourgoing, Cop, and St André, were to be contributors to the Bourse Française which, after 1550, provided financial assistance to the poorer French religious refugees.[66]

An examination of the notarial records provides the clearest proof of this change. The first thing that is apparent is the almost total lack of active business involvement on the part of the earlier ministers. The most noticeable exception is Marcourt who was owed a debt of 500 florins, a sum equal to Calvin's yearly wage.[67] Of the earlier ministers, Marcourt is the only one who would have fitted into the same social and educational group as the later ministers. In general though, Marcourt, Bernard, Ecclesia, De la Mare, and Megret were involved only in a few contracts, other than as witnesses. But even this activity is significant, since it shows the extent to which these ministers remained involved in the lives of other Genevans; this was true even after their deposition or resignation. This is especially true of Megret but perhaps understandable when one notices his marriage into the Roset family, one of Geneva's more prominent.[68] Obviously, the removal of these men from Genevan pulpits did not end their activity in the city; many Genevans had formed connections with their exiled pastors which endured. This level of continual contact could well explain the constant complaints of the later ministers about the activities and sermons of the former Genevan pastors who had found new posts just inside Bernese territory.[69]

Even so, an examination of the economic activity of the later ministers produces a striking contrast. Bougoing and Cop evidently possessed funds well above their yearly salary of 240 florins as they were able to offer substantial sums of money to purchase the houses which the city had provided them.[70] Even Petit, a humble rural minister, was active economically.[71] The obvious difference is that these ministers ceased being passive witnesses to contracts and became actively involved in the business life of Geneva. Equally importantly, their economic power, as a group, freed them from the almost beggarly dependence on the magistrates which had been the lot of the earlier ministers.

In contrast, there is a notable absence of later ministers, as witnesses, from wills and marriages. One might normally expect to see them in this role. What this may suggest is that the social standing of the newer ministers had the potential to increase the separation from their parishioners already arising from their ethnic differences. This would have made them less likely to have had intimate contact with local Genevans. This conclusion is strengthened by the fact that of the three cases in which the later ministers witnessed wills only one, involving Petit, may have been Genevan.[72] The other two were for prominent religious refugees.[73]

What one sees then is a clear tendency after 1545 to hire better qualified, more experienced Frenchmen of prominent backgrounds. The result of this process was that by 1546 Geneva was equipped with what would prove to be a stable, unified Company of Pastors. These ministers were marked by education, proven religious zeal, noble birth, fiery preaching, and a measure of independent wealth.[74] No single person exemplified all of these characteristics but it is clear that as a body, the new ministers noticeably differed in these areas from their predecessors.

Nevertheless, this did not complete the reformation of the Genevan ecclesiastical structure. The Company of Pastors, while influential through their position and control of the pulpits, were also part of the Consistory. This latter body was composed of all the ministers and representatives of the magistracy. For obvious geographical reasons the city ministers would have found it easier to attend the weekly meetings. The rural ministers of Armoy and Draillians were usually prohibited from attending by Berne which prevented them from crossing through Bernese Thonon, which separated the two distant parishes from Geneva proper.[75] This situation favoured the more prestigious city ministers: Calvin, Chauvet, Bourgoing, and Cop. But it was also important for the final triumph of the new ecclesiastical polity that this body, with its prominent lay and magisterial element, become as stable and as unified as the Company of Pastors.

The Consistory's magisterial members were comprised of one

presiding syndic, two senators and nine elders drawn from the Council of Sixty and of Two Hundred. This arrangement was designed to allow the magistracy to control this potentially powerful body; on at least three occasions the Senate was also forced to assert its authority over the Consistory in the issue of excommunication.[76] Senatorial control remained paramount until Calvin's political triumph in 1555.[77] The syndic and senatorial representatives did not function as long-term members and in only a few cases served for consecutive years. Indeed none served for more than three years in this capacity. However, this is obviously not the case when one examines the other elders. By 1546, the Consistory had managed to attract a core of seven elders who would serve for the next seven years; another, Jehanton Genod, was added in 1547. Thus, in the eldership, there was a process similar to that found among the ministers whereby significant individuals were recruited and remained in their posts, as a group, for a number of years.

Thus, after 1546, the Consistory consisted of a group of ministers and elders who continued to serve as a stable, unified body for at least the next six years. This gave a stability to the Genevan ecclesiastical structure in marked contrast to the chaotic situation which had been the hallmark of previous decades. The most significant fact is that these elders represented the establishment of a unified and stable magisterial element in the Consistory. To this then was added a similar group of pastors. Together these men, in regular contact with one another, provided Geneva with a united and secure ecclesiastical structure. This intimate contact welded the ministers and elders into a powerful force in Genevan society and politics.

Hitherto, the discussion has focused almost wholly upon the Company of Pastors and the political machinations involved in collecting qualified ministers. Undoubtedly this is the most important group to consider when discussing Geneva's ministry. However, Calvin's ideals placed emphasis upon a much broader understanding of the work of the church. Not only was he concerned to provide Geneva with an excellent preaching ministry but he was also determined to establish institutional control over morals and social behaviour: this was achieved through the operation of the Consistory. Moreover, both Calvin and the city saw the need for providing care for the poor and education for all. The problem of poor relief had been solved, for the most part, by the requisitioning of the goods of the old church to the new Hospital, and the establishment for the refugees of the Bourse Française. Also, by 1546, a unified group of lay elders had been gathered in the Consistory.

This ambitious programme upon which Calvin had embarked in Geneva put considerable demands on the time of the small cadre of ministers which numbered from nine to sixteen during Calvin's ministry. The need to educate the Genevan citizenry in the new faith was paramount. To achieve this goal, and to assist the small Company of Pastors, the work of the Consistory, as it developed, showed a decided emphasis on education. Along with the catechism, the Consistory strove to inculcate among all Genevans the public and private practices and precepts of the new faith. The catechism and Consistory formed the core of Geneva's religious education, totally overshadowing the efforts of the state and private schools and tutors.

In the rural parishes this educational work was assisted by the co-operation which existed between Geneva's Consistory and those in the neighbouring Bernese rural areas. On different occasions Geneva became aware of improper behaviour by Genevans through reports from the Consistories in Morges, Ternier, and Gex.[78] This watchfulness was supplemented by a programme of rural visitations. The local Genevan officials, the châtellains, were charged with enforcing Geneva's religious settlement in the rural parishes in co-operation with the parish ministers. The visitation committees, composed of two magistrates and two city ministers, examined each rural inhabitant, without the châtellain or rural pastor being present. The system was designed to correct the beliefs and practices of the peasantry and to gauge the quality of Geneva's local representatives and the effectiveness of their application of Geneva's ecclesiastical regulations.[79]

In the city, Calvin, and to a lesser extent the magistrates, were concerned that an adequate educational programme should be established. But, as with the ministry, the state showed an unwillingness to pay to implement its good intentions. A school had been started as early as 1536 but as late as 1552 the regent was bemoaning, as had his predecessors, the ruinous state of the buildings and the inadequate wages provided.[80] Even Guillaume Franc, who had been hired to teach the new metrical psalms, begged to be released from his contract as his salary was insufficient to sustain him.[81] In general, the state preferred education to be supplied by private tuition; for example, Geneva granted permission for a foreign couple, Jean le Maystre and his wife, to open a school for boys and girls in 1545.[82] The process of education did not actually begin to progress until after Calvin's political victory in 1555; rural schools were established, in 1557, in Peney, Cartigny, and Chancy.[83] By 1558, the Senate was beginning serious discussions about founding the Collège.[84]

With the founding of the Academy in 1559, the programme for renovating Geneva's religious structure and life was substantially complete. Geneva had a distinguished Company of Pastors, a powerful and supportive Consistory, a thorough education programme, an effective system of poor relief, and its rural parishes were supplied with ministers and magistrates dedicated to the Reformation; Calvin's Reformation had reached its institutional culmination. Maintaining this position now became the premier task. Geneva's ability to sustain the quality of its ministry for subsequent decades is a credit not only to the enduring fame of Calvin and the Academy and the events in France but also to the fully integrated system in Geneva which came to fruition after 1555. In later years, the Consistory and Academy would decline in fame and utility somewhat but the Company of Pastors remained a truly distinguished body for decades even in the rural parishes.

It is also noteworthy that the ministers remained overwhelmingly French well into the seventeenth century. No city pulpit was filled by a native Genevan until 1594 when two ministers, Abraham Grenet, of French refugee extraction, and Abraham de la Maisonneuve, of Genevan descent, were appointed.[85] Most rural parishes saw native pastors in 1570–71 though De la Maisonneuve broke the barrier in two and his brother, Louis, in a third.[86] Satigny was served by Frenchmen until 1609.[87] A similar pattern was apparent in the Academy; Pierre Chevalier, of Genevan ancestry, and Jean Diodati, a refugee's son, became the first native-born professors in 1589 and 1599 respectively.[88] The state accepted its continued reliance upon imported ministers and professors as late as 1616 when the Senate specifically exempted their posts from a decree reserving state positions for citizens.[89]

From 1525 to 1546, Geneva's church, Catholic and Protestant, was marked by constant instability, dissension, and disruptive changes in personnel. In practical terms this meant that Genevan society was very visibly out of control. With the arrival of the new ministers and the gathering of a committed body of lay elders in 1546, Geneva's ecclesiastical structure entered a period of stability not seen for over two decades. Political stability was finally achieved a decade later with Calvin's triumph over his opponents in 1555. It is not unfair to see these events as a continuing part of the same process: in a very real sense the resolution of the political crisis in this year represented an opting by the city's electorate for order over disorder.[90] After 1555, the state finally added an educational programme that reached down into the peasantry and upwards to educated Protestants throughout Europe. In this respect, the renovation of the ministry in Calvin's Geneva had effected a very real, and very obvious, transformation of society. The Reformation had seen the removal of the non-resident priests, the political hierarchy around the Bishop, and the financial burden of Geneva's extensive monastic structure. In their place had arisen a new order, as foreign as the Savoyard clerics and as deeply involved in politics but also an order in which even distant rural parishes enjoyed the pastoral efforts of some of the best French-speaking ministers of the day. The Reformation, at least in Geneva, had seen a permanent and profound change in the ministry provided to the average person. Deacons administered the Hospital, elders assisted in an independent Consistory, doctors taught in the various schools and men of learning and ability served and preached in Geneva's parishes; this edifice, to an amazing degree, represented Calvin's vision of a Reformed society made reality.

Notes

1 H. Naef, *Les Origines de Genève* (2 vols, Geneva, 1936), II. pp. 44–50. E. W. Monter, *Calvin's Geneva* (London, 1967), p. 15. Jeanne de Jussie, nun of Ste Claire, related that the 'gens de longue robbe' began to depart in 1526.
2 Political resistance to Calvin arose from a desire by the Genevans to avoid a return to ecclesiastical rule. R. Kingdon, 'Calvin and "Presbytery"': The Genevan Company of Pastors', in *Pacific Theological Review*, 18, 2 (winter 1985), p. 44. P. Martin, 'L'Emancipation Politique de Genève 1519–1536', in *Almanach Paroissial* (Geneva, 1925), p. 31.
3 Monter, *Geneva*, p. 12.
4 J. Gaberel, *Histoire de l'Eglise de Genève* (3 volumes, Geneva, 1858), I, p. 57. L. Binz, *Vie Religieuse et Réforme Ecclésiastique dans le Diocèse*

de Genève, 1378–1450 (Geneva, 1973), pp. 501–3. Similar figures are reported for the Pays de Vaud: 160 parishes, 24 monasteries, 35 convents. H. Vuilleumeier, *Histoire de l'Eglise Réformée du Pays de Vaud* (Lausanne, 1927), pp. 6f.

5 Monter, *Geneva*, p. 31.

6 M. Roset, *Les Chroniques de Genève* (Geneva, 1894), pp. 13f. Also, Monter, *Geneva*, p. 10; Naef, *Origines*, I, p. 5; P. Martin, 'L'Emancipation', pp. 27f.

7 Monter, *Geneva*, pp. 10, 14.

8 L. Binz, *Vie Religieuse* (Geneva, 1973), pp. 489f.

9 L. Binz, *Vie Religieuse*, p. 495. A. Froment, *Les Actes et Gestes Merveilleux* [Geneva, J. Girard, 1554], modern edition (Geneva, 1854), p. 1: 'les chanoynes, prebstres et moynes en grand nombre estans en leur auctorité'.

10 P. Martin, *Histoire de Genève des Origins à 1798* (Geneva, 1951), p. 227.

11 Monter, *Geneva*, pp. 13, 21, 32; F. Fleury, *Les Confréries de Genève* (Geneva, 1869), pp. 1f; A. Babel, *Histoire Economique de Genève des Origins au Début du XVIe Siècle* (Geneva, 1963), pp. 252f.

12 Froment, *Actes*, p. 52; Roset, *Chroniques*, p. 170.

13 Monter, *Geneva*, p. 45.

14 Roset, *Chroniques*, p. 221; G. Goyau, *Une Ville-Eglise Genève* (Paris, 1919), I, p. 22. Cf., Monter, *Geneva*, p. 11; F. Grenus-Saladin, *Fragmens Biographiques et Historiques* (Geneva, 1815), p. 2.

15 Monter, *Geneva*, p. 54; Gaberel, *Histoire*, I, pp. 66f. Cf. Tremey, 'Obituaire des Cordeliers de Genève', in *Memoires et Documents Publiés par l'Académie Salésienne*, 28 (Annency, 1904), 237.

16 J. Flournois, *Extraits Contenus tout ce qu'il y a d'Important dans les Registres Publics de Genève* (Geneva, 1854), p. 105.

17 Gaberel, *Histoire*, I, p. 74.

18 Gaberel, *Histoire*, I, pp. 70f; Flournois, *Extraits*, pp. 101–5.

19 Roset, *Chroniques*, p. 146. A. Head-König and B. Veyrasset-Herren, 'Les Revenus Décimaux à Genève de 1540 à 1783', in J. Goy and E. Ladurie (eds), *Les Fluctuations du Produit de la Dîme* (Paris, 1972), p. 166.

20 F. Bonivard, *Advis et Devis sur l'Ancienne et Nouvelle Police de Genève*, 2 vols (Geneva, 1865), II, pp. 45f.

21 Roset, *Chroniques*, p. 185.

22 Roset, *Chroniques*, p. 188.

23 Roset, *Chroniques*, p. 196.

24 Roset, *Chroniques*, pp. 196f; Grenus-Saladin, *Fragmens*, p. 1.

25 Roset, *Chroniques*, pp. 200f.

26 Roset, *Chroniques*, p. 210; Martin, 'L'Emancipation', p. 30; B. Lezcase, *Sauver l'Ame Nourrir le Corps* (Geneva, 1958), pp. 56 f.

27 Roset, *Chroniques*, pp. 214f.

28 Monter, *Geneva*, pp. 18, 78.

29 H. Heyer, *L'Eglise de Genève* (Geneva, 1909), pp. 226, n. 1; 228, n. 2.

30 Heyer, *L'Eglise*, p. 211.

31 Heyer, *L'Eglise*, pp. 206, n. 1; 228.

32 Heyer, *L'Eglise*, pp. 203; 212, n. 3; 215, n. 1; 220, n. 2. T. Claparède, 'Les Collaborateurs de Calvin à Genève', in *Histoire de Genève Varia*, AEG 2012 (14).

33 RC 35, fol. 193 (5 May 1541); RC 37, fol. 62 (16 April 1543). Volumes used: 30 (1536–37), 34–43 (1540–49), 45–8 (1550–55), 52–4 (1556–59), 115 (1616).

34 RC 37, fol. 58v (13 April 1543).

35 RC 36, fol. 23 (26 May 1542); RC 37, fols 204 (27 August 1543), 217v (10 September 1543), 226v–227 (24 September 1543).

36 RC 36, fol. 94v (14 August 1542).

37 RC 38, fol. 226v (30 May 1544); RC 40, fol. 144v (11 June 1545).

38 RC 39, fols 27 (4 November 1544), 68 (12 December 1544).

39 RC 41, fols 164 (3 August 1546), 166v (6 August 1546).

40 RC 40, fol. 29v (19 February 1545).

41 RC 34, fol. 382v (16 August 1540).

42 RC 37, fols 185 (7 August 1543), 188v (10 August 1543).

43 Grenus-Saladin, *Fragmens*, p. 5 (11, 12 May 1538).

44 J. Bergier, 'Salaires des Pasteurs de Genève au XVIe Siècle', in *Melanges d'Histoire du XVIe Siècle offerts à Henri Meylan*, in *Bibliothèque Historique Vaudoise*, 43 (Lausanne, 1970), 165–8.

45 RC 35, fol. 324 (13 September 1541).

46 The city had already shown a tendency to allow its senior minister such freedom. The hiring of Calvin by Farel is a perfect example; so little importance was attached to the man, and the event, that the magisterial records simply noted Calvin as 'ille gallus'. RC 30, fol. 51 (5 September 1536).

47 For details on Geneva's preaching and teaching minstry see T. H. L. Parker, *The Oracles of God* (London, 1947), and E. Mülhaupt, *Die Predigt Calvins* (Berlin, 1931).

48 *CO*, XI. col. 378f (letter to Myconius, 14 March 1542).

49 The former priests worked in the rural areas only. RC 34, fols 388 (20 August 1540), 452v (21 September 1540). After Morand's departure, the Senate ordered that 'ung home scavant' should be found to replace him; Calvin is not mentioned until Marcourt's resignation a month later.

50 RC 36, fols. 94 (14 August 1542), 178 (27 November 1542), 184 (5 December 1542).

51 RC 40, fols. 72 (6 April 1545), 74v (7 April 1545), 79 (11 April 1545).

52 RC 40, fols. 134v (1 June 1545), 159 (23 June 1545).

53 *RCP*, I pp. 109f (April 1549).

54 RC 37, fol. 226v (24 September 1543). Gaberel, *Histoire*, III, p. 282, discusses concerns about the ministers' salaries.

55 RC 36, fol. 72 (16 July 1542).

56 RC 36, fol. 76 (22 July 1542).

57 RC 38, fol. 309 (1 August 1544).

58 RC 39, fol. 53v. (1 December 1544).

59 RC 40, fols 135 (1 June 1545), 141 (8 June 1545), 358 (26 Jan 1546). Roset, *Chroniques*, pp. 311f, 315; *RCP*, I, p. 200.

60 Kingdon, *Geneva and the Coming of the Wars of Religions in France, 1555–1563* (Geneva, 1956), p. 6, discusses the ministers' noble origins.
61 RC 48, fol. 72v (12 June 1554).
62 RC 41, fols. 123–131v (28 June 1546).
63 M. Prevost et al. (eds), *Dictionnaire Biographique Française* (Aa-Joncoux, Paris, 1933–91), VI, col. 1500 (Bourgoing); VIII. col. 914f (Chauvet); IX, col. 555 (Cop); X. col. 1353 (des Gallars).
64 RC 46, fol. 152 (11 February 1552).
65 Monter, *Government*, p. 17 f, discusses Geneva's ecclesiastical revenues.
66 J. Olson, *Calvin and Social Welfare: Deacons and the Bourse Française*, (Sellingsgrove, PA, 1989), pp. 120–6. Roset, *Chroniques*, p. 309.
67 AEG/Minutes des Notaires [Min], J. du Verney, VIII (1543–45), fols 405 (27 September 1544), 410v (11 October 1544). Bergier, 'Salaires', p. 168; Grenus-Saladin, *Fragmens*, p. 8. Calvin's higher wage was because of 'son grand savoir'.
68 Vandert, Champereau, Treppereau, and Moreau witnessed one document apiece. AEG/Min, P. Bally, I. (1537–47), pt 2, fol. 32v (purchase by Bernard; 19 Mar 1543); B. Neyrod, II, (1556–57), fol. 59 (debt of Ecclesia; 6 February 1557); F. Vuarrier, V (1537–67), fols 82, 84 (Marcourt's daughter married J. de Lonnex, citizen; 1 May 1553); J. du Verney, V (1541–46), fol. 43 (De la Mare and family in dispute; 23 November 1542); G. Malliet (single volume, 1541–44), fol. 71 (will of Megret's wife, daughter of F. Roset, citizen; 2 January 1542).
69 *RCP*, I, pp. 60–2 (3 June 1547).
70 RC 46, fol. 191 (Bourgoing offered 1,000 florins; 19 April 1552); RC 48, fol. 141v (Cop offered 1,500 florins; 1 November 1554).
71 AEG/Min, G. Patru, I, (1548–96), fol. 7v (association; 4 May 1551); C. Blecheret, I (1548–51), fols 13v (sale; 24 November 1551), 176 (cession; 26 April 1550); II (1552–5), fol. 101 (exchange; 5 December 1552); III (1551–54), fol. 24v (purchase; 29 Mar 1553).
72 AEG/Min, G. Messiez, VI (1544–62), fol. 41 (J. Malard's will; 1 December 1545).
73 AEG/Min, P. du Verney, I (1553–70), fol. 16 (will of Françoise, widow of Sr de Chavalle in Vienne; 29 October 1557); J. Ragueau, II (1556–58), pt 2, p. 22 (will of J. Chaperon of Normandy; 28 June 1557).
74 The connection between education and wealth is important. J. Dewald, *The Formation of a Provincial Nobility* (Princeton, 1980), pp. 133f, notes costs which were incurred in education. From 1550 to 1568, Nicolas Romé spent around 24,000 florins on his education. In 1520–30, Charles de Bourgeville spent over 350 florins *per annum* on his education.
75 RC 45, fols 153 (22 December 1550), 218v (9 March 1551); RC 46, fols 29v (7 August 1551), 309 (21 November 1552).
76 RC 37, fol. 37v (19 March 1543); RC 2, fol. 72v (31 March 1547); RC 47, fols 197v–198 (21 December 1553).
77 RC 48, fol. 182v (24 January 1555).
78 RC 40, fols 35 (18 January 1546), 345 (11 November 1546); RC 42, fol. 355 (28 November 1547); RC 43, fols 174 (24 August 1548), 176v (27 August 1548).

79 RC 42, fols 36v (24 February 1547), 183–183v (22 July 1547); RC 45, fol. 147v (15 December 1550). Monter, *Studies*, pp. 79f.
80 Roset, *Chroniques*, pp. 232f; RC 46, fols 233–233v (5 July 1552).
81 RC 40, fol. 202v (3 August 1545).
82 RC 40, fol. 28v (19 February 1545).
83 RC 52, fol. 234v (1 February 1557); RC 53, fol. 125 (4 May 1557).
84 RC 54, fol. 48 (17 January 1558).
85 Heyer, *L'Eglise*, pp. 449, 471f.
86 Heyer, *L'Eglise*, pp. 205 (Célligny, 1571), 207 (Genthod-Moëns-Chollex, 1577), 213 (Dardagny-Russin-Malval, 1598), 215 (Chancy-Cartigny-Valleiry, 1572), 221 (Bossey-Neydans, 1570), 226 (Jussy-Foncenex, 1572).
87 Heyer, *L'Eglise*, p. 211.
88 Heyer, *L'Eglise*, pp. 235f. Professorships of non-theological chairs, e.g., philosophy and Greek, were held by Genevans at earlier dates.
89 RC 115, fol. 84v (5 April 1616).
90 I expand upon this theme in chapter 8 of my doctoral dissertation, 'Calvin and the Consolidation of the Genevan Reformation' (St Andrews University Ph.D. thesis, 1992).

7

Education and training for the Calvinist ministry: the Academy of Geneva, 1559–1620

Karin Maag

The Ecclesiastical Ordinances of the city of Geneva, published in 1541, contained a section which boldly affirmed the importance of education, and the need for a new institution to facilitate these goals. 'The function closest to ministry and to the governing of the Church is teaching in theology, preferably the Old and New Testaments. But because one cannot profit from such teaching unless one is taught languages and humanities first, and because we need to sow seeds for the future so as not to leave a deserted Church to our children, we will have to establish a college to teach them, to prepare them as much for ministry as for civil government.'[1] Yet in fact it would be almost another two decades before the provisions of this resolution became reality with the foundation of the Genevan Academy.

The years between 1541 and 1559 were filled with many problems which effectively ruled out the establishment of Geneva's own institution of higher education. For many years Calvin was preoccupied primarily with the threat posed by internal opposition; in addition there were problems finding qualified professors, and other financial commitments were more pressing.[2] By 1555, however, most of these problems were close to resolution. In this year internal opposition was effectively stilled, with the defeat and exile of Calvin's most vociferous Genevan opponents. The Calvinist victory of 1555 also provided an opportunity to solve the financial problem, since the Genevan authorities were able to auction off the estates of the exiles, channelling the resulting funds towards the costs of constructing the new buildings of the Academy.[3] Equally providentially, the problem of finding capable personnel was resolved by the arrival in 1559 in Geneva of the greater part of the teaching staff of the neighbouring Academy of Lausanne, the first, and until the creation of the Genevan Academy the only, French-language training centre for Reformed ministers.[4] Thus, on 21 March and 22 May 1559 the Genevan Small Council was able to record this windfall and endorse the Genevan ministers' proposals for the first professors of the new Academy: Antoine Le Chevalier as professor of Hebrew, François Bérauld as professor of Greek, and Jean Tagaut as professor of philosophy.[5] Another former Lausanne professor, Theodore Beza, became professor of theology alongside Calvin, and was also named as first Rector of the new institution.

One of the main aims of the new Academy was to train young men for the Reformed ministry. This was not a new initiative, for Geneva had been training and sending out young ministers, particularly to France, several years before the Academy was founded.[6] The training of ministers in Geneva prior to 1559 was however relatively informal, at least in terms of academic work. Calvin and Farel gave public exegetical lectures in the Old and New Testaments, and this, along with listening to sermons and practical work as temporary ministers in smaller parishes around Geneva, seems to have been the sum total of theological training available in Geneva until the Academy was founded.[7] It is no surprise then that the creation of the Academy was greatly desired in order to provide ministerial candidates with the greater intellectual and scholarly training which were deemed necessary in the new churches now being established across northern Europe.

In this respect, the Academy had clear objectives. But the history of its first half century would show that these were not so easy to carry through. The aims of the ministers were not shared by all in Geneva. Others among the city's ruling elite, particularly among the magistracy, hankered after a more conventional institution of higher education, based on the model of the Humanist university. These conflicting perspectives produced a tension at the very heart of the new institution. On the one hand, the training of ministers remained important, even up until the first decades of the seventeenth century.[8] On the other hand, pressure from local and foreign dignitaries, and from foreign students, led the Academy to conform more and more to the university model, in order to attract students from outside the city and to raise its profile on the European educational scene.

The history of the Academy thus indicates the difficulties that would attend the establishment of a specialist training seminary within the context of conventional expectations of sixteenth-century higher education. It also reveals a second dilemma which went right to the heart of the Reformed ministry: what made a minister, practical training or scholarship?

Interestingly enough, if one compares the Ecclesiastical Ordinances of 1541 and 1576, the foundation of the Academy made little impact on the examination criteria required by the Company of Pastors for candidates for the ministry. The passages detailing the examination of candidates by the Company of Pastors remain essentially the same. In both cases, the candidate was to be examined at length on his doctrine and on his 'good and sound knowledge of Scripture'. The second part of the examination dealt with his character and morals.[9] There is no mention in 1576, for instance, of any academic requirements to be fulfilled prior to ordination as a minister.

The Academy's developing curriculum, however, reflected the constant pressures for an ever more scholarly approach to education. During the course of the century the magistrates sanctioned and found funds for the creation of new, more specialist chairs, and focused on aspects of the Academy which would bring it into line with the practice of established universities elsewhere. The teaching of law in the Academy began in 1566.[10] Owing to the poor calibre of those teaching, namely Henry Scrimger and Pierre Charpentier, the law courses were interrupted and then restarted in 1572, when the St Bartholomew's Day massacre brought talented refugees to Geneva, among them François Hotman and Hugues Doneau, who agreed to teach law in the Academy.[11] A chair of medicine was established in 1567, but the professor, Simon Simonius, quarrelled with the minister of the Italian church of Geneva, was dismissed from his post, and was forced to leave the city in the same year. No further attempts were made to create a chair in the first sixty years of the Academy's existence.[12] In 1584, a matriculation fee, a common feature in contemporary universities, was imposed on all students apart from Genevans and those from Switzerland. The funds raised were intended to pay the salary of the third professor of law.[13]

The broadening of the curriculum reflected by and large the priorities of Geneva's secular rulers. With the establishment of these new fields of study, Geneva could now boast an institution of higher education on a par with many of the longer established universities and colleges in the Protestant world. Yet Calvinist churches continued to look to Geneva above all for practical training for their ministers, and their concerns were not answered by this concentration on broadening the academic curriculum. Their expectations in fact necessitated the maintenance of a second structure of examination and control run directly by the Company of Pastors. In this respect the Academy continued to represent only one aspect of ministerial training even in a period of greater concern for formal academic qualifications.

In the beginning, the Genevan Academy had four chairs: one of theology, one of Hebrew, one of Greek, and one of philosophy. This last covered various disciplines such as Latin eloquence, rhetoric, logic, and physics. At first attention was focused mostly on theology and its related areas. Starting in 1559 and until Calvin's death, the chair of theology was held simultaneously by Calvin and Beza, who taught each on alternate weeks. The course content was essentially only scriptural exegesis, although students could apply in the theology lectures skills and knowledge which they had gained in other courses, particularly Hebrew. Thus on 22 November 1574, having notified the Company of Pastors, Beza began to expound the Book of Genesis in the Academy.[14] The Greek course focused more on Classical Greek literature than on the language, since it was expected that students would have acquired their linguistic knowledge of Greek in their earlier schooling.

After Calvin's death in 1564, Beza remained the mainstay of the chair of theology until 1599.[15] During that period, Beza was assisted by various colleagues, including prominent Genevan ministers such as Lambert Daneau, Jean-Baptiste Rotan, and Antoine de la Faye. The increase in number of theology professors led to a division of duties. By 1587, the Small Council of Geneva recorded that the Company of Pastors wished to have three people teaching theology: one teaching the Old Testament, one teaching the New Testament, and one teaching a corpus of doctrine, known as the *Loci Communes*, which were generally drawn from Paul's Letter to the Romans.[16] Previously, Calvin and Beza had provided doctrinal teaching and scriptural exegesis within the same lecture: these were not considered as two components of theology which could be taught separately, and until the 1580s, exegesis had remained the central focus of theological teaching.[17] The change in emphasis in the 1580s, from scriptural exegesis, where the aim was to make passages clearly understandable, and to draw from them the central themes and elements of doctrine, to a focus on doctrine itself, is thus an important one. Indeed, the transformation reflects the change in expectations among contemporary scholars regarding the necessary elements of theological training for future ministers. While in the years when the Reformed church was still growing in places such as France and the Netherlands attention was focused on being able to expound scriptural passages clearly and competently, and on opposing the Catholic understanding of various key passages which were the underpinnings of rites and practices, in later years the Reformed approach changed. By the 1580s and afterwards, as the Catholic church began gaining territory and allegiances again, the Reformed ministry needed to have a systematic and coherent body of doctrine at its fingertips, in order to be able to keep the members it had, and to repulse the Catholic attacks. In other words, training in scriptural exegesis corresponded to a period when the Reformed church was gaining ground, when Reformed clergy and lay people through their more thorough knowledge of Scripture could attack the fabric of the old church at a point when it was still vulnerable. Training in the *Loci Communes* and the elaboration of a cohesive body of doctrine corresponded to the later period, when the Reformed church was on the defensive, and felt it needed to establish a corpus of doctrine to assert and prove logically the validity of its existence.

One must not conclude, however, that there was no coherent doctrine prior to the 1580s nor that scriptural exegesis, with its more text-centred approach, came to an end in the 1580s. Indeed, to a large extent these two perspectives existed simultaneously. However, it does seem that the focus of attention shifted during the 1580s. The pressure for more intensive theological training did not come from the ministers and professors alone. On 2 March 1604, the Registers of the Company of Pastors stated, 'It has been noted that apart from the teaching of the theology professors, the students also wish to hear lectures on the commonplaces, especially on the catechism. Be it resolved that a decision will wait until a more favourable moment, given the difficulties of the present time.'[18]

Apart from attending the lectures in theology, candidates for the ministry engaged in academic exercises called *disputations* and *propositions*, during which a student would defend orally a thesis set by one of the professors in theology or by a minister. These exercises took place on separate days and in different languages, the Latin *disputations* being chaired by a professor in theology and the French *propositions* by each of the ministers of the city in turn. At times, problems arose because the *propositions* were falling into disuse, or because students who were not yet sufficiently competent academically were none the less engaging in these exercises, to the annoyance of their more advanced fellow students.[19] A further problem arose in the early years of the seventeenth century. The Company of Pastors and the French churches noticed that students were beginning to place a greater emphasis on style rather than on content. The French churches noticed this change in new ministers' sermons, and the Genevan ministers noticed the same change in the theology students' thesis defences. On 20 June 1606, the Registers of the Company recorded its concern: 'As regards the *proposition* of the theology students, it appears that there is a problem, which may have serious consequences if it is not dealt with. Some, taking only one verse, or half a verse, and sometimes only one word, are inclined to be verbose, and often stray from the point, so that one sees more affectation than solidity.'[20]

Because the Genevan Academy had no power to grant degrees, as it had no papal nor imperial charter, there were also no examinations. Students who wished could request a testimonial letter from the Rector of the Academy, detailing their record of attendance and participation in classes, and their behaviour. This testimonial was available to students in all fields, and was a matter for the Rector. However, students in theology who were training for the ministry often received testimonials from the Genevan Company of Pastors instead. The Company of Pastors found out from the Rector and the professors the nature of the student's academic record, and then proceeded to examine his fitness for the ministry themselves. It is worth noting that the practical elements of training for the ministry, such as preaching in Geneva's rural parishes, remained important factors in a candidate's preparation. On 9 December 1584, the Company of Pastors wrote to an unnamed church, providing a testimonial letter for a ministerial candidate, Jean Valeton.

As regards the witness which we can and must give concerning him, we testify to you that thanks to God, after having heard him expound several passages of Scripture and even having given him practice in preaching in one of the parishes of our territory, we have always found him to hold a pure and complete doctrine. He also has not a little talent to teach and make himself heard [. . .]. And as regards his morals, he has always behaved in a Christian and peaceful fashion among us, so that we cannot but hope that he will bear good fruit.[21]

The Company of Pastors took these practical matters into consideration as well in its testimonial letters, even though preaching experience and proficiency do not appear in the Ecclesiastical Ordinances as criteria for ordination.

The other area of the Company's responsibility lay in its supervision of the morals of candidates for the ministry. The emphasis on good conduct is understandable, since ministers were the representatives *par excellence* of the Reformed church. In addition, given that the administration of discipline played such an important role in the life of Reformed communities, high behavioural standards were expected of ministers as much as or more so than of lay people. Therefore the Company of Pastors insisted that especially those studying for the ministry had to maintain high moral standards. Those who did not do so could find that the Genevan authorities used their correspondence network to inform the home churches about troublesome students' behaviour. In extreme cases student ministers could even lose their funds if their sponsors lost patience with them, as was the case with Jean Verneuil who had been in trouble with the Genevan authorities in 1604 and 1605 because of his dissolute lifestyle. The Company of Pastors acknowledged that his academic performance was good, but they felt that his morals left a lot to be desired. His sponsors, the church of Bordeaux, wrote to Geneva in 1605 announcing that Verneuil would no longer be receiving any funds from them.[22]

The nature and status of the letters conveying the opinions and recommendations of the Company of Pastors about theology students training for the ministry are somewhat difficult to assess, mainly because of the uncertainty surrounding ordination procedures. In many cases, it seems that the churches who had sent students to Geneva requested Geneva to assess their performance and readiness for ministry before sending them back: in certain cases, Geneva's positive assessment of a student's capacities for ministry was understood by the churches to be equivalent to ordination. At the very least, the churches' ready acceptance of the letters of recommendation shows in what high regard Geneva and its church were held.

At times, lack of academic ability ruled out a candidate before he had progressed very far. On 2 January 1601, a certain Mr Felis, who came from Paris and had been recommended to the Company of Pastors, was told, after having received funds to study for two months, that 'he should look for something wherever God gives him the opportunity, for the Company cannot support him any further, given that there is little hope of him being able to serve [as minister], given that he has neither the knowledge nor the languages [required]'.[23]

It is difficult to dissociate the academic training that ministerial candidates received from their practical training, mainly because both aspects of that training were overseen by Geneva's Company of Pastors. The Company of Pastors, whose members were the ministers of the city and of Geneva's rural areas, as well as the professors of the chairs of theology, Hebrew, Greek, and philosophy, was the linchpin of the ministerial training scheme. Letters requesting ministers were sent to the Company, as were letters recommending students coming to Geneva to study. The Company was responsible for seeking out and interviewing potential candidates for chairs in the Academy, for supervising students' conduct, in particular that of ministerial candidates, and for organising and allocating teaching loads. In a certain sense, therefore, this article should perhaps be called 'The Genevan Company of Pastors and training for the ministry'. And yet the Academy was important enough for the ministers to put its survival before their own, so that in 1586, when the Small Council of Geneva considered closing down the Academy because of the blockade from Savoy, the ministers suggested that instead some of the ministers of the city could cease receiving salaries, and remain on a voluntary basis. The ministers also described the Academy as a nursery for ministers,[24] a phrase which recurs in letters from foreign churches.[25]

The churches which despatched ministerial candidates to Geneva also had very definite ideas concerning the training which they expected their students to receive, and the characteristics which they looked for in a minister. In many cases, those sending students to Geneva provided them with a letter addressed to the

Company of Pastors, recommending the student to the Company's care, and providing a testimony of the student's conduct up until his departure. Thus, the church of Rouen, writing to Geneva on 24 September 1613, recommended an unnamed student, stating,

> The letter carrier is sent by us to finish his studies in your Academy. He is a candidate of our church, to which he has dedicated his labours for the holy ministry with the grace of God. We ask you to take him as being recommended [. . .]. We can testify than he is full of piety and has good morals, and that he has been this way since he was small'.[26]

The Colloquy of Aulnis, in France, writing to the Company on 21 May 1615, warmly recommended their student Pierre Joutin to Geneva's care: 'We implore you very affectionately not to deny him anything which your usual piety ordinarily provides for the good and the progress of those who, like him, are sent to you.'[27]

In their letters, the churches also indicated the areas on which their students should focus in their training. For instance, the church of Aubeterre wrote to the Company on 8 January 1565 detailing the course of study which they were hoping their student Jean Boutellant would follow:

> He is in Geneva to study and profit not only from the languages and doctrine of the Word of God, but also from the practice of doctrine and good order which can bolster ecclesiastical discipline, which is a most necessary thing [. . .]. Please have him practise in some village, so that he will be less of a novice when he comes to lead the flock in this area.[28]

The church of Rouen's letter, quoted above, also contains a request for specific training for their student.

> If such a thing is allowed among you, we would ask that he could have entry to your consistories, to learn that good order which was first born among you and then spread to the churches of France. We also ask you to use him sometimes, as you do others of the same status, to preach in the villages of your area, so that by speaking in public, he may be able to train his voice and grow in confidence.[29]

Both these letters indicate how important practical matters of training, such as knowledge of discipline and practice in preaching, were to the churches. The Company of Pastors itself encouraged practical training by making use of students as occasional preachers in rural Genevan parishes, for such a scheme meant that Geneva had the resources to fill gaps in ministerial ranks, at least temporarily, until a permanent minister could be found. There was then less likelihood of worshippers falling away, as there might have been if the pulpit were left vacant for long periods. At the same time, this occasional preaching provided an opportunity for student ministers to try their homiletic skills on captive congregations.

The churches' requests for ministers display the same interest in practical elements of training. Particularly in the early years, in the 1560s and 1570s, the lack of ministers was acute, and thus it may be that churches were less choosy about potential recruits, as their needs far outstripped the availability of pastors. Thus, the church in Nîmes reported to the Genevan Company of Pastors in a letter dated 12 May 1561 that at the recent provincial synod of Saintes, there were ten ministers for 54 churches, and they begged to be sent some pastors.[30] But later in the sixteenth century and early seventeenth century, the churches were in a position to be more discerning, and could lay out with increasing emphasis the qualities which they sought in their ministers. Thus, the French church in Basle wrote to the Company of Pastors on 22 May 1592, requesting Monsieur Arnoult as their minister, 'as much because of his great piety and learning, as because of God's gift of Italian, Spanish, and other languages to him, which are very useful in this place which many people from those nations pass through each day'.[31] On the same subject of languages, the church of Metz requested a minister from Geneva in January 1615, stating, 'He should, apart from the necessary talents, be willing to work with us at the work of the Lord and should have a loud voice, to fill our assembly.' Discussing the two candidates who might be appropriate, the Metz church continued, 'if you judge the aforesaid de Marsal to be as suited as Tissenil, we would prefer the first one, because firstly as a native son we will get permission more easily from Milord the Duke d'Epernon to employ him, and because of his knowledge of German, which is very useful around here on many occasions.'[32] Again, practical considerations appear to prevail.

The same was true in the case of the Rouen church's request for a minister from Geneva on 30 October 1613. Evidently, the Company of Pastors had already suggested some possible ministers, but Rouen's criteria were not being met, and they had little qualms in letting Geneva know that the possibilities did not meet with their approval. The Rouen church wrote,

> We will say to you frankly and we hope you will take it in good part, that the choice you offer us of two people whom you have named as possible choices for us do not quite match our wishes. It is not that we reject your judgement as regards the excellent testimony which you give us regarding both these men. But the first one, you say, can only promise us 18 months of service, which we find much too short. It would be a shame to have him make such a long trip, in winter as well, only to send him back after 18 months. We also hear that he has a large family, which would also be difficult. As for the second one, who you say was born and raised in your church and whom you used for a while as a replacement to preach in an extraordinary assembly near the city, because we are not sure of the strength of his voice, we fear it will not be heard by the four to five thousand people who make up this church, a point which we raised specifically when we wrote to two of the members of your company. You do not mention this matter when speaking of this man, but only recommend his morals and learning. This church, more than any other in the province, needs to be led by ministers who are doctrinally able and prudent, having knowledge of the world, able to speak out when needed to the government and magistrates about various problems which arise relatively often here.[33]

Apart from the oversight of the students whom churches sent to Geneva, the churches' other expectation vis-à-vis the Company of Pastors was that it would carry out an assessment of students' performance, if and when asked to do so. Thus, the church of Nantes on 1 April 1565 asked the Company of Pastors to evaluate the performance of François Loyseau, to gauge his ability to serve the church of Nantes. The church added that if he were found to be unsuitable, Geneva should try to obtain another student for the Nantes church.[34] On 11 April of the same year, the church of Loubens wrote via the Seigneur of Sausseux to Geneva to find out whether their student, Antoine Faure, was ready to be sent to them.[35] On 5 August 1584, the churches of Vert and Tonneins wrote to the Company to explain that they could not afford to keep Elias Neau, their student, in Geneva for any longer than six months, and that this period was coming to an end. Therefore, they requested the Company to examine him, and 'finding him capable and able to teach, as we hope you will do, please send him back to us with your testimony and laying-on of hands, so that our churches may benefit from his ministry from his arrival onwards.[36]

All told, the churches were interested in practical matters above all, even as regarded studies for the ministry. Financial constraints, or the large size of a building in which the new minister would be preaching, could become more important than the length of study and calibre of training potential ministerial candidates received. Yet the students themselves also had a voice in their training, and it may be worthwhile at this point to consider the students, and their reasons for coming to Geneva to study.

Students who came to Geneva to study for the ministry came mainly from France. The proportion of Frenchmen among the ministerial candidates remained significantly large up until 1620, though it did diminish somewhat throughout the sixty years under discussion.[37] The proportion of those studying for the ministry out of the entire student body, meanwhile, remained relatively constant, at about a third of the total number of students.[38] Between 1559 and 1620, a total of 2,674 students are known to have attended the Genevan Academy, and out of that number 729 are known to have become ministers. Because the Genevan matriculation list is incomplete, the total number of students may be higher. In addition, in spite of arduous research on the part of the Stelling-Michaud team, little is known about certain matriculated students apart from their name and place of origin.[39] Thus, it is probable that the real number of those who became ministers after their studies in Geneva is larger than the number indicated. In the early years, until the turn of the century, Geneva's appeal lay at least partly in the fact that it was one of the few established French-language centres of training for Reformed clergy. The Genevan Academy had much to recommend it as a centre of training: as it was outside French territory, French anti-heresy laws could not touch those who took refuge and were students there.[40] Geneva was close enough to France both geographically and in terms of its leadership to be able to make a considerable impact on the French religious situation, since nearly all of Geneva's ministers were French in the latter half of the sixteenth century, and the Company of Pastors' interests led them naturally to focus on the churches in their homeland. The geographic proximity between France and Geneva allowed for the two-way traffic of students coming to Geneva to train for the ministry, and of ministers being sent out, often secretly for fear of discovery and execution, to French congregations. Lausanne, the other possible French-language academy in the vicinity, took many years to recover from the blow of losing most of her professors to Geneva, and the main Huguenot academies in France, which did provide ministerial training, were nearly all founded around or after 1600, too late to be able to have an impact on the expansion of French Protestantism in the sixteenth century.[41]

Very occasionally one can catch glimpses of the students' own perspective on their studies in Geneva. Their expectations regarding their studies in Geneva are rarely explained, chiefly because only a very few letters written by Genevan students survive. Those alumni that did express views on Geneva often did so after their training was over, and, in many cases, they painted their studies in a favourable light, either because of the fond memories which they held from that period, or because they were asking Geneva for a favour in their letters, in which case a negative assessment of their studies would have been counterproductive. Those who did report on their studies seemed to value especially the atmosphere of learning which they felt permeated the Academy. Nicolas Le More, a young French minister, wrote plaintively to the Company of Pastors on 1 November 1561, asking to be allowed to return to the Academy, as he was having difficulty obtaining the respect of his congregation. He wrote, 'Please remember that I am still an apprentice, and that I am still very young, and that I really need to return to my studies . . .'[42] In a few instances, however, a less glowing picture is provided of the Academy by students who for one reason or other felt they had been badly treated by the Genevan authorities. Such, for example, was the case of Pierre Vert, a student minister from Metz. Metz had provided a number of students for Geneva, and many of the Metz ministers had been trained there, so that there was a long history of contact between Metz and Geneva regarding training and ministry. Vert got into trouble in Geneva, according to a letter sent by the Company of Pastors to the church of Metz on 28 July 1618.[43] In its letter, the Company stated that, far from being a model student, Vert had spent his time hanging around town and playing games of chance. He also managed to quarrel violently with a Flemish nobleman over a game of tennis, so much so that

Vert provoked the nobleman to a duel. As duels were forbidden in Geneva, Vert could not put his plan into practice, but instead whenever he met the nobleman, would 'tease, torment and threaten him, saying he would give the nobleman a beating'. Things went from bad to worse, as Vert taunted the nobleman once too often in broad daylight on a city street. The nobleman used his stick on Vert, and, as the Company remarked, 'the scandal was not small'. It was eventually decided that both parties should meet before the Consistory. The Flemish nobleman obeyed the summons, but Vert had by then fled town, and, from Metz, wrote reproachfully back to the Genevan minister Etienne Mollet, blaming the Company for his woes.

> Your assembly was as much against me as you are, or at least a part of it was, (for I know there are honourable people among you). It spoke so uncharitably against me to those who were to have me work for them [as their minister], that they believed you as easily as certain people spew out venom to my disadvantage, and they accepted someone else. I ask you, is it right to prevent the reception of a young man without legitimate cause?

'After this', he continued plaintively,

> who will have the courage to use up a large part of his means to meet the costs of study, since even having done nothing, he can be disgraced by those in authority, and by being blocked by them finds himself stopped short at the end of his race? Indeed, if I believed that your assembly had a voice everywhere, I would despair of ever being able to serve, because I know that your company knows how to preserve its enmity against those it dislikes. I saw many examples of this among you, which confirms my views. I pray God, however, that your enmity will not spread further, and that I will be the last to have felt it.[44]

Vert's letter shows, albeit in a negative light, what influence Geneva had, not only during a student's course of study but also afterwards, in terms of placement in parishes. Vert acknowledged reluctantly that Geneva's word carried weight.

As Vert pointed out, one of the main problems which confronted students for the ministry was that of funding. The difficulty lay not in the fees, since education in Geneva was completely free until 1584, when a modest matriculation fee was imposed on all students apart from Genevans and those from Switzerland. The main expenses were lodging, food, clothing, and books. In response to this the Company of Pastors set up a sponsorship scheme, hoping to alleviate such problems. A church, a wealthy individual, or a city provided funds for a student from their area to spend a period in Geneva, sometimes for as little as six months, as the churches of Vert and Tonneins explained.[45] In certain cases, the funds were sent directly to the Genevan authorities to have them disburse the money to their student in a controlled fashion, lessening the risk that the student might use the money for other purposes. Thus, on 11 October 1596, the Registers of the Genevan Small Council recorded that a letter had been received by the Council from the States of Friesland in the Netherlands, requesting that Joannes Bogermann, a student in theology, be provided with a bursary of 150 gold florins. The States suggested that the money should be taken out of the 300 florins which Geneva owed to Friesland as annual interest on the Frisian loan of 5,000 florins to the Council, a loan contracted two years previously in response to the request of the Genevan Councillor Jacob Anjorrant, then touring the Netherlands in search of funds for the city.[46] The Council decided to give Bogermann 150 florins then, and the other half in six months, if he agreed to the arrangement and was satisfied.[47] Yet at times the Genevan authorities did not fulfil their responsibilities as well as they might. In November 1598, two Dutch students, Hadrianus Cornelius Drogius and Nicolaus Grevinchof, had to write to the Genevan Small Council to complain that their scholarship, which the States of Holland had given the Genevan authorities to administer, had been cut short. They were supposed to receive 26 écus each per quarter, but had only received 20. However, by 17 January 1599 they had received the full amount.[48]

The students benefited from the scheme by receiving enough funds to maintain themselves and profit from their stay in Geneva without financial worries or distractions from their studies. Geneva profited from the arrangement by knowing that through sponsorship, the Academy would be furnished with students able to support themselves, who would not run into financial difficulties and turn to the Genevan authorities for assistance. As well, the Genevan church would not then be depleted of all its own ministers when answering requests of other churches. In consequence the Company actively encouraged sponsorship schemes and scholarships. Writing to the church of Metz on 28 October 1579, the

Company noted, 'The other point is that if possible, you should
provide maintenance for a few promising students, whom you could
use if need be. If you employ our services for the purpose, we will
try our best to cultivate the young plants which you will send to
us, so that you can gain from them the fruit which you need.'[49] In
a more concrete fashion, the Company wrote to the church of Metz
on 6 April 1580, organising Metz's sponsorship of François de
Combles's studies. The Company even outlined the amount which
it felt Metz should pay de Combles per year, namely 50 écus sols.[50]
On 27 January 1581, nearly a year later, another student, François
Buffet, was sponsored by Metz, and Geneva recommended increasing the scholarship to 60 écus sols a year, perhaps in the light of
de Combles's experience, or because of the increased cost of living
in Geneva.[51] The Company of Pastors also attempted to organise,
seemingly with less success, scholarships which were to be provided by the Small Council, in order to create a body of young
ministers who were tied to the city and who would pledge themselves to serve it in return for the financial support which they
received during their studies. In 1574, 1578, and again in 1583,
the Company proposed students' names to the Small Council,
asking for them to be given funds. In 1583, one of the students in
theology, Pierre Châtillon, had to subscribe to the following promise: 'Pierre Châtillon [. . .] promises to serve the *Seigneurie* during
his whole life, wherever the Council sees fit to send him'. In
exchange, the Council promised him 160 florins a year.[52] Unfortunately, these scholarships provided by the Council were not
repeated.

As in this case, the provision of scholarships to students in
the ministry was intended to benefit the sponsors as well, because
students receiving funds from them had to promise that once their
studies were completed, they would serve as ministers those who
had given them financial support. The Company of Pastors kept
particular watch over students who were sponsored, so as to be
able to report back to the sponsors on their protégés' progress. On
21 May 1602, the Company of Pastors decided 'that the Rector will
keep the letters from churches who recommend to us the students
that they are sending here, and that he will keep a particular eye
on them, and call them in to watch over their studies and
behaviour, and exhort them to do their duty, since the said
churches recommend the students to us and rely on us'.[53] Of

course, the system was not perfect since from time to time various participants tried to withdraw from their commitments, as did the church of Lyons, which in 1571 suddenly stopped providing funds to its students in Geneva, without any explanation. The Company noted students' complaints 'that for several months they have received nothing, and some, very little, so that they have had to borrow and get into debt, and are still in need'. The church of Lyons eventually replied that it had no more funds and that the students should seek funding elsewhere.[54] Yet by and large, the sponsorship scheme was a success, as it provided the necessary financial stability and oversight which made training more effective. Out of 729 students who became ministers, 108 students, or nearly 15 per cent of the total, are known to have received funds for their Genevan training, from churches, city councils, or nobles and princes scattered from London to Utrecht via many of the French churches.[55] The willingness of such groups and individuals to provide money for students to come to Geneva indicates something of the Genevan Academy's stature in Europe as a training centre for ministers.

In preparing students for the Reformed ministry, Geneva judged their aptitude in three areas: their assiduity for and ability in their studies, their moral behaviour, and their practical training as preachers. Even after the establishment of the Academy the Company of Pastors remained the institution in the city most competent to monitor students' progress in these three areas. Although established with the goal of creating a capable, trained, preaching ministry, the Academy was increasingly distracted from these purposes by pressures to provide a more broad-ranging curriculum which reflected contemporary expectations as to the purpose of institutions of higher education. Such pressures were reinforced by Geneva's secular rulers, keen to attract students of social distinction, who were more likely to be interested in secular disciplines (especially law) than theology. On the other side, churches continued to value practical skills – proficiency in preaching and knowledge of church organisation, which had no place inside a university curriculum.

Training for the ministry in Geneva thus remained a curious mix of the formal and informal, in which the practical expertise of the Company of Pastors played as important a role as the scholarly training provided by professors of the Academy. It was a pragmatic response to the need to provide a core of preaching ministers who could also offer leadership through their personal example to congregations in a variety of different and trying circumstances in the Calvinist churches of Europe.

Notes

1 *Ordonnances Ecclesiastiques de 1541*, reprinted in H. Heyer, *L'Eglise de Genève 1535–1909: Esquisse historique de son organisation* (Geneva, 1909), p. 266.

2 E. W. Monter, *Calvin's Geneva* (New York, 1967). The fullest interpretation of these events is now to be found in William Naphy, 'Calvin and the Consolidation of the Genevan Reformation' (St Andrews University Ph.D. thesis, 1993).

3 E. W. Monter, *Studies in Genevan Government (1536–1605)* (Geneva, 1964), p. 25. He presents figures from the Treasury accounts, totalling disbursements of over 36,000 florins in 1559 from the regular Treasury, and another 11,178 florins from the special account of the Arche in 1560, for a total of over 47,000 florins for those two years. Monter points out that these figures represented an increase in spending of about a third, as compared with the budgets of 1558 and 1561. However, he also notes that receipts for 1559 amounted to 30,129 florins received by the regular Treasury, and 31,582 florins received by the Arche in 1560, and concludes that these very high receipts were the result of the auctioning of the property of Calvin's opponents after their exile.

4 The professors of the Lausanne Academy, founded in 1537, had sided with their colleagues in the ministry in the city in opposing the attempts of their Bernese overlords to impose the exercise of discipline and the liturgy along Bernese rather than Genevan lines. Faced with the refusal of the Lausanne clergy to conform to Bernese instructions, the latter dismissed some of the leading clergy who were followed into exile by the majority of their ministerial and professorial colleagues, as well as by an indeterminate number of students. Charles Borgeaud, *Histoire de l'université de Genève* (4 vols, Geneva, 1900–59), I, pp. 38–41.

5 RC 55, fol. 21, 21 March 1559; fol. 48, 22 May 1559.

6 R. Kingdon, *Geneva and the Coming of the Wars of Religion in France 1555–1563* (Geneva, 1956), pp. 14–15.

7 T. Parker, *Calvin's Preaching* (Edinburgh, 1992), pp. 38–9.

8 In 1559, out of the 68 students who matriculated, 37 are known to have become ministers (54.4 per cent). In 1560, out of 52 students, 21 became ministers (40.4 per cent). In 1561, 8 out of 19 students became ministers (42.1 per cent). In 1562, 6 out of 22 matriculated students went on to the ministry (27.3 per cent), and in 1563, 26 out of 95 students followed the same path (27.4 per cent). In comparison, in 1616, 15 out of 27 students matriculated in Geneva's Academy became ministers (55.6 per

cent), in 1617, 16 out of 37 did the same (43.2 per cent), in 1618, 28 out of 104 students went on to the ministry (26.9 per cent), in 1619, 17 out of 71 students are known to have entered the ministry (23.9 per cent), and in 1620, 12 out of 30 students became ministers (40 per cent). Overall, the percentage of students entering the ministry from among the total student body remained relatively constant. Data from Sven and Suzanne Stelling-Michaud, *Le Livre du recteur de l'académie de Genève 1559–1878* (6 vols, Geneva 1959–80).

9 *Ordonnances Ecclésiastiques de 1541* and *Ordonnances Ecclésiastiques de 1576* in Heyer, *L'Eglise de Genève*, pp. 262–3, 278–9.

10 RC 61, fol. 100, 22 October 1566.

11 RC 67, fol. 164, 13 October 1572.

12 Borgeaud, *L'Université de Genève*, pp. 96–7.

13 RC 79, fol. 135, 6 October 1584.

14 *RCP* III, p. 152.

15 Paul-F. Geisendorf, *L'Université de Genève 1559–1959: Quatre siècles d'histoire* (Geneva, 1959), p. 69.

16 RC 82, fol. 166, 4 September 1587.

17 Borgeaud, *L'Université de Genève*, p. 228.

18 *RCP* IX, p. 13.

19 *RCP* VII, p. 79, 28 October 1597. The registers noted that the students of theology were called together to be told that the *propositions* would be restarted, and that 33 students were present, most of them from the city. The complaints about less able students participating in the *propositions* can be found in *RCP* IX, p. 215, 17 October 1606.

20 *RCP* IX, pp. 199, 215.

21 *RCP* V, p. 305.

22 *RCP* IX, pp. 67, 265.

23 *RCP* VIII, p. 57.

24 RC 81, fol. 159, 6 August 1586; fol. 229, 18 October 1586.

25 For instance, see BPU Manuscrits français (hereafter Ms. fr.) 422, fols 29–30, 8 August 1614, letter from the church of Metz to the Company of Pastors: 'your church and school, having been for many years like a nursery for ministers, and having produced so many excellent people who served well elsewhere and who now enjoy the crown of life. . . .'

26 BPU Ms. fr. 421, fol. 99.

27 BPU Ms. fr. 422, fol. 57.

28 *RCP* III, p. 165.

29 BPU Ms. fr. 421, fol. 99.

30 BPU Ms. fr. 197a, fol. 92.

31 *RCP* VI, p. 268.

32 BPU Ms. fr. 422, fols 42–3.

33 BPU Ms. fr. 421, fols 105–6.

34 *RCP* III, p. 166.

35 BPU Ms. fr. 197a, fol. 208.

36 *RCP* V, p. 293.

37 In 1559, 29 out of the 37 students in the Academy who went on to become ministers came from France (78.4 per cent). In 1560, 17 out of

21 student ministers came from France (81 per cent). In 1561, 5 out of 8 future ministers were from France (62.5 per cent), whereas in 1562, 5 out of 6 student ministers were French (83.3 per cent). In 1563, 19 out of 26 future ministers came from France (73.1 per cent). By 1600, the proportion of French students studying for the ministry had dropped, so that in 1600, 2 future ministers out of 12 came from France (16.6 per cent), in 1601, 4 future ministers out of 10 were French (40 per cent), in 1602, 4 out of 11 future ministers were from France (36.4 per cent), in 1603, one future minister out of 4 was French (25 per cent), and in 1604, 6 out of 17 future ministers came from France (35.3 per cent). Data from Stelling-Michaud, *Le Livre du recteur* (the calculations are my own).

38 See note 7.
39 Stelling-Michaud, *Le Livre du recteur*.
40 Kingdon, *Geneva and the Coming of the Wars of Religion*, p. 1.
41 Henri Meylan, 'Collèges et académies protestantes au XVIe siècle', in Henri Meylan, *D'Erasme à Théodore de Bèze* (Geneva, 1976), pp. 196–7.
42 *BSHPF*, 46 (1897), 466–8.
43 The account of Vert's conduct is found in the letter from the Company of Pastors to the church of Metz, 28 July 1618. BPU Ms. fr. 423, fol. 22.
44 Letter of Pierre Vert to the minister Etienne Mollet in Geneva, 26 June 1618. BPU Ms. fr. 423, fol. 21.
45 *RCP* V, p. 293.
46 Anjorrant's report of his fundraising activities is reprinted in H. de Vries de Heekelingen, *Genève, pépinière du calvinisme hollandaise*, 2 vols, (The Hague, 1916–24), II, pp. 372–81. A translated extract in A. Duke, G. Lewis, and A. Pettegree (eds), *Calvinism in Europe 1540–1610. A Collection of Documents* (Manchester, 1992), pp. 237–42.
47 RC 96, fol. 198.
48 Letter from Hadrianus Cornelius Drogius and Nicolaus Grevinchof Roterodamus, November [1598], to [Small Council,] Geneva, and receipt made out to the two students from the syndic Jean de Villars. In AEG, Requêtes et rapports au Conseil: écoles. RR: écoles.
49 *RCP* IV, p. 296.
50 *RCP* IV, p. 320.
51 *RCP* IV, p. 357.
52 *RCP* V, p. 18.
53 *RCP* VIII, p. 148.
54 *RCP* III, p. 30.
55 Data in Stelling-Michaud, *Le Livre du recteur*; *RCP*; Zurich Staatsarchiv, Album in Tigurina schola studentium (Matriculation list of Zurich's academy). The calculation is my own.

8

The demands and dangers of the Reformed ministry in Troyes, 1552–72

Penny Roberts

The establishment of an organised Calvinist church in France was undertaken in the face of increasing persecution and civil strife. Each year, in response to requests from individual churches and beginning with Poitiers in 1555, Geneva despatched ministers to the cities of France in ever greater numbers. These men would all have undergone the rigorous theological training expected of Calvinist ministers. Confident exposition and vocal projection were much valued as attributes for the pulpit and, in addition, the minister was required to have led a morally upright life. Having passed these tests, the examinee was then entitled to accrediting letters allocating him to serve a specified church in France.[1] The Genevan Company thus ensured that the ministers charged with instructing and increasing the Calvinist presence were of the highest calibre, and that the influence and discipline of Geneva would be felt throughout the French church.

However, between 1555 and 1562 only eighty-eight ministers are officially recorded as having been sent out from Geneva, despite an estimated total of over a thousand French Reformed churches, many of which would have required more than one pastor.[2] Although this may simply be a result of under-registration, it is clear that the Genevan organisation was only part of the story. Other centres, such as Lausanne and Neuchâtel, and the Reformed church of Paris, also played an important role in the training and supply of ministers. Even so, the demand was such that many churches were initially forced to rely on the services of dubiously qualified, self-styled ministers, often to the detriment of their congregations. Even when a church was fortunate enough to acquire professionally trained pastors, the demands and dangers they faced

The Province of Champagne

in carrying out their ministry could be considerable. Moreover, factors such as the attitude of regional authorities and the location of sites for worship could be crucial for the well-being of the church and the burden placed upon its ministers. Such were the problems confronting the Reformed church at Troyes in Champagne, from its inception in 1552, through a period of expansion and decline over the subsequent two decades. The chance survival of an outstanding contemporary source, the memoir of a leading member of the church at Troyes, Nicolas Pithou, also provides a rare insight into the experience of the ministers as they attempted to perform their duties, often in adverse conditions.[3]

Troyes was well placed to receive the attention of the propagators of the French Reformation. Its location, three days' ride south-east of Paris, ensured that the city was favoured as a convenient stop-over by preachers and booksellers passing between Paris and Geneva. In 1558, the preacher Jean de Gannes, who stayed on the outskirts of Troyes on his way back from Geneva to Paris with a bundle of books of Holy Scripture, was seized and imprisoned. Even from a prison cell he was able to edify the Reformers, and to scandalise the Catholics, who came regularly to visit and discuss matters of faith with him. Soon afterwards, the Genevan minister, Jean Macard, on his return from a spell preaching in Paris, urged the Reformers of Troyes to re-establish a ministry to serve their spiritual needs and to maintain them in the faith. Later, the first minister of the Parisian church, Jean de La Rivière, promised to do all he could to provide the church at Troyes with a suitably qualified man from the theological debating forum for aspiring young ministers which had developed in the capital.[4]

The ministers who served the church at Troyes, though from outside the city, were all native Frenchmen and, in general, allocated to Troyes by the church where they had received their formal training. Girard de Courlieu, from a notable Angoulême family, who arrived in Troyes at the beginning of 1559, was to be the first of three Genevan-trained ministers sent by the Reformed church of Paris; the others being Paumier, in March 1560, and Jean Gravelle, a native of Dreux in Normandy, in January 1561. Paumier was to be the only one to come officially designated, not only to Troyes but to the entire province of Champagne, by the Genevan Company of Pastors.[5] Jacques Sorel, who was sent to assist Gravelle in 1561, was dispatched from the church at Neuchâtel, initially for six months. Neuchâtel was responsible for sending a substantial number of pastors to work in the provinces of Burgundy and Champagne, conveniently situated as it was on the other side of the Jura. Pierre Fornelet, for example, a contemporary of Sorel at Neuchâtel, became minister to the Reformed church at Châlons-sur-Marne.[6] Calvin himself was said to have interceded to secure Sorel's appointment. This suggests that Sorel, like Fornelet, had to travel to Geneva in order to obtain the necessary letters of accreditation before he could take up residence in Troyes. A native of Brie, Sorel expressed his delight at returning to his native region, and the congregation seem to have listened to his sermons all the more attentively as one of their own.[7] This illustrates the advantage for the 'native' minister when establishing relations with his allotted congregation, avoiding the initial complication of having to deal with alien customs and the difficulties of the local *patois*.

In common with many other fledgling churches, the Reformed church at Troyes first emerged under the guidance of one who was not formally trained for his pastoral role. Michel Poncelet was a wool-carder from Meaux, the so-called 'cradle of the French Reformation'; his credentials were his knowledge of and ability to argue from Holy Scripture and his devotion to God's cause.[8] The well-established trading links between Troyes and Meaux must have provided ample opportunity for merchants and artisans in search of work to pick up something of the religious fervour which had characterised the movement at Meaux for several decades. Poncelet took up his duty as a result of an entreaty from local Protestants as he passed through Troyes on his way to Geneva in 1551. He was to serve the church at Troyes for six years.

The interest which the arrival of Poncelet aroused among those sympathetic with the Reformed faith in Troyes, reveals that both artisans and notables had been discussing the new ideas in private, but were previously ignorant of each other's existence. Pithou tells us, 'those who had some knowledge of the religion behaved so covertly, that there were few who communicated one with another, so much did they fear being found out and recognised for what they were'.[9] On Poncelet's return from Geneva at the beginning of 1552, the Huguenots of Troyes were encouraged to begin meeting regularly together for worship. Whatever instruction Poncelet may have received on his brief trip to Geneva, it was insufficient to qualify him to administer the sacraments. Catholic baptismal registers covering the period of his ministry reveal that Huguenots were continuing to have their children baptised in local parish churches.[10]

As with other Huguenot communities in the 1550s, meetings were initially held clandestinely in private houses, at which Poncelet would give an exhortation and lead a small group in readings, psalms, and prayers. The hosts were usually drawn from the better-off members of the congregation, such as the doctor, Berthélemy Allyon, and the royal official, Pierre Girardin, no doubt because of the size and relative privacy of their residences.[11] The disclosure of Girardin's servant alerted the authorities to the presence of a minister in the town in 1555, and papers seized at the house revealed the identity of some long-suspected Huguenots who had been attending the assemblies.[12] For larger gatherings, and those accessible to other Reformers in the district, the meadows and fields around Troyes were the venue. This also allowed those curious about the new religion, but not yet prepared to commit themselves, to attend discreetly. The existence of such secret sympathisers helps explain why Reformed churches throughout France were able to expand so rapidly when political circumstances permitted. Although despised by Calvin, such 'Nicodemites' represented an important potential source of strength for the church when official persecution eased.[13]

The years of political turmoil which followed the death of Henry II in 1559, provided the context in which the French churches were able to thrive. In Troyes, Girard de Courlieu was able to preside over the establishment of a more ordered *église dressée*, or 'gathered' church, appointing elders to assist him by co-ordinating assemblies of the faithful. He also began administering the sacraments, baptising two infants soon after his arrival and celebrating the first Lord's Supper.[14] Catholic baptism and attendance at Mass would no longer be tolerated among the faithful, as de Courlieu demonstrated by leaving his lodgings when, contrary to his instructions, his host's child was baptised at the parish church. In May 1561, under the ministry of Jean Gravelle, as confidence and numbers grew, open-air services were held in streets and cemeteries despite the attempts of the royal *bailli* to sabotage them.[15] By the end of the month, so great had the demands on Gravelle's time become that (as he wrote to Beza) 'the number of those who invoke the name of the Lord here is so great, that I cannot provide for them'. He requested the sending of another pastor to assist him in his duties.[16] His plea did not go unheeded, and he was soon joined by Jacques Sorel. By November, as private houses could no longer accommodate the rapidly expanding congregation, the Huguenots rented a barn in which to hold services. This was in common with other towns in the province, such as Vassy and Céant-en-Othe, where the Protestant community did not have sufficient leverage to be able to take over an existing Catholic church, nor the wherewithal to undertake the construction of a *temple* of their own.[17]

By the autumn of 1561 there were three active Reformed ministers at Troyes. Gravelle and Sorel were joined by Pierre Le Roy, an ex-Carmelite and former minister of the Reformed church at Dijon. At the beginning of 1562, if we are to include the controversial bishop of Troyes, Antonio Caracciolo, who requested and was accepted into the Reformed ministry (although he was to conduct only one full service himself at Lent 1562), then the church could boast four ministers attending to the needs of its burgeoning congregation on the eve of the civil wars. Le Roy did not endear himself to the congregation because of his open hostility to the popular acceptance of Bishop Caracciolo into the ministry, a theme which dominated his sermons. On one occasion when Le Roy was conducting a service, his stance upset so many of his audience that they demonstrated their disapproval by walking out.[18] Even Pithou, who was also staunchly opposed to the bishop's appointment, thought that Le Roy's behaviour was rash because of the unnecessary divisions it caused within the church.

The bishop's conversion would have represented a notable coup for the Calvinist church, both at the local level in Troyes and for the leaders of the movement in Geneva. Nevertheless, since his appointment as bishop in 1551, Caracciolo had frustrated both Protestants and Catholics by his inconsistency and prevarication in religious affairs. It was apparently at the Colloquy of Poissy of September 1561 that the bishop decided to declare once and for all for the Reform, doubtless prompted by the impressive Calvinist contingent led by Beza, and the realisation that he was not the only member of the episcopate sympathetic to Reformed ideas. On his return to Troyes Caracciolo presented himself before the Reformed consistory, declared his repentance, begged forgiveness, signed the confession of faith, and sought admission to the ministry.

A dispute ensued in the general assembly held to discuss the issue, but the majority remained in favour of accepting Caracciolo's appointment.[19] This decision was later ratified by Peter Martyr, and more, reluctantly, recalling the fickle nature of the bishop, by Calvin. Calvin's eventual decision grudgingly allowed for Caracciolo's admission, although he also remarked that such individuals ought to be content to favour the Reform as great lay lords rather than as ministers.[20] However, the honeymoon was to be short-lived; Caracciolo's resignation from the bishopric and departure from Troyes came just before the outbreak of the wars in the spring of 1562.

Although he would later try to re-enter the Calvinist ministry, Caracciolo was to play only a peripheral part in the future of the Reformed church at Troyes.[21] His election may have been misjudged, but an evangelically-minded bishop was a less manifestly unsuitable choice than many men who proposed themselves for the ministry at this time. In a period of rapid expansion, with churches springing up all over France, the demand for ministers was such that some churches were less scrupulous than they might otherwise have been in accepting any likely candidate. Many of these men were former monks or priests more concerned to safeguard their future in a time of highly uncertain prospects than genuinely committed to the Gospel. The most notorious of these cases were dealt with by successive national synods, which published lists of ministers deposed because of their licentious behaviour or unorthodox views, of whom churches were advised to beware.[22] Whilst the shortfall in trained ministers continued, the attempt to root out these charlatans could be only partially successful. In this context the quality of the men who served Troyes is all the more striking. All the ministers were capable and articulate men and, apart from the artisan Poncelet, had connections with the centres of French exiled Protestantism in Switzerland. The attention paid to the provision of able pastors to Troyes illustrates the importance attached by the church leadership in Geneva to the maintenance of the faith in these strategic northern urban centres.

Even for the most able and experienced of Calvinist missionaries, the establishment of churches in France was a hazardous undertaking. In Troyes, as elsewhere, the church had a rather erratic existence as ministers, as a result of persecution or short-term contracts, came and went. In Troyes there was a year's gap between the departure of Poncelet and the arrival of de Courlieu, and another hiatus between de Courlieu and Gravelle. Although congregations grew dramatically after the death of Henry II, persecution was to continue unabated under Francis II and the regime dominated by the duke of Guise. The minister Paumier was in Troyes for only two months before he was arrested, shortly after conducting his first service, in May 1560.[23] As ministers were the primary target of the authorities still bent on suppression, it was crucial to keep their identity and location secret, since if caught they were invariably sentenced to death. Aliases were common among Genevan missionaries as just one of the precautions taken to avoid detection. Thus Poncelet was known as 'Le Picard', Gravelle as 'Dupin', and Sorel as 'Ponterreuse'. It was useful, also, if a minister could pass as a local tradesman, as frequently occurred among the artisan ministers of the first generation in the Netherlands. Michel Poncelet maintained his cover as an ordinary craftsman, so much so that when sergeants undertook a search in a house where he had been conducting prayers, he was able to greet them without fear of recognition.[24] Even if a minister evaded capture, once recognised, it was too dangerous for him to return.[25]

To prevent the discovery of Protestant assemblies a number of measures were taken. One such was to ensure a regular rotation of venues.[26] Ministers, too, were forced to change their lodgings frequently to avoid suspicion. Girard de Courlieu's experience illustrates the difficulty for ministers in keeping their identity secret in an environment where there was little privacy and a stranger's presence would be remarked upon. Pithou claims that it was, 'the nature of the citizens of Troyes, curious to find out about the affairs of their neighbours, . . . and quick to put their nose to the window as soon as they heard their neighbours' shutters creaking, to discover what they were up to'.[27] Danger was heightened by an increasing awareness among the inhabitants that secret gatherings were being held in the town. De Courlieu's first lodging proved to be rather too close for comfort to the house of the Cordeliers, as the minister could be seen from the library of the convent writing at his desk. Those who handled the affairs of the church insisted that he should move to another residence, despite the fact that its owner, a pharmacist, was the most renowned Huguenot in the city. Here, de Courlieu persuaded his

hosts not to decorate their house at Corpus Christi 1559, a provo-
cation to those who took part in the processions which occurred
on that day, and one that ran the risk of the minister being dis-
covered by drawing attention to his hiding-place.[28] De Courlieu
was finally arrested and imprisoned following a search for stolen
property; an incident quite unconnected with the suppression of
services. Some important papers were also seized, including a list
of those who had attended the recent synod in Paris, and other
incriminating documents containing the names of those in the
church at Troyes.[29] The keeping of such lists presented another
risk requiring great prudence on the part of church-goers.

Thus, ministers often had to operate under dangerous and
difficult conditions, both because of the hostility of local authorities
and because of the repercussions of official persecution. Poncelet
relinquished his charge as a result of the growing fears of his
congregation following the rue Saint-Jacques affair in Paris in 1557
(when about 130 Huguenots attending a service were arrested) and
the subsequent royal edict of 1558. As a consequence of these
events, the minister was sent to a place of safety outside Troyes.
The greater vigilance and activity of the secular authorities in
uncovering clandestine services at this time, combined with the
invective of Catholic preachers against them, seems to have
deterred the Huguenots of Troyes from carrying out their devotions. Poncelet found that on his return from his refuge, the congregation was so cool towards him and the continuation of his ministry
that, disillusioned, he left for good.[30]

The repercussions of a clamp-down in Paris following the
treaty of Câteau-Cambrésis which ended the Habsburg/Valois wars
in 1559 prompted a search of the houses of Huguenot suspects by
the Troyen authorities. The principals of the Reformed church
responded by sending the then minister, de Courlieu, to a château
fifteen miles distant, although the minister criticised this move, as
had Poncelet before him, saying that it displayed their fear and set
a poor example for other churches.[31] The Reformed church benefited from the new adherents de Courlieu attracted by preaching
in his new location, but his followers in Troyes itself took a dim
view of the elders depriving them of their minister, as they saw it.
De Courlieu was arrested on his return and was sentenced to be
burned, but appealed and had his case referred to the Paris Parle-
ment. On his way to the capital to be tried in November 1559, he

was rescued by a group of masked men of unknown identity. This was not an isolated incident, the same having happened to Jean de Gannes only seven months before.[32] The relative frequency of the rescue of condemned ministers suggests both that there was an efficient Protestant network in operation, and that sixteenth-century prisons and prison guards were not always reliable. It may also be that there was a degree of collusion on the part of the local authorities, reluctant to risk the unrest that might accompany the execution of such a prominent figure. Similar circumstances were to surround the imprisonment of minister Paumier.

Paumier arrived in March 1560 in the wake of the Conspiracy of Amboise, and was consequently advised to lie low. However, frustrated by his enforced idleness, he went with a group from the church to hold a service at the house of a merchant just outside the city. The royal *bailli* was tipped off and his sergeants arrested the men, incriminated by the discovery of some of Paumier's books including Calvin's commentaries on St Paul.[33] The Huguenot prisoners, except for Paumier and two others who refused to compromise their faith, were able to benefit from the recent edict which provided an amnesty as long as they agreed to live henceforth as Catholics (as this clause expressly excluded pastors Paumier's stance was perhaps not so admirable as Pithou would have us believe). In fact, the remaining three prisoners were able to escape before they were brought to trial. On this occasion the escape of the minister caused ripples further afield. The municipal council received letters from both the governor, the duke of Nevers, and the dowager duchess of Guise, expressing their discontent at the escape of the 'seditious stranger', and that they held the council responsible in future for 'guarding the honour of God and His faith'.[34]

The daring nature of such escapes and the growing defiance of the Huguenots are an indication of the general air of confidence which pervaded the movement as the political mood appeared to swing in their favour. This confidence was reinforced by the rapid growth of congregations throughout France. Pithou states that at the time of de Courlieu's arrest in November 1559, there were 310 communicating members of the church at Troyes, 'as many men as women, all natives of Troyes'.[35] Two years later, Sorel put the figure closer to five hundred.[36] However, by Pentecost 1562, Pithou claimed that as many as eight to nine thousand attended communion (equivalent to nearly one-third of the population of Troyes), although this figure was swelled by the suites of the dukes of Nevers and Savoy, and the inhabitants of villages in the vicinity.[37] Such an inflated figure may be treated with some caution, but even so there had evidently been a dramatic increase in the size of the congregation at Troyes during the Huguenot 'wonderyear' of 1561–62, and this was in line with the growth of other urban churches on the eve of the civil wars.[38]

Behind these figures lies the fact that the ministers at Troyes were expected to serve the spiritual needs of an ever-increasing and widely scattered congregation. For the demands for their services came from far beyond the city walls, from other provincial centres and the rural estates of the local nobility. The church at Troyes thus had a considerable catchment area, as was true for other churches in the province. Pierre Fornelet, minister at Châlons, wrote to Neuchâtel expressing the urgent need for more ministers, as 'there is more than enough work for them'. In a letter of October 1561, Jacques Sorel spoke excitedly of the rapid growth of the congregation and that services were being held day and night despite royal prohibition of such assemblies. He went on to say that the church required all three of its present ministers, as one was always needed in the countryside to serve the rural communities 'because there are many places round about which are deprived of ministers and which have to rely for preaching on the ministers of this city'.[39] As Sorel had been sent on a temporary basis, a common position in the early 1560s, the church was in danger of losing not only him but also Le Roy, both of whom could be reallocated at any time. Indeed, in December, the church was to appeal unsuccessfully to prevent Le Roy's departure for Bordeaux.[40]

Sorel's letter also reveals some of the hardships experienced by Calvinist missionaries. The rigorous round of duties they were expected to perform, in an area where their numbers were insufficient to meet the demand, was detrimental to many a pastor's health. The ministers at Troyes were forced to undertake an exhausting circuit of the district with little chance of respite. The risks of their occupation also meant that missionaries were usually forced to leave wife and children behind. Sorel was eager to be joined by his family in the event that he was permitted to extend his ministry at Troyes. His ultimate fate, however, was in the hands

163

of his superiors in Neuchâtel; they evidently conceded his request, and his wife was soon able to join him.[41] Sorel's value went beyond simply sharing the burden of ministerial duties. In response to the need for easier access for agricultural workers, anxious about the attitude of their Catholic employers if they attended services within the town, the church council decided to convene an assembly outside the walls on 1 April 1562, to be conducted by Sorel because of his strong voice.[42]

Sorel's petition to be allowed to continue in his charge was reiterated by pleas in two further letters, from the minister Gravelle and the consistory, to retain his services indefinitely. It was also hoped that the church of Neuchâtel might allocate them 'yet more to send to our neighbours who, through lack of ministers, remain without knowing God, however much they desire to'.[43] The demand upon the ministers to serve communities in the vicinity of Troyes was nothing new. Shortly before his arrest in 1559, Girard de Courlieu had conducted marriages on the estates of the local nobility.[44] Involvement with churches in other centres in the province, aside from providing for and ministering to the inhabitants of outlying villages, demonstrates that the church at Troyes formed part of a provincial network. The church at Vitry-Le-François was established by the de Vassans, a merchant family native to Troyes and allies of the Pithous.[45] Representatives from the churches of Châlons-sur-Marne, Sens, and Meaux, were sent to Troyes to confer on matters of mutual concern, such visits probably forming meetings of the local colloquy. The colloquy played a vital role in the organisation of the French Reformed church as a local supervisory body, but the paucity of surviving documentation prevents a reconstruction of its functions in any detail. Thus, the scattered references we do have take on added importance.

Delegates from the church at Châlons visited Troyes in October 1561. Pierre Fornelet, minister at Châlons, mentions that he had written to Jacques Sorel, 'via one of our elders, who left last Sunday to go to Troyes to confer with those of its Church, about some matter that we have been looking at concerning the welfare and advancement of both our churches.'[46] In November 1561, minister Morel, also from Châlons, preached and performed a baptism in the houses of two Huguenots in Troyes.[47] On the day of the massacre at Sens in April 1562, the leader and guardian of the city's Reformed church was in Troyes to discuss strategy.[48] Highest in everyone's mind was probably the appropriate course of action following the attack on their near-neighbours at Vassy. For, by the end of 1561, it was with the community at Vassy that the Troyen church had forged its closest links.[49] Jean Gravelle was responsible for setting up the church at Vassy in October 1561, organised to serve until such time as the congregation should obtain a minister of its own. In December Gravelle was confronted whilst giving a sermon by the bishop of Châlons, who had been sent by the Cardinal of Lorraine to root out this emergence of heresy within Guise territory. An argument ensued between the bishop and the minister over the status of the episcopate, and Gravelle was said to have outwitted and humiliated his opponent.[50]

Unfortunately this period of prosperity and growth was to prove all too brief for the churches in Champagne. In the same month that the church at Vassy was established, Sorel requested that the pastors at Neuchâtel 'pray to the Lord for us, and for the churches nearby which are in the midst of many dangers, for we have many enemies surrounding us'.[51] Prayers were not sufficient, however, to prevent the massacres at Vassy and Sens in the spring of 1562, nor that in Troyes itself later in the year. The events of the first civil war resolved the religious uncertainty in many parts of France; in the north, decisively in favour of the old religion. The massacres in Champagne made the position of the ministers in Troyes increasingly untenable. Assemblies continued in the face of growing hostility until Gravelle conducted the final service outside the town on 2 August; he and many of his congregation would not return.[52] Sorel made a much more dramatic escape on horseback, running the gauntlet of Catholic gunfire. Two days later, an effigy of the minister and the pulpit from which he had conducted services were burned in the marketplace, symbolic of the fate awaiting the minister who was captured.[53]

The relationship between minister and congregation was crucial for the recruitment and continuing allegiance to the Reformed faith. The minister represented the congregation's spiritual lifeline, guiding his flock in the ways of the new religion and its most visible connection with the leaders of the Calvinist church, whether in Paris or in Geneva. Deprived of a minister, often for a year or more, there are reports of Reformers going astray and neglecting both devotions and discipline, despite the best efforts of their lay leaders. However, the minister, too, sometimes had difficulties in communicating his message; because of local circumstances, a lack of enthusiasm, or simply a clash of opinion or personality. Le Roy, as we have seen, proved unpopular because of his stance against Bishop Caracciolo; he had already been forced to move on from Dijon because of disagreement with the church there.[54] Minister de Courlieu had no illusions about the abilities of his congregation, describing them thus: 'the majority of the faithful [are] poor people, rude and ignorant, unversed in Holy Scripture'.[55] Taken out of context this statement hardly suggests a fond rapport between minister and congregation, but, in fact, de Courlieu was defending his flock against the claim that an ability to argue from passages of Scripture was an essential prerequisite for salvation. Thus he stressed the priority of faith, stating that, despite their ignorance, those who believe 'are acknowledged by God as His own'.

If a congregation was dependent on its minister for spiritual guidance, ministers were also reliant on the members of their congregation for support. They were provided with lodgings and a salary, and granted some form of travel expenses for attending synods and fulfilling duties at nearby churches. Unfortunately, the evidence for determining just how much ministers were paid by their congregations is sparse. In Troyes, it seems a communal fund met all costs, including contributions to the Protestant war effort, renting buildings in which to hold services, and purchasing land for a cemetery in 1571. There were some disputes over contributions when richer members, who had acted as creditors to the rest of the church, sought repayment of loans for causes which it was felt had not been approved by the whole congregation.[56] Ministers were further assisted in their work by the appointment of elders. De Courlieu was the first to organise the church at Troyes along these lines in 1559. Later that year, the first national synod of the French Reformed church, held in Paris under Genevan supervision, produced a confession of faith and forty articles concerning church discipline to be observed by all the churches of France. As a result, those elders in Troyes who continued to attend mass and outwardly conform with Catholic ritual were replaced.[57]

It was not until 1561 that a formal council was established at Troyes to support the ministers in dealing with church affairs. This was in line with the articles of 1559, and in imitation of the Genevan model, with the appointment of elders and deacons. There were twelve elected elders on the council who met regularly to discuss church business, and each elder had a deputy who was responsible for informing the congregation of when and where an assembly was to be held. The consistory was made up of the twelve elders plus the ministers.[58] In Geneva, and French cities in which Calvinists formed the majority, such as Nîmes, the consistory worked closely with the local authorities, although the relationship was not always harmonious. In Troyes, as in other centres, the consistory appears to have been dominated by merchants, lawyers, and doctors, as was the membership of the local administration. Several of the elders had previously held municipal or royal office before their exclusion as followers of the Reformed faith.[59]

In 1564, the elders began distributing a special token or *méreau* which acted as a pass for admission to communion; a system first suggested by Calvin in 1560, and later recommended by him to the faithful in France.[60] It was to be withheld from any unregenerates whose behaviour was thought to be bringing the church into disrepute. The token bore an insignia, a palm and a 'T' for Troyes, to distinguish it from those carried by Reformers from other churches in the region. In the mid–1560s, when the provision of ministers had become erratic and the allegiance of many was wavering in the face of recent persecution, the elders believed that an increasing number of the congregation were behaving irreverently and irresponsibly. In particular, concern was expressed regarding members who were socialising with Catholic clergy. Pithou entered into a correspondence with Theodore Beza about the morality of gambling and games of chance in 1566, and complained how standards among the congregation in general had declined. Beza himself wrote that he was 'astonished that at such a calamitous time Christians can think to amuse themselves with such vanities'.[61] Such issues reveal some of the tensions present between the elders and members of the congregation. Nor was the relationship between the ministers and the council always entirely cordial, as can be seen in the over-protective attitude of the elders towards their pastors at times of intensified persecution.

In addition to administrative assistance, ministers also sought help with their pastoral duties. Deacons were specifically instructed to visit the poor, prisoners, and the sick, and to catechise church members in their homes. The need for Troyens to step in and minister to the infirm and to give religious instruction became even more crucial later in the 1560s when ministers were refused access to the town.[62] In such circumstances some of the pastor's functions could be taken over by the church's lay ministers; deacons were able to conduct prayers and give a reading from the Bible.[63] Other members of the congregation were assigned to instruct Huguenot children in the faith; by 1568 the Edict of Longjumeau permitted teaching at designated sites and in private houses.[64] Although none of the congregation at Troyes was trained formally to become a minister, some of its members were encouraged to indulge in theological discussion, possibly with a view to entering the ministry; they included a lawyer, Claude Girardin, a doctor, Jacques Douynet, and a joiner, Jean Le Febvre.[65] The inclusion of Le Febvre is a unique example of an artisan within the notable-dominated ranks of the church hierarchy in Troyes.

The story of the Reformed church at Troyes during the first decade of the civil wars is one of continual attempts to have their rights of worship observed and the site of their services moved to a more convenient location in closer proximity to the city. In the 1550s, the Catholic authorities had viewed the prevention of Protestant assemblies, and the identification and capture of the ministers conducting them, as a priority. Clandestine gatherings had been unearthed in private houses and in the fields around Troyes, often incriminated by the possession of 'heretical' literature, and attempts made to bring the participants to justice.[66] With the advent of open-air services in 1561, local officials and members of the clergy continued to intimidate Huguenots, setting up ambushes and provoking confrontations. However, it was between the crises and bloodshed of 1562 and 1572 that the dispute over the location of services, and the provision and accessibility of Reformed worship for the city's Huguenots, came to dominate relations between the faiths.

The Peace of Amboise of March 1563 designated one official site for Reformed worship in each *bailliage*. The choice of location was to be vital for the future of Huguenot congregations, and the Reformers at Troyes had good cause to welcome the nomination of the suburbs of the city. However, they were too much weakened by recent persecution to ensure its implementation, faced by the determination of Catholic officials to pursue a relentless campaign against the exercise of Reformed worship in or near Troyes. Services were resurrected only in 1564 following the designation of Céant-en-Othe, a site eighteen to twenty miles from Troyes.[67] It was a measure of Geneva's concern to retain a presence in the region that the Company sent François Bourgoing, one of their most senior pastors who had been trained alongside Nicholas des Gallars in the 1540s.[68] His services had been secured by Sorel and those Huguenots from Troyes who had taken refuge in Geneva. Assisted by Sorel, Bourgoing re-established the church and its administrative bodies on 30 April; it was under his ministry that the *méreau* was introduced. Bourgoing was to serve the church at Troyes for only a year and a half until his death in November 1565, reputedly brought on by exhaustion due to ill-health and overwork.[69]

Ministers were faced with the considerable task of encouraging a disgruntled and fearful congregation to brave the dangers and inconvenience involved in attending services at Céant. There were complaints regarding the loss of trade and revenue because of the time spent travelling, and the risk to the lives of new-born babies carried so far in order to be baptised.[70] The situation cannot have been aided by the exclusion of ministers from the city, preventing a direct appeal to recalcitrant or reluctant participants. In the summer of 1567, the local authorities were alerted to the fact that regular clandestine assemblies were being held in the city at the houses of two leatherworkers.[71] Apparently if artisans were refusing to attend official services, some of them at least were maintaining their own form of communal worship.

The provision of protection for assemblies on the estates of the local nobility, involving less cost and inconvenience than trips to Céant, was an important step towards the rejuvenation of the Reformed church at Troyes. Whatever the validity of their claims to freedom of worship, as only those nobles specified in the 1563 edict were granted such a right, these lords seem to have acquired a certain immunity from prosecution.[72] In 1565, Huguenots from Troyes attended a service and baptism at Dosches, only five miles from Troyes, at the house of Jacques Ménisson.[73] Another member of the Ménisson family, Antoine, seigneur of Saint-Pouange, upset the authorities by granting access to services on his estates between 1566 and 1571, despite official attempts to prohibit him from doing so. There were repeated complaints to the *bailli* concerning Huguenot activities at Saint-Pouange, for instance from the clergy of

Troyes, 'in view of the disturbances which arise every day from certain sermons and assemblies'.[74]

The provision and turnover of ministers had become erratic once again. A request to the Company of Pastors for the return of Pierre Le Roy to Troyes in 1566, came to nothing.[75] Jean Chassanion, alias 'La Chasse', was sent to administer to the church at Troyes by the ministers of Lausanne and Geneva in 1570. He was based at Saint-Mards, twelve miles to the west of Troyes, on the estates of Odard Piedefer.[76] This followed the disastrous designation of Villenaux for the Reformed churches of Champagne in the recent edict of pacification. Not only was Villenaux situated even further from Troyes than Céant, but its inhabitants were hostile to the Huguenots who gathered to worship there, killed one of their preachers, and drove them away.[77] Meanwhile, the provision in the edict of Saint-Germain for worship in the homes of those nobles with rights of high justice, endorsed the legality of the services held at Saint-Mards and deprived the authorities of any redress against their host.

In April 1572, La Chasse was preaching and conducting services at an even closer site at Isle, owned by Marie de Clèves, future wife of the prince of Condé. The city council sought to prevent certain of its members, who were also elders in the Reformed church, attending assemblies at Isle.[78] Pithou informs us that the magistrate arranged a visitation of all those 'of the religion' in their homes, but they were not to be deterred from attending the Sunday service the following day, despite the presence of officials sent to witness those who had contravened the prohibition.[79] Some fines and imprisonments resulted.[80] The services at Isle were still a serious bone of contention between the faiths when news of the St Bartholomew's massacre in Paris reached Troyes, forcing La Chasse to flee. The edict of pacification of 1576 allowed churches to be reconstituted in many areas, but insufficient enthusiasm was shown by those Huguenots remaining in Troyes to retain the services of La Chasse, who went instead to Metz.[81] Thus, it was the indifference of church members rather than the pressure of mounting odds which finally persuaded the ministry to withdraw. Persecution had resulted in a dwindling congregation, of which the most committed members had been forced to seek freedom of conscience in exile, whilst the remainder showed a lack of religious zeal. Consequently, despite the efforts of a series of conscientious ministers, the twenty-year battle to sustain a church in a hostile environment had been lost.

In the uncertain circumstances of the religious wars pastors had to minister as best they could to the needs of the churches to which they were allocated. It was their role to ensure that members of the congregation were given the correct instruction and discipline, and encouraged to persevere in their faith despite persecution. The task of the ministers in maintaining the morale of church-goers despite adverse conditions, as well as risking their own lives in the cause of their faith, should not be underrated. That the Reformed church was able to maintain itself at all in staunchly Catholic areas like Champagne must be largely attributed to the tenacity and commitment of its ministers. It also reflects a conscious decision on the part of the Reformed leadership to give a high priority to the establishment of strong churches in strategically placed French cities. It was, therefore, vital that the missionaries sent to such locations were of a consistently high calibre; an advantage not enjoyed by all French churches, many of which took pot-luck in order to secure a minister in their formative years. For the demand for ministers rapidly outstripped the supply of eligible men at a crucial time for the implantation of the Reform in France. The experience of the first generation of ministers was shaped by fluid and dangerous circumstances, posing a challenge which the Reformed church was only partially successful in meeting.

Notes

All translations are the author's own.

1 The official line was first stated in the *Ordonnances Ecclésiastiques* of 1541, in *RCP* I, p. 2. Also see R. M. Kingdon, *Geneva and the Coming of the Wars of Religion in France, 1555–63* (Geneva, 1956), pp. 25–9.

2 Kingdon, ibid.; Mark Greengrass, *The French Reformation* (Oxford, 1987), p. 40.

3 BN Dupuy, MS 698, Nicolas Pithou, 'Histoire ecclésiastique de l'église réformée de la ville de Troyes', 515 fols [hereafter Pithou].

4 Pithou: on de Gannes, fols 108v–9r, 114–15, 117v and 120v–3r; on Macard, fol. 109; and on de La Rivière, fols 115v–16. Also see *Histoire ecclésiastique des églises réformées au royaume de France*, ed. G. Baum, E. Cunitz, and R. Reuss (3 vols, Paris, 1883–89) [hereafter *Hist. ecc.*], I, p. 163.

5 Kingdon, *Geneva and the Coming*, p. 55.

6 Ibid., p. 27 on Fornelet, and p. 81 on Neuchâtel.
7 'Le Protestantisme en Champagne, 1561', *BSHPF*, 12 (1863), 354, Sorel to Neuchâtel; and 356, Jacques Duchat on behalf of the church at Troyes.
8 On Poncelet, see Pithou, fols 66–8r; *Hist. ecc.*, I, pp. 101 and 135. Cf. Metz, where a carder from Meaux first preached the new ideas in 1523, *Hist. ecc.*, III, p. 526. D. Nicholls, 'The Nature of Popular Heresy in France, 1520–42', *HJ*, 26 (1983), 268, on Meaux as a centre of heresy instrumental in spreading the Reformation elsewhere.
9 Pithou, fol 67.
10 Archives de la Bibliothèque Municipale de Troyes [hereafter BM Troyes], Boutiot GG IV supplement, baptismal registers of the church of Saint-Jean, regs 4 (1553–56) and 5 (1557–60).
11 Pithou: on Allyon, fol 78; on Girardin, fols 80v–1r.
12 Ibid., fols 82v–3r; also Kingdon, *Geneva and the Coming*, p. 57.
13 Pithou, fols 89v–90r. For a similar positive re-evaluation of such discreet evangelical sympathisers within the Dutch context, see Guido Marnef, 'The Reformation in Antwerp', in Gillian Lewis et al. (eds), *Calvinism in Europe* (Cambridge, 1993).
14 Pithou, fols 116v–17 and 124v; *Hist. ecc.*, I, pp. 163–4 and 333–5.
15 Ibid., fols 144v and 171–2; *Hist. ecc.*, I, p. 848.
16 Bèze, *Correspondance*, III, p. 109.
17 Pithou, fol 183v. The congregation at Vassy was worshipping in a barn at the time of the massacre in 1562: S. Mours, *Le Protestantisme en France au XVIe siècle* (Paris, 1959), p. 177.
18 Pithou, fol 179.
19 Ibid., fols 178v–80; *Hist. ecc.*, I, pp. 849–51. On Caracciolo's career, see J. Roserot de Melin, *Antonio Caracciolo, évêque de Troyes (1515?–1570)* (Paris, 1923).
20 Bèze, *Correspondance*, III, pp. 209, 213–14 and 216–17. Pithou, fols 181v–3.
21 Pithou, fols 357v–8r. Bèze, *Correspondance*, V, pp. 34–5.
22 For examples, see John Quick, *Synodicon in Gallia Reformata*, 2 vols (London, 1692), I, pp. 42, 46–7 and 74.
23 Pithou, fol 162.
24 Pithou, fol 83r.
25 Kingdon, *Geneva and the Coming*, pp. 38 and 49.
26 The system is suggested in the letter of minister Sorel in 'Le Protestantisme en Champagne, 1561', *BSHPF*, 12 (1863), 352–3, although by this period the problem was with numbers rather than maintaining secrecy.
27 Pithou, fol 149.
28 Ibid., fols 124v–5r.
29 Ibid., fols 144v–6. Lists of members of the church were also seized with Pierre Girardin in 1555, Pithou, fols 82v–3r.
30 Pithou, fols 101–2.
31 Ibid., fols 130–1.
32 Ibid., fols 146–8; on de Gannes, fols 122–3r.
33 Ibid., fols 161v–4; *Hist. ecc.* I, pp. 335–6.
34 BM Troyes Boutiot A 13, 19 and 30 August. Pithou, fols 164–8r.

35 Pithou, fol. 149r. The origin of those affiliated to the Reformed church was a sensitive issue and a cause of lively debate between the authorities, out to discredit the movement, and the Huguenots, determined to prove their citizenship.

36 'Le Protestantisme en Champagne, 1561', 352.

37 Pithou, fols 215v–16r.

38 Cf. D. L. Rosenberg, 'Social Experience and Religious Choice: A Case Study, the Protestant Weavers and Woolcombers of Amiens in the Sixteenth Century' (Yale University Ph.D. thesis, 1978), p. 14; and Philip Benedict, *Rouen during the Wars of Religion* (Cambridge, 1981), p. 53.

39 'Le Protestantisme en Champagne, 1561', 352–5 (Sorel) and 362 (Fornelet).

40 *RCP* III, p. 210, suggests that this was Bordeaux near Caen.

41 'Le Protestantisme en Champagne, 1561', 352–4.

42 Pithou, fol. 198v.

43 'Le Protestantisme en Champagne, 1561', 358. Also see Kingdon, *Geneva and the Coming*, p. 32, on temporary loans of ministers as common practice in 1561, and on these ministers usually being requested to stay on.

44 Pithou, fol. 144r.

45 *BSHPF*, 40 (1891), 474–8: 'The Church at Vitry, like that at Vassy, seems to have been a daughter of that at Troyes' (476).

46 'Le Protestantisme en Champagne, 1561', 362.

47 Pithou, fol. 183v.

48 *Mémoires de Claude Haton*, ed. F. Bourquelot, 2 vols (Paris, 1857), I, pp. 193–4.

49 R. Crozet, 'Le Protestantisme et la Ligue à Vitry-Le-François et en Perthois', *Revue Historique*, 156 (1927), 4.

50 Pithou, fols 181v and 185–7r; *Hist. ecc.*, I, pp. 805–6.

51 'Le Protestantisme en Champagne, 1561', 353.

52 Pithou, fol. 226r; *Hist. ecc.*, II, p. 466.

53 Pithou, fols 229v–32; *Hist. ecc.*, II, pp. 468–9.

54 Pithou, fol. 179.

55 Ibid., fol. 144v.

56 This fund is mentioned only briefly in Pithou, fols 8–9 (1552), 315 (1565), 364r (cemetery, 1571), and 421v–42r (1576), usually because of its abuse or a reluctance to contribute.

57 Pithou, fol. 143v. For a standard text of the confession and articles see *Hist. ecc.*, I, pp. 201–20; also Pithou, fols 125v–9.

58 'Le Protestantisme en Champagne, 1561', 353.

59 H. Heller, *The Conquest of Poverty: The Calvinist Revolt in Sixteenth-Century France* (Leiden, 1986), p. 143; R. A. Mentzer, 'Disciplina nervus ecclesiae: the Calvinist Reform of Morals at Nîmes', *SCJ*, 18 (1987), 90–1; J. M. Davies, 'Persecution and Protestantism: Toulouse 1562–75', *HJ*, 22 (1979), 50.

60 Pithou, fol. 308. For descriptions of *méreaux* used by other churches see *BSHPF*, 37 (1888), 205–8 and 316–18; and their use in Nîmes, Mentzer, 'Calvinist Reform of Morals', 96.

61 Pithou, fols 309v–10 and 328–31r; Bèze, *Correspondance*, VII, pp. 59–61.
62 Pithou, fols 324–7 and 331.
63 From the text of the articles of 1559 in *Hist. ecc.*, I, p. 218, cf. Pithou, fol. 127.
64 Pithou, fols 331 and 338r.
65 Ibid., fols 183v–4r.
66 For examples, see Pithou, fols 80–5r, 97v–9r and 102v–3.
67 Ibid., fols 290r and 308.
68 R. Kingdon, *Geneva and the Consolidation of the French Protestant Movement, 1564–1572* (Geneva, 1967), p. 19; *RCP* I, p. 21.
69 Pithou, fols 323v–4r; *Hist. ecc.*, I, p. 849, which erroneously places Bourgoing's arrival in Troyes in 1561.
70 Pithou, fols 298–9r.
71 BM Troyes Boutiot BB 14 ii. nos 13 and 14.
72 Pithou, fols 313–14.
73 Ibid., fol. 317.
74 BM Troyes Boutiot BB 14 i, no. 47, and ii, nos. 7–9 and 11.
75 *RCP* III, pp. 209–10.
76 Pithou, fol. 357. I suspect that La Chasse is one and the same as Jean Carbon, formerly pastor at Sainte-Marie-aux-Mines, mentioned in *RCP* III, p. 231, and V p. 310.
77 *Mémoires de Claude Haton*, II, pp. 605–7.
78 BM Troyes Boutiot BB 14 ii, no. 41.
79 Pithou, fol. 366.
80 BM Troyes Boutiot BB 14 ii, nos. 42 and 43.
81 Pithou, fols 421–2r.

9

Building a Reformed ministry in Holland, 1572–1585

Richard Fitzsimmons

On 1 April 1572, the *Watergeuzen*, or Sea Beggars, rebel supporters of the exiled William of Orange, descended on the island
of Voorne in Zeeland and took the small fishing town of Den Briel.
Overcoming the small garrison of only six hundred troops, the
Beggars took the town, destroying the churches and issuing the
proclamation that all would be treated well 'except priests, monks,
and papists'. By August a large part of Holland and Zeeland was
controlled by the rebels.[1] Of the major towns, only Amsterdam
remained in government control; even conservative Gouda went
over to the rebellion.

Few amongst the city magistrates embraced the revolt with
any semblance of enthusiasm; many were at best apathetic, not
only to the *Watergeuzen*, but also to the demands which the Reformed were now making for churches in which they could begin
holding services. In July 1572, the States of Holland, prompted by
Philip Marnix, representative of William of Orange, had agreed and
declared that religious freedom would be extended to 'Reformed or
Roman Catholic, in public or in private, in church, or in chapel'.[2]
But this was a situation which could not be maintained: from 1573
only the Reformed were permitted to worship in public.

The Reformed church in Holland now became a 'public'
church. But this 'public' church was *not* a state church. The Roman
Catholics and Anabaptists were free to worship, but in private. As
the Reformed church was the only legal one, it had to accommodate
the fact that it was the only place where the citizens of Holland
could legally worship in public and request the sacraments. Anyone
could attend services there, have their child baptised, or marriage
solemnised. Many went along to the Reformed services, not

because they wished to join the church, but because they believed that they could still perform their devotions to God in the same way as before, that nothing had changed for them except the name of the service and the language in which it was said. Accordingly, the Reformed church in Holland ended up a twofold church; a 'public' church for everyone to attend, and a 'voluntary' church in which a confession of faith was required to receive the Lord's Supper.

The Reformed church also inherited the Catholic church organisation at the local level – the parish, with a congregation which expected sacramental services and which retained property accumulated from gifts to the church. But the day-to-day running of the parish lay in the hands of the churchwardens, who were appointed by the town magistrates, and who frequently were not Reformed. The States felt a responsibility to support the public exercise of religion and they reorganised pastoral properties to guarantee a minimum salary for each Reformed minister. In 1578 the Geestelijke Kantoor or Spiritual Office was set up in Delft by the States to receive all funds from pastoral properties. This was to provide the salaries of all the ministers of south Holland.

This persistence of the parish organisation had both its advantages and its hindrances. First, the Reformed church could demonstrate continuity with the previous church. The Reformed minister replaced the Catholic priest, and the parish 'provided the Reformed church with almost immediate legitimacy'.[3] Secondly, because of the Geestelijke Kantoor, the Reformed ministers remained financially independent of the parishes, patrons, and local authorities. However, the drawbacks included the running of the churches' buildings by potentially hostile churchwardens. Initially, poor relief was also outside the hands of the Reformed deacons. Finally, it posed the question, who chose the minister for the parish? This would be a major point of collision between the church and the particularistic magistrates.

In most of the Holland towns which had gone over to the revolt after April 1572, the Reformed had already assumed control of the monastic churches and chapels by August. At Delft, the Reformed gained the use of the Nieuwe Kerk within a week of the town going over; at Dordrecht, the Reformed gained the use of the Augustijner Kerk; in Den Haag, the Dominican Kloosterkerk and in Gouda the Onze Lieve Vrouwekapel.[4] Inevitably, as these churches were made ready for Reformed worship, the new communities had a real need for organisation. Amongst the many cries which went out from these communities to the exile churches was the plea from the minister Bartholdus Wilhelmus at Dordrecht to the London Dutch church. He wrote, 'As very few people at Dordrecht know anything about the Reformation of the church, ministers acquainted with church government are wanted.'[5] This plea was echoed by many others during the course of 1572 and 1573. The exile churches responded by sending many of their own ministers, and many of the ministers who had gone into exile in 1566/7 also repaired back to their former congregations. The minister Jan Arendsz returned from Emden to Alkmaar in 1572 along with his erstwhile colleague Pieter Cornelisz. Pieter Gabriel, Arendsz's former colleague at Amsterdam, returned from Emden to look after the growing church at Delft. The former priests, Andreas Cornelisz from Den Briel and Andries Dircksz van Castricum from Enkhuizen, returned from Emden to their former charges. This is just a small sample of those who made their way from Emden and East Friesland; it would seem that as many as 33 ministers returned from the principal German exile centre during the course of 1572.[6] Other ministers came from the exile communities in England. The ministers of the London church, Bartholdus Wilhelmus, Joris Wybo, and Godfrey van Winghen, all crossed to south Holland to lend a hand in the church-making. From the community at Sandwich came Isbrand Balck and from Thetford Carolus Rijckwaert, both of whom became ministers at Rotterdam.[7]

That the newly arisen churches were desperate for ministers is shown by the avalanche of letters to the exile churches in England pleading for the communities there to send whatever ministers they had, even to the detriment of their own communities. The appeal of Gerardus Gallinaceus the minister at Delft in September 1572 is typical:

> We can never thank the Lord sufficiently for opening such a large door to his Holy Word everywhere, and especially in Holland. But we want ministers to interpret His Gospel and administer the sacraments. The community at Schiedam request me to add my letter to their own, in order to induce Pieter Carpentier to accept the ministry among them. And we also pray you to persuade him to comply with our request, or send us another if he cannot come.[8]

The church at Schiedam followed up this appeal with one of their own in October, again asking for Carpentier, but if he were not available, Joannes Cubus would do instead.[9]

Despite the early success which the churches had in exhorting their co-religionists in England and Emden to send ministers, inevitably the churches also began to attract ministers of a rather dubious quality. Arnold Steur was one such case. Steur had been a *ziekentrooster*, or visitor of the sick, in London when he obtained a post in Holland. Bartholdus Wilhelmus, the new minister of Dordrecht, now informed his new church that Steur had left London under a cloud. Dordrecht wrote to London requesting information as to why Steur should be removed or suspended from the ministry. Wilhelmus's complaint was that Steur had left London without testimonial and had been forbidden to preach at Vlissingen. Steur had been requested to cross over to England to be reconciled with the London community, but he refused to have anything to do with the consistory.

Steur himself wrote to the London church from Den Briel in June 1573 to give his own account of these tangled events.

> I am very sorry that I left London without testimonial and that I did not marry my wife in the ordinary way in the London church, which I omitted because M. van Swieten could not remain in London until the banns had been proclaimed. But the moment that I arrived in Vlissingen, a minister married us secretly in the presence of Captain Fransoocis and others who have now all been killed before Amsterdam, wherefore I could not give any proof of my marriage to Bartholdus on his arrival at Dordrecht. As the latter had suspicions on the point, I travelled to Zeeland and was married there once more in the presence of witnesses, but in secret so as not to offend anybody. I have done no wrong, but I hope you will forgive me.[10]

Steur was not allowed to take up a post at Den Briel because of the condition laid down by Orange that no one could preach without a testimonial from his last congregation. Yet notwithstanding the uncertain circumstances surrounding Steur's departure from London, a number in Holland would take up his cause, among them the minister of Zierikzee, Herman Moded.[11] Moded wished to retain Steur in the ministry despite him having been declared unworthy of service by Dordrecht and London. The *coetus* and consistory of Zierikzee was in full agreement with Moded, not wanting to discharge Steur until all the facts were fully known, despite the evident and suspicious irregularities in Steur's marriage. It would seem that the case was resolved, at least temporarily, as Steur became minister at Sommelsdijk in south Holland in 1574, although he was disciplined by the south Holland synod for some unspecified 'misconduct'.[12] He went on to leave Sommelsdijk in 1575 to go to Zwijndrecht in the classis of Dordrecht, but with a testimonial from the classis of Den Briel on this occasion.[13]

This whole sorry case proved why there was a need for ministers to have testimonials from their former communities; if a minister had a valid testimonial, it was an indication that he was a respected member of a Reformed community and had given that community valuable service. What it did not do was guarantee that the minister was of the highest educational and moral calibre.

Steur's case illustrates the churches' reluctance to accept men who had fallen below strict standards of personal morality, but cases of doctrinal unorthodoxy could prove equally troubling. This was illustrated by the controversy that surrounded the installation of Pieter de Zuttere as minister in Rotterdam. De Zuttere settled in Rotterdam in 1574 having moved there from Emden. On the death of the Rotterdam minister Jan Isebrantsz earlier in the year, it was proposed by some of the town council that he should be appointed minister to fill the vacancy.[14] However, the Reformed community led by the minister Aegidius Johannes Frisius was opposed to his appointment. The burgomasters summoned Aegidius to tell him that it was their wish that de Zuttere should be allowed to preach, whereupon Aegidius informed them that it was out of the question, as it was forbidden under the church's ordinances. The case was adjourned when Aegidius threatened to protest to Orange about the burgomasters' actions.[15] The case of de Zuttere was discussed at the provincial synod at Dordrecht in June 1574. It was decided that he should not be allowed to preach 'dewijle men hem voor suspect houdt' until the opinions of Heidelberg and Emden were sought.[16] The consistory of Rotterdam itself wrote to Emden informing the consistory there of the events which had taken place. Aegidius had been summoned again by the burgomasters where he presented the twelfth, thirteenth, and seventeenth articles of the recent Dordrecht synod concerning the choosing and attestation of ministers. According to Aegidius, de Zuttere could not be allowed to preach without contravening all of these articles. The articles stated that to avoid confusion caused by election from the common folk, the consistory would elect the minister, that all ministers would be examined openly in the meeting of the classis, and that a minister coming from another church should not be accepted without a letter from the former classis or consistory, or, if there were none, a letter from ministers who could be believed.[17] Whilst de Zuttere had an attestation, it had been signed by just one of the Emden ministers, not by the consistory.[18]

In the end, de Zuttere was not appointed by the Rotterdam magistrates, although he did move them to insist that they had the right to appoint ministers over and above the right of the consistory. This was dangerous indeed, for, as Aegidius wrote to Emden, 'if this should come to pass, it could be poison for all the Reformed churches in Holland, wherever the authorities are not yet wholly godly, not mentioning the same division and disturbance among our citizenry'.[19] In the interests of avoiding the suspicion of being partisan, the Rotterdam council, whilst not appointing de Zuttere, also decided to dismiss his principal opponent, Aegidius. The vacancy caused by the death of Isebrantsz was now filled by Pieter de Bert from IJsselmonde.[20]

These two episodes with their contrasting causes serve as a demonstration that, although ministers were being found for the newly created churches, it was one thing to provide ministers, but another to provide a settled ministry. Without appropriate controls anyone could enter the ministry on their own terms or on the terms of the civil authorities who were by-and-large still at best ambivalent towards the Reformed church. In this way it was possible to bypass the conditions which the Reformed wished to impose in terms of standards of morality and doctrine for their ministers.

Inevitably, in the first days of church-forming, the best and most respected ministers were quickly taken by the churches of the larger towns. Rotterdam, Delft, and Dordrecht all competed for ministers, often offering inducements above the normal salaries.[21] However, even the larger towns were hard pressed for ministers: in 1572, Rotterdam, a town of 8,000 people, had only two ministers; Delft, a town of 14,000 people in 1573, had three ministers; Dordrecht, also in 1573, had two ministers for some 13,000 people.[22] Whilst the position was difficult in the towns, it was nearly impossible to find ministers for the smaller communities. Many years went by before many rural churches had ministers.[23] As a result, the churches had to compromise on the high standards they might have wished to demand of their pastors. The clear theoretical precepts concerning ministry, calling and the relationship with the community had to be balanced against the pressing practical necessity to provide some sort of ministry for every community. But did the Reformed church have to lower its admission standards, so that scores of uneducated and problem-causing men found their way into its ranks?

It is possible to offer some answers to these questions with the help of a prosopographical survey. Biographical information for some 275 ministers has been assembled, serving in both north and south Holland during the years 1572 to 1585. Much of the early information for each minister is unfortunately incomplete: date and place of birth, possible education, occupation, whether lay or former cleric, all these details are often lacking. Yet despite the obvious lacunae, an overall picture can be drawn about the composition of the ministry.[24]

Of the ministers identified, the occupation, of roughly 36 per cent are known: of these 99 ministers, the vast majority were ex-Roman clergy – a total of 80 monks, clerics, and priests. The majority of the rest comprise what may loosely be called members of the artisanal class – glassmakers, weavers, basketmakers, fishmongers etc. This ties in well with what we know about the process whereby ex-Roman clergy sought to enter the ministry. But it would perhaps be clarified still further if the educational background of the ministers was clearer. The educational qualifications of the ministers are largely unknown; information exists for only sixteen in the period to 1585. Of these, nine had been to the University of Heidelberg, two to Cologne, two to the Catholic university at Louvain, two to Geneva and one to Goch.

The Reformed church did accept many men without conventional educational qualifications, including many ex-Catholic clergy, into the ministry – it had no other option if it was to fill churches in the short term. This included those known as 'Duitse Klerken', generally ex-schoolmasters and artisans with no knowledge of the classical languages. Perhaps Caspar Coolhaes, the Leiden minister, was accurate in his description of his colleagues as 'tailors, shoemakers, weavers, lock-makers, in short all kinds of artisans doing it more for a lazy life and a secure income than for God's honour and the building of Christ's church'.[25] Or, 'for the most part mass priests and monastics, who had not so much deserted, as been deserted by the papacy'.[26]

The provincial synod of Dordrecht in 1574 proclaimed that its criteria for a good minister included godliness and humility, eloquence and good understanding and discernment.[27] But 'as the demand for ministers fast outstripped the supply of such paragons, the synods had to choose between admitting a significant number of former priests and renegade monks to the ministry, or leaving many villages bereft of doctrinal instruction and pastoral care'.[28] Even so, in 1582 the minister Werner Helmichius estimated that there were barely 50 ministers in the whole of Holland.[29]

The classis of Dordrecht tried to sort out the problem of finding suitably qualified clergy for its many parishes: it instituted training for those already in the ministry, it established a theological school at Dordrecht, and the Reformed church, along with the magistrates, reformed the Latin school there.[30] To improve preaching, the classis assigned half of the ministers present to deliver sermons at the meetings, with a critique to follow the presentations.[31] Above all, it laid emphasis on the practice of sermon technique. This process, known as *proponeren*, was geared to filling gaps in a young minister's training.

Each proponent was to expound a passage of scripture to the classis under the correction of the ministers and elders present. When the proponent had finished, the other candidates would be asked what they had to add, if anything, with the proviso that they should not repeat anything already said, or stray from the point. If there were errors or evidence of misconstruing the text, 'infelicities of speech, or unsuitable gestures or actions', the proponent was admonished. If the proponent was accepted for the ministry, his life and doctrine were to be examined closely according to I Timothy chapter 3. The newly accepted minister would sign the Confession of Faith and subscribe to the use of the Heidelberg Catechism.[32]

This process of training within the circle of the established ministry, rather than formal university education, was responsible for forming the first generation of an 'educated' Dutch ministry. Although the University of Leiden was established in 1575 to provide a flow of candidates for the ministry, the theological faculty did not really get up and running until the founding of the States

College in 1593. Even when it did get sorted out, the faculty still did not teach homiletics, or the writing and delivery of sermons.[33] Nor did the Reformed universities abroad make as large a contribution as might have been expected. Heidelberg was closed to Reformed candidates for part of this period because of the ruler's brief flirtation with Lutheranism. Meanwhile, it was possible that the expense of education in Geneva made that an option of which only a few could take advantage. According to Jaanus, the number of ministers with academic training in the northern Netherlands could be counted on the fingers of one hand and it is certain that the small number of ministers from the academies lasted at least until 1600.[34]

In his analysis of the late sixteenth-century Reformed church, Rogier saw a desire for a strictly systematic theological education for the ministers arising naturally from what he saw as Calvinist emphasis on dogma as the main factor promoting the forceful expansion of Calvinist propaganda. There may have been a thorough theological 'grilling' of proponents in the training provided by the classes, but there is no sign that a graduate clergy was being pursued with an active zeal. The requirements which the classes put before ministers were different to those which lay at the core of the training at Leiden or any other academy of the period, laying greater emphasis on the practical application of preaching and theological skills as opposed to a broader Humanist and literary training. Ultimately, 'the church was not impressed by academic training if it considered someone to be unreformed or unfit'.[35]

According to the processes laid down in the earliest Reformed synods, the process of choosing a minister was fourfold. First, a candidate had to show a letter of attestation from the last place where he had lived. Primarily this was in an effort to safeguard the church against heresy and men of doubtful morality such as Arnold Steur. Secondly, the candidate would be asked if he subscribed to the Dutch Confession of Faith. Thirdly, he would be examined on the principal points of the Reformed religion, probably along the lines of the Heidelberg Catechism. Finally, the candidate would be given two or three passages of scripture to propound in the presence of fellow ministers.[36] To tackle the problem of appointments in places where there had previously been no church, no one could be appointed without the advice and recommendation of a neighbouring church. Once a network of classes had been established, all of this process would take place there, but until this time the consistory would suffice.[37] The Convent of Wesel also defined the ministers' tasks: teaching, admonition of sinners, comforting of the sick or bereaved, expounding God's word, administering the sacraments.

The Wesel decisions were further refined at the Synod of Emden in October 1571, which laid the firmest foundations for the establishment of a church organisation and ministry. The synod divided the Dutch churches into classes or presbyteries, groups of churches in geographical order, each to meet every three or six months 'as seems expedient and necessary'.[38] The synod provided that ministers were to be chosen by the consistory with the advice of the classis, or neighbouring ministers. Ministers would be presented to the congregation whose consent to the appointment would be indicated by silence.[39] Ministers would be examined by those who chose them. If found suitable, they would be confirmed in office 'with fitting prayers and with the laying on of hands, though the latter is not obligatory and should be done without superstition'.[40] Ministers could not preach in another charge without the permission of the minister or consistory of that charge.[41] This would ensure against ministers leaving their own ministry for another without permission, though in some cases it did happen. Any minister who chose to ignore this constraint would first be admonished by the consistory, and, if this did not stop him, he would be spoken to by other ministers of the classis; if he were still obstinate, he could be declared schismatic and anyone who attended his services would be severely dealt with by the consistory.[42]

The synod also made provision for the training of future ministers. 'In the larger churches those who give promise of entering the ministry of God's Church at some stage may be trained in preaching. A minister should preside at the exercises to see that order is kept.'[43] Crucially, the Emden synod seems to have anticipated the training of potential ministers in the classis rather than setting up a separate organisation for the purpose. The classical meeting was to be opened by one of the participating ministers preaching a sermon which would be considered by the others present who would say how it could be improved, if at all. At a later stage, the president would raise a doctrinal point at variance with the Catholic teachings and lead a discussion on it so that the ministers might be spurred on to study.[44]

This church order would be modified in future years, not only by future national synods, but also by the provincial synod of Dordrecht in June 1574 which reaffirmed many of the resolutions of the Emden synod, but which also carried a few of them further. By 1574 the political situation had changed. The organisation which had been formulated at Emden, a meeting which took place in an exile town, was now being asked to perform in a totally different context. The church had to cope with both a vastly increased demand for ministers and a far greater pool of potential recruits. Ministers now needed an attestation from their classis in order to move from one church to the next, rather than from their former community.[45] The laying on of hands at the induction of a minister was now regarded as being liable to lead to superstition and was to be replaced by prayer only.[46] All those who offered themselves as ministers without undergoing any formal examination could be examined by the nearest classis. If they were proved to be adequate, they would be allowed to remain.[47] If these were former monks or priests, for example a priest who might be prepared to remain in his parish to preach the 'nieuwe leer', the synod took a firmer line. For these, a rigorous examination of doctrine was necessary to see if they had forsaken popery and if they were willing to submit to the new Calvinist discipline.[48] In the short term there was really no alternative except to accept such willing albeit unsatisfactory recruits at least for the villages, and hope that the in-service training provided by the classis would bring a gradual improvement. In the case of ministers who were in service without a lawful calling, the classis was to examine them as if they had never been in service. Those who were found inadequate were to be suspended until they could be re-educated. If they were found adequate, they would preach a sermon, sign the Confession, and be presented by the ministers of the classis.[49]

Clearly the synod regarded the classis as the central institution of Calvinist organisation with regard to the regulation of the ministry. The meetings, beginning with questions to establish the functioning of an effective ministry and discipline in each community, and a prolonged discussion of the state of individual churches, ended with the *censura morum*, a process whereby the ministers examined mutually their morals and theological standing.

It was the classis who supervised the daily running of the churches. It was responsible for the arrival and dispatch of ministers, ensuring that only those of sound doctrine were appointed; it ensured that every church had a duly constituted consistory and it instituted synodal decisions on procedure and discipline. To all intents and purposes, the classis took over the functions performed previously by exile churches. So much so that Professor van Deursen has justifiably identified the classis as 'pre-eminently the instrument of Calvinisation'.[50] The leading role in this was taken by the ministers of the larger towns where the classical meetings took place: for example in south Holland at Dordrecht, Den Haag, Delft, and Rotterdam; in north Holland, Enkhuizen, Alkmaar, and later Amsterdam. They took a major role in the organisation of the churches in the rural areas and effectively became mother churches to these nascent communities, encouraging the churches to elect consistories and pressuring the civil authorities to uphold the privileges which the States of Holland had given the Reformed church.

At the national synod of Dordrecht in 1578 the only significant change to existing procedure was that 'all those examined by the University of Leiden, or any other university of our religion, need no further doctrinal examination'. Ministers chosen in this way were to be presented to the reformed civil government and to the community for fourteen days. If no objections were forthcoming the election would proceed.[51] Questions were to be posed of candidates for the ministry: whether they felt properly called, whether they held by the Scriptures as the sole Word of God, whether they would subject themselves to Christian discipline. If the answers were satisfactory, they would then be instituted with the laying on of hands or with the right hand of fellowship.[52]

By 1578 then, the churches in Holland had built up a system whereby the ministers would be guaranteed a minimum income, they would be trained 'in house' if need be, and they could meet together to maintain doctrinal and moral standards. This was a considerable achievement in such a short space of time, but had they succeeded in building up a ministerial cadre equal to the challenges of the new church? What sort of problems could they face in the parishes?

Above, I have outlined the early struggle of the nascent Reformed communities to have a minister installed in the parishes of the larger towns. This was largely accomplished by 1576, but in the rural parishes, the process took much longer, and it was on the classis that the main burden fell. This burden is described by the letters of the Zoetermeer minister Winandus Beeck Gerardi to the Delft minister Arent Cornelisz. They catalogue a woeful mix of obstruction and ignorance.

> I cannot help but tell you of the wretched and distressing state we live in, especially (though you, no doubt, know this better than I) in the countryside. First of all, believe that a very great and common abuse and contempt has arisen which has led to the whole population holding the community fast-days in contempt and abuse. The leaders and officers themselves can do little about this contempt and abuse (for the most abuse came from them) . . . I cannot conceal that people got drunk on the fast day, they spoke slanderously of God's Word and much trade took place. This makes me so sad that I cannot refrain from telling you such things. I hope God will hear your and my prayers and effect a good remedy . . .
>
> [There is] no word of God in the land, for all blasphemy, fornication, permissiveness, adultery, and incest have taken the upper hand . . . I am caused great pain by the contempt for the Sabbath or the despicable breaking of Sundays via the buying and selling in the morning before the service, during or after it, through drinking, playing, and frivolous practices or by dancing . . . In sum there is little seen of the shame of Joseph, one leaves Lazarus lying and little is thought of Christ's wounds.'[53]

Obviously Gerardi was having serious problems as the letters complaining about his parish continue.

> I cannot in conscience conceal from you that on the fast day appointed for 18 June last, an officer of my lord, the *baljuw* of Rijnland, was here and the same entered the house of a smith, by name, Master Jacob from Brabant, who was then advising a large number of peasants how to sell and sharpen their farming implements (as he also does every Sunday). To the best of my knowledge nothing much was done because the aforesaid sergeant is a very papist (the aforesaid smith is likewise very papistical and an enemy of the truth) . . . Besides the aforesaid officer also freely takes, so it is said here, bribes. The minister of Hazerswoude has also complained to me that on the said most recent fast-day the secretary, on his way to oversee the partition of some estate, rode through the village of Hazerswoude in a wagon with some others, in the presence of many peasants, at the same time as the bell to announce the sermon was rung for the third time. . . . I do not know

what they intend by this, but drunkards and other frivolous persons, along with all the tavern keepers or tapsters, congregate in large numbers during the Sunday sermon.

And I can scarcely find words to describe the superstitious practices used by the papists when they bury their dead. They have so many strange fancies about making the shroud, they place the body in this way or that in the charnel house, go to the graveside or to the church to pray, or kiss the bier and many make unprofitable pilgrimages for the benefit of the deceased and, after the funeral, they lay on a veritable feast . . . In short, unless the papists are curbed, they will eventually do as they please, if nothing is done to improve matters.'[54]

These letters encapsulate just about all the problems with which the rural ministers had to deal: Catholic local magistrates and authorities who were, if not hostile to the Reformed, then at best apathetic; a general lack of respect for the Lord's Day; the tenacity of 'superstitious' practices, which the Reformed church had made a point of trying to eradicate; finally, the realisation that Catholicism had not been pushed back in the minds of the ordinary person and that the Reformation was not going to be as swift as the ministers, and some historians, would have liked.

The burden of trying to eradicate the problems which Gerardi was obviously finding in the rural setting, fell on the classis. The minutes of the classes of Dordrecht and Rotterdam pullulate with the complaints that the papists were obstructing the work of the ministers; not only the ordinary people, but also the former priests who may have remained in the vicinity of their former parishes.[55] It is therefore not a surprise to learn that the Reformation in the countryside was a slow and painful event. The classis of Dordrecht comprised some thirty villages and towns – by 1580 only five had consistories, and by 1590 only fifteen.[56] But to attribute the small and slow growth of the churches to the opposition of the magistrates and people alone would be a mistake. We have already seen that the Reformed church had a shortage of ministers of any quality in the early years. They were beset by deficiencies of training and, in some cases, by moral infelicities.[57]

The meeting of the Dordrecht classis on 4 March 1578 noted the state of the communities under its control: its investigation reported that drinking took place in the taverns during the Sunday service and that ill-discipline and 'whoredom' abounded in the villages. In addition to this, there was opposition and competition from Anabaptists and other sects. The ministers were instructed to watch carefully over their flocks and instruct negligent parents of the importance of infant baptism.[58] Writing to Arent Cornelisz in 1579, Hendrik van der Corput complained that the Anabaptists were passing out books such as almanacs, claiming that they could convert the world with three or four sermons.[59] Between 1574 and 1610, the consistory of Dordrecht saw 28 cases of *lidmaten* (i.e. full members) interested in the Mennonites. Of these, 23 left to join the Anabaptists.[60]

In a follow-up report on 2 September 1578, the classis recommended that letters be sent to the local sheriffs Nieveld and Winzen to admonish them to do their duty as Sundays were filled with 'work, fornication, whoredom, drunkenness, gambling, dancing, and other unedifying things'.[61] The Reformed were forced to accept a seven-day agricultural working week in the rural parishes. This was not really an issue for them, instead their focus was on the popular culture of amusement which was expressed by and large on Sundays. The Reformed aimed at closing down the taverns for at least the duration of the church service and eliminating the dancing enjoyed at Sunday afternoon wedding celebrations. In most villages, the tavern was close to the church and therefore posed an automatic and immediate threat to the Sunday service.

This attack on the taverns and associated practices such as dancing, 'lewd behaviour', and prostitution formed the major part of the Reformed assault on popular culture and its attempt to 'Protestantise' public life and piety. Allied to this was the Reformed emphasis on the preached Word, based on observance of Sunday as the day of worship. A schoolmaster would read portions of text before the service and, following the opening of the service, the congregation sang from Dathenus's psalter. There followed short simple prayers and then the focus of the service, the sermon. Hand in hand with the prescribing of regular Sunday services and the regulation of the taverns was the Reformed insistence on an end to funeral sermons and other 'superstitions'. There were mixed results in abolishing these *lijkpredicaties*: at Dordrecht they were stopped in 1578, but at the village of Ridderkerk not until 1584. But given the pressure put on ministers in the rural parishes, to abolish funeral sermons permanently would be impossible. Instead a compromise was arrived at whereby the minister could agree to give a sermon, but also admonish those attending from the Heidelberg Catechism and the Bible. To avoid the appearance of superstition, all sermons had to be preached from the pulpit rather than the graveside.[62]

What conclusions may we draw regarding the Calvinist ministry in Holland during these years? The inference seems plain that, at least for the earlier period 1572–6, ministers who came from exile communities were called by reputation, as a result of whatever significance they may have had there, rather than any desire to search either for graduates or those especially well qualified in terms of academic training. These ministers from exile tended, initially, to go into service in the larger cities and towns such as Rotterdam or Dordrecht, not merely because of the greater salaries, but because of their experience of church government and organisation in this period of church-building. Those ministers who had found refuge in London or Emden before 1572 had had the opportunity to see Reformed churches in action: the regular meetings of ministers and elders in the consistory, the weekly gathering of ministers in the *coetus*. Aside from this experienced elite, the new churches had little alternative but to rely on the existing clerical professionals to fill their parishes. Throughout the first fifteen years members of the ex-Catholic clergy who had submitted to the authority of the Reformed church remained in a numerical majority among those appointed by the classes, although the rigorous examinations and safeguards imposed suggest the churches' continuing uneasiness regarding men of this sort. In this context windfall reinforcements, such as the arrival of a large group of expelled ministers and schoolteachers from the Palatinate, were especially welcome.[63]

As the backgrounds of most of the ministers remain obscure, it is difficult to establish with anything approaching statistical accuracy the overall quality of the ministry: many simply leave a first name in the classis and synodal records, and were never mentioned again. Groenhuis in his study of the clergy in the early seventeenth century, concluded that the general quality of Reformed ministers improved only after 1600.[64] He is right only in the narrow sense of formal educational qualifications. By 1600 almost all the ministers had to undergo training at the University of Leiden, as well as training in the classis. Yet such an assessment greatly underestimates the effectiveness of the mechanisms of in-service training,

centred on the classis, established in the first years of church-
building. These achieved a considerable amount in producing a
committed and capable ministerial cadre in a short period of time.

If quality of ministry can be judged by the number of ministers who were disciplined by their classis, then the ministry
1572–85 acquits itself well, when subjected to scrutiny in cases of
moral and theological uncertainties. The classis of Dordrecht, for
instance, in the period 1573–90 disciplined only ten ministers in a
total of nearly 70 serving in the classis.[65] The cases I have cited
such as that of Steur tended to be the exception, an inevitable
result of the uncertainties of the early days of the ministry's establishment and the overwhelming demand for ministers during these
years. The rapid development of the classis swiftly improvised a
system of control that made cases of this sort much less likely to
happen in the future. By 1590 the Dutch church had already
achieved a considerable success in imposing doctrinal orthodoxy
and discipling erring colleagues. Despite the hostility or indifference of many in the magistracy, the Dutch ministry compares by
no means unfavourably with the ministry in France or Scotland in
this same early period of church-building. It was an achievement
in which the founding fathers of the Dutch church could take
considerable pride.

Notes

1 Geoffrey Parker gives an account of the fall of the various towns to the
revolt. Parker, *The Dutch Revolt* (2nd edition, London, 1985), pp. 137–9.
2 Parker, *Dutch Revolt*, p. 151. A. C. Duke and R. L. Jones, 'Towards a
Reformed Polity in Holland, 1572–1578', *Tijdschrift voor Geschiedenis*,
89 (1976), 376. Reprinted in Duke's *Reformation and Revolt in the Low
Countries* (London, 1990).
3 J. P. Elliott, 'Protestantization in the Northern Netherlands, a Case
Study: The Classis of Dordrecht, 1572–1640' (Columbia University
Ph.D. thesis, 1990), p. 99. This and the preceding paragraph are based
on pp. 90–102.
4 H. J. Jaanus, *Hervormd Delft ten tijde van Arent Cornelisz* (Amsterdam,
1950), pp. 30–1; *Uw Rijk Kome. Acta van de kerkeraad van de Neder-
duits Gereformeerde Gemeente te Dordrecht, 1573–1578*, ed. T. W.
Jensma (Dordrecht, 1981), p. x; for Den Haag, see Duke and Jones,
'Towards a Reformed Polity', 380; for Gouda, C. C. Hibben, *Gouda in
Revolt* (Utrecht, 1983), p. 84. The article by Duke and Jones gives an
excellent account of the process of church-building in Holland.

5 *Ecclesiae Londino-Batavae Archivum*, ed. J. H. Hessels, 3 vols in 4 (Cambridge, 1889–97) [hereafter Hessels]. Here, III, i, no. 206.

6 The estimate is my own derived from *NNBW*, Emden consistory minutes and other church records. For Arendsz *NNBW* I, 165–8 and H. A. Enno van Gelder, 'Hervorming en Hervormden te Alkmaar', *Oud-Holland*, 40 (1922), 92–123. For Gabriel, *NNBW* VI, 541–2 and Jaanus, *Hervormd Delft*, pp. 31–5. For Cornelisz at Den Briel, W. Troost and J. Woltjer, 'Brielle in Hervormingstijd', *Bijdragen en mededeelingen betreffende de geschiedenis der Nederlanden*, 87 (1972), 307–53. For Castricum at Enkhuizen, *NNBW* I, 587.

7 For information regarding Balck, *NNBW* I, 227–30 and Hessels III, i, nos 205, 207, 211. On Rijckwaert, *NNBW* III, 114–116. On their ministry in Rotterdam, H. ten Boom, *De Reformatie in Rotterdam, 1530–1585* (Hollandse Historische Reeks, 7, 1987), p. 155.

8 Hessels III, i, no. 207.

9 Hessels III, i, no. 210.

10 Hessels III, i, no. 251.

11 The church at Den Briel also testified on Steur's behalf. Hessels III, i, no. 253.

12 *NNBW* 3, 1201–3. See also *Acta der Provinciale en Particuliere Synoden gehouden in de Noorderlijke Nederlanden gedurende de jaren 1572–1620*, ed. J. Reitsma and S. V. van Veen, 8 vols (Groningen, 1892–99). Henceforth, RV. Here II. p. 141.

13 Classis Brielle, fo. 10v. Information kindly supplied by Dr A. C. Duke.

14 For Pieter Hyperphragmus, *NNBW* IV, 1049–50. Also ten Boom, *Rotterdam*, pp. 159–63.

15 A letter was sent from the Rotterdam consistory to Emden explaining the events concerning de Zuttere. It is reprinted in *Brieven uit Onderscheidene kerkelijke archieven* ed. H. Q. Janssen and J. J. van Toorenenbergen (*WMV*, III, ii, Utrecht, 1878), pp. 14–17. Rotterdam to Emden, 5 October 1574. Signed by the minister and the consistory.

16 RV II, pp. 151–2.

17 RV II, pp. 130–1.

18 *WMV*, III, ii, p. 17. Letter of the Rotterdam consistory to Emden. The attestation of de Zuttere had been signed by Borsumannus, one of the Emden ministers. See also Andrew Pettegree, *Emden and the Dutch Revolt* (Oxford, 1992), pp. 199–200.

19 *WMV*, III, ii, p. 17. Letter of the Rotterdam consistory to Emden.

20 Ten Boom, *Rotterdam*, p. 166. For more information about Aegidius Johannis Frisius see Classis Brielle, fol. 12v. He was a minister in this classis by the summer of 1575. See also 'Aanvullingen en verbeteringen op de naamlijst van Predikanten in Zuid-Holland', ed. W. M. C. Regt in *NAK*, 28 (1936), 176. For P. de Bert see *NNBW* I, 319–20 and *Biografisch Woordenboek van Protestantsche Godgeleerden in Nederland*, ed. J. P. de Bie and J. Loosje, 5 vols (The Hague, 1919–49), I, 434–5.

21 Hessels III, i, no. 312.

22 Ten Boom, *Rotterdam*, p. 155; for Delft and Dordrecht see Parker,

Dutch Revolt, p. 153. His description is based on the article by Duke and Jones cited above.

23 The process of church-founding can be closely followed in the classis of Dordrecht. For an excellent account of this process, see A. C. Duke, 'The Reformation of the Backwoods: The Struggle for a Calvinist and Presbyterian Structure in the Country-Side of South Holland and Utrecht before 1620', in his *Reformation and the Revolt in the Low Countries*, pp. 227–68. See particularly note 92, p. 247.

24 The biographical information has been derived from entries in *NNBW*, Emden consistory minutes and other church records, particularly classis minutes. Use has also been made of 'Aanvullingen en verbeteringen op de naamlijst van Predikanten in Zuid-Holland', ed. W. M. C. Regt in *NAK*, 28–30 (1936–8).

25 Quoted by A. Th. van Deursen, *Bavianen en Slijkgeuzen* (Assen, 1974), p. 36. The original came from H. H. Kuyper, *De Opleiding tot den dienst des Woords bij de Gereformeerden* (The Hague, 1891), p. 267.

26 H. C. Rogge, *Caspar Coolhaes de Voorlooper van Arminius en der Remonstranten*, 2 vols (Amsterdam, 1856–58), I, p. 37.

27 *Acta van de Nederlandsche Synoden der Zestiende eeuw*, ed. F. L. Rutgers (*WMV*, 1st series, 4, 1899). Henceforth *Acta*. Provincial synod of Dordrecht, June 1574, p. 140.

28 Duke, 'The Reformation of the Backwoods', p. 242.

29 *WMV*, III, iv, p. 32. Wernerus Helmichius to Arent Cornelisz, 13 February 1582.

30 Elliott, 'Protestantization in the Northern Netherlands', p. 173.

31 *Classicale Acta, 1573–1620. Particuliere Synode Zuid-Holland. Vol. I, Classis Dordrecht, 1573–1600*, ed. J. P. van Dooren (The Hague, 1980), p. 65, article 11. Hereafter *CAD*. Elliott, 'Protestantization in the Northern Netherlands', p. 173. C. Tukker, *De Classis Dordrecht van 1573 tot 1609* (Leiden, 1965), p. 155.

32 *Acta van de Colloquia der Nederlandsche Gemeenten in Engeland, 1572–1624*, ed. J. J. van Toorenenbergen. (*WMV*, II, i, 1872), pp. 17–20.

33 Elliott, 'Protestantization in the Northern Netherlands', pp. 172–3.

34 Jaanus, *Hervormd Delft*, p. 159.

35 C. A. Tukker, 'The Recruitment and Training of Protestant Ministers in the Netherlands in the 16th Century', in *Miscellanea Historiae Ecclesiasticae*, 3, ed. D. Baker (Cambridge, 1970), p. 199.

36 *Acta*, Convent of Wesel, article 8, p. 32.

37 *Acta*, article 10, p. 32.

38 *Acta*, articles 10 and 11, pp. 59–60.

39 *Acta*, article 13, pp. 61–2.

40 *Acta*, article 16, p. 63.

41 *Acta*, articles 17 and 18, pp. 63–4.

42 *Acta*, article 18, pp. 63–4.

43 *Acta*, article 52, p. 86.

44 *Acta*, Chapter 2, pp. 105–9.

45 *Acta*, article 17, p. 138.

46 *Acta*, article 24, p. 138.

47 *Acta*, pp. 140–1.

48 *Acta*, pp. 141.

49 *Acta*, pp. 159–60.

50 A. Th. van Deursen, *Bavianen en Slijkgeuzen*, p. 9. For a good description of the working of the classis, see pp. 5–11.

51 *Acta*, article 4, p. 235.

52 *Acta*, article 5, p. 235–6.

53 Letter of 29 August 1583. Printed in L. Knappert, 'Stukken uit den stichtingstijd der Nederlandsche Hervormde Kerk', *NAK*, 7 (1910), 249–52.

54 Letter of 6 July 1586. Knappert, 'Stukken', 259–61.

55 Duke, 'Reformation of the Backwoods', pp. 229–30. He gives the example of the former priest of Houten who warned the people not to attend the Reformed services on pain of eternal damnation. The Reformed minister had to put up with conversation during the service, the local magistrates advised the people to avoid the services, and the local sexton ran the tavern, having left the church to serve his customers.

56 Ibid., p. 247.

57 In March 1575 Johannes Simonsz, minister at Westmaas, was suspended for a 'disorderly life'. *CAD*, p. 33. In October 1580 Laurentius Copicanus was deposed from his charge for adultery. *CAD*, p. 94.

58 *CAD*, p. 51.

59 Letter of 15 November 1579. Printed in *WMV*, III, ii, pp. 118–22.

60 Elliott, 'Protestantization in the Northern Netherlands', p. 255.

61 *CAD*, p. 59.

62 This paragraph is based on Elliott, 'Protestantization in the Northern Netherlands', pp. 462–88.

63 A list exists in the Collectie Arent Cornelisz in the Gemeentearchief Delft detailing some 80 ministers from the Palatinate employed either as preachers or schoolmasters in the Classis of Dordrecht.

64 G. Groenhuis, *De Predikanten. De sociale positie van de Gereformeerde predikanten in de Republiek der Verenigde Nederlanden voor ± 1700* (Groningen, 1977).

65 Elliott, 'Protestantization in the Northern Netherlands', pp. 189–94, 236–7. As a comparison with the Dordrecht classis, in Zurich over the period 1532–80 something like a third of ministers were subjected to disciplinary procedures. See B. Gordon, *Clerical Discipline and the Rural Reformation*, pp. 209–13. The Dutch ministry in the Dordrecht classis certainly compares favourably with this settled church.

10

'A Faythful Pastor in the Churches': ministers in the French and Walloon communities in England, 1560–1620

Andrew Spicer

The exodus from France and the Netherlands during the second half of the sixteenth century resulted in refugee communities being established in the German Empire at Cologne, Frankenthal, and Aachen, at Emden in the county of East Friesland, and in England. The reverses suffered by the rebels in the Netherlands in 1567 and the subsequent closure of the Calvinist churches resulted in waves of new emigrants. Furthermore fluctuations in the fortunes of the Huguenot cause in France, such as the Massacre of St Bartholomew's Day, resulted in the daily arrival of boatloads of refugees.[1] At least fifteen thousand refugees are estimated to have come to England. The growth in the London stranger community and the settlement of aliens at ports of entry such as Rye alarmed the authorities who considered their settlement to be a threat to security. The government as a result attempted to disperse the refugees in order to reduce this threat. Sir William Cecil was also keen to exploit the economic advantages that these refugees offered, in particular their skills in the 'new draperies', in the hope that these new settlements would help to revitalise several flagging urban economies.[2] The first such community was established for Flemish refugees at Sandwich after negotiations between the ministers of the Dutch congregation and the government. With the growing numbers of refugees, further communities were established, for example at Norwich (1565) and Maidstone (1567). A Walloon community was established in Southampton in 1567. Exiles from France had settled in Rye from about 1562 and also at Winchelsea. The French community at Canterbury also became firmly established in 1575 after earlier tentative beginnings, with the migration of the Walloon community at Sandwich and French exiles at Winchelsea to the city at this time.[3]

Ministers were particularly conspicuous amongst the refugees who came to England. This was perhaps not surprising in view of their vulnerability as they attempted to preach and conduct services in the Reformed communities in their homelands, often in the face of fierce official persecution. Even after the establishment of official toleration, a sudden reversal of policy might result in summary expulsion. With the outbreak of the Third Civil War in France in 1568, Huguenot ministers were given fifteen days to leave the country. The Huguenot ministers were again expelled after Henry III's reconciliation with the Catholic League in 1585. Nineteen French ministers were recorded in London in 1568 and a further fifteen fled from Normandy to Jersey.[4] In the wake of the Massacre of St Bartholomew's Day no fewer than sixty French ministers were registered in London.[5] Ministers also appeared in some of the smaller communities, such as Rye and Southampton.[6] While some refugee ministers settled permanently in England, sometimes taking up positions in the universities or in the cathedral chapters,[7] for many of these ministers their exile was temporary, before they returned to their flocks in France and the Netherlands.

These exiled ministers were therefore a very transitory group and their experiences of exile clearly differed from those of ministers who settled permanently in England to serve the foreign congregations. Despite a very partial survival of records it is possible to say quite a lot about the men who served these churches. They were a diverse group, reflecting the very different demands placed on men who put their services at the disposal of an exile church. The ministers' role was defined as being 'annoncer la parole de Dieu, par icelle endoctriner, admonester, exhorter et reprendre tant en public qu'en particulier, administrer les sacremens, et commun (avec les aultres anciens choisis pour surueiller sur les moeurs et conduire leglise) mectre en vsage avec charité chrestienne les admonitions et censures eclesiasticques à lendroit de ceux qui destourneront de leur debuoir'.[8] But as if this was not enough – and one must remember that these ministers served a congregation outside the normal parochial structure and spread throughout the town – the ministers were often also required to assume a prominent leadership role, in representing the interests of the immigrant community to the local authorities. A harmonious relationship between a respected minister and sympathetic magistrates could play a vital role in protecting the community from the jealous hostility of local inhabitants.

What can one say about the men called upon to perform these demanding and diverse functions? First, there is a clear contrast in the calibre of the ministers who served the French-speaking church in London and those in the provincial communities. Three of the four principal pastors who served the Threadneedle Street church during the sixteenth century were aristocrats: Nicholas des Gallars, Sieur de Saules (1560–63); Pierre Loiseleur, Seigneur de Villiers (1574–79); Robert le Maçon, Sieur de la Fontaine (1574–1611). The only exception was Jean Cousin who served the church between 1563 and 1574. Their origins were French rather than Walloon and they had served in some of the more important Huguenot churches such as Caen and Orléans.[9] The appointment of Nicholas des Gallars, one of the leading figures in Geneva, was a recognition of the importance which Calvin attached to sustaining the London church. Furthermore the appointment of men of such status provided the church with an advantage in their relations with the English government as well as in their dealings with continental reformers. Robert le Maçon de la Fontaine was the confidant of the King of Navarre, and a correspondent of Mornay and Theodore Beza.[10] The ministers could also play an important diplomatic role at court, representing the interests of the Huguenot nobility and the Prince of Orange. Des Gallars was also valuable to the English government through providing reports on the Colloquy of Poissy and negotiating with the Huguenot leaders in 1562.[11]

In contrast, the earliest provincial ministers were generally men of much humbler stock. Two, Anthoine Lescaillet and Walerand Thevelin, were lay preachers who had taken part in the Troubles of the Wonderyear, the first part of the Dutch Revolt (1566–67). Lescaillet was initially the minister of the Walloon community at Sandwich, and after their migration to Canterbury he became the minister there until his death in 1596. He was a shoemaker's son who had begun to preach in June 1566 and continued to preach at La Gorgue, Lestrem, and Estaires and later was present at the battle of Wattrelos.[12] Walerand Thevelin became the minister in Southampton in 1568 after being banished from the southern Netherlands by the Council of Troubles in September

1567. He had been chosen as the preacher at Tourcoing in August 1566 at the same time as the establishment of a formal consistory there. He had publicly celebrated the Lord's Supper in the market place at Tourcoing, attended 'en grande nombre et avecq armes'. In October 1566 Thevelin was one of the Walloon ministers present at the Synod of Ghent where discussions took place about buying their religious freedom from the king. This came to be known as the Three Million Guilders Request and ultimately provided an excuse to raise money for the rebel forces when the attempts to buy their religious freedom failed.[13] Phyllis Mack Crew, who studied 149 lay preachers active during the Troubles of 1566, concluded that such men were generally obscure priests or laymen mainly from the artisan class and of limited education.[14] Yet both of these refugee ministers appear to have been literate, and the first minister of the French community in Norwich, Johannes Helmichius, had studied Hebrew at Lausanne. He had also been involved in the Troubles, returning from Lausanne to the Netherlands to preach at Ghent and Antwerp. He died at Norwich in 1568.[15]

The ministers who initially served the communities established at Rye and Winchelsea are more comparable with those of Threadneedle Street. The first minister at Rye was François de Saint Paul, who served several Huguenot churches before being sent from Geneva to be the minister at Dieppe. Like Des Gallars, he had attended the Colloquy of Poissy. De Saint Paul arrived in Rye with some of his congregation in November 1562 but he returned to celebrate the Lord's Supper in Dieppe by Christmas.[16] He appeared again in Rye after the publication of the edict against the Huguenot ministers in 1568, again accompanied by refugees from Dieppe, who included his assistant Nicholas le Tellier and Hector Hamon de Bacquerville who served the community at Winchelsea.[17]

The second generation of refugee ministers in the provincial churches reflected the growing trend towards a better trained and educated ministry. Philippe de la Motte, the second minister in Southampton, was typical of this development. He had been born to Catholic parents at Tournai but had been converted after being apprenticed to a Reformed silk-weaver. He matriculated as a student of theology at the Genevan Academy in June 1581 and was ordained by the Walloon synod in the Netherlands after an examination of his religious doctrine and his lifestyle. He acted as the secretary to the Walloon classis held at Leiden in October 1584 and was unsuccessful in the disputed election to serve the church at Leiden in the following month. Although he was directed to serve the church at Oostende, de la Motte had arrived in Southampton by May 1585, probably accompanied by his wife and her family.[18]

A similar move towards a more educated ministry can also be seen amongst the ministers who were born in England or became exiles when they were young. In a number of cases they were the children of ministers or church officials, such as Aaron Cappel, the son of one of the elders of the French church in London, or the son of Nicholas Basnage, the minister in Norwich. These young men initially studied at Cambridge, three of them (John Bulteel, Philippe Delmé, Timothée Blier) at Emmanuel College which had been founded by Sir Walter Mildmay for 'rendering as many persons as possible fit for the sacred ministry of the word and sacraments; so that from this seminary the Church of England might have men whom it may call forth to instruct the people and undertake the duty of pastors'.[19] The students continued their education at Geneva, Leiden, or Heidelberg; in some cases they studied at several centres. The ministers also appear to have served for a short period as an assistant minister, presumably learning the practical side of their role before they became the principal minister in a community.

Aaron Cappel and Samuel le Chevalier were typical of the students who were financed by the French church. Aaron Cappel's father had been one of the first elders of the French church in London and Samuel was the son of Anthoine-Raoul le Chevalier of Normandy who had lectured in Hebrew at Cambridge and later in Geneva during Mary's reign. Cappel was born in London and le Chevalier in Geneva. They both studied at Peterhouse, Cambridge; Cappel matriculated in 1581 and Le Chevalier graduated with a Bachelor of Arts degree in 1582–83. They both went to study theology at the Academy in Geneva in 1583, le Chevalier remaining there until 1589 while Cappel matriculated at Heidelberg in 1586. The two were consecrated in London in 1589 and presented to the people in 1591. Cappel temporarily served the church at Norwich before becoming the minister in London, while le Chevalier served as an assistant to the church in Canterbury before succeeding Anthoine Lescaillet in 1596.[20] These two contemporaries were not isolated examples. The careers of John Bulteel and Philippe Delmé were similar although they studied at Leiden.[21]

The education of these students for the ministry was on occasions financed by collections raised among the members of the French-speaking churches in England. In 1583 the French churches decided to collect funds in order to finance students for the ministry, the fund to be administered by the Threadneedle Street church in London. The student would then be assigned to a church with a particular need.[22] The French church in Southampton made specific arrangements for the house-to-house collection of money every three months by the elders and deacons in order to finance students. The accounts for the collections which were made in Canterbury have survived for the years 1599–1601.[23] These particular collections probably funded the education of Timothée Blier and Daniel Tuvel. Initially Blier was financed by the French church in London but the consistory records reveal that this was viewed as only being a temporary measure. Pledges of financial support for Blier and Daniel Tuvel were made in July 1601 by the communities at Norwich (£10), Canterbury (£12), Southampton (£7 11s.) together with £3 pledged by his father.[24] The Threadneedle Street church resigned their rights to Blier in 1603, on condition that the French-speaking churches of Norwich, Canterbury, and Southampton continued to fund his training until he was considered to be fit for the ministry. These churches would then decide in which he should serve and be employed to the best advantage. They also undertook from time to time to fund a further scholar.[25]

Such financial support could also be extended to the widow and orphans of former ministers. The son of the late Jean Marie was educated at the expense of the French churches. Nathaniel Marie must have shown rare promise, since the church at Norwich showed some anxiety that he should not be lured away by promises of support from the Walloon churches of Holland and Zeeland because he would be obliged to serve in one of their churches. The Norwich consistory therefore offered 'quelque somme pour l'entretenir à Cambridge pour un an, jusques a tant qu'il ait trouvé meilleure condition de continuer ses études'.[26] The exiled French churches were not always successful in engaging the students whom they had financed to serve in their churches. Mathieu du Scarron who had studied at Geneva at the same time as Cappel and le Chevalier and also at the expense of the French church refused to return to England and after several years of correspondence it was agreed that he should repay the consistory in 1595.[27] Daniel Tuvel failed to complete his studies and in 1603–4 was ordered by the Colloquy to repay the costs of his education, up to £40 with quarterly payments of 20s.[28]

The demands of the exile churches for ministers to serve their congregations could also disrupt the education of ministers. The case of Timothée Blier provides an interesting example of this. In spite of promising to work diligently at his studies in 1600, by March 1604 Blier had been appropriated by the church in Southampton. The Colloquy of the French churches agreed to Blier's service there as a temporary measure, due to the ill-health of their minister, but they censured the church for its action. The Southampton church was criticised in particular for encouraging Blier to abandon his studies, since the representatives of the Canterbury church had wanted Blier to complete his training at Montauban. The church was also attacked for conniving at Blier's marriage; he had married the sister-in-law of Philippe de la Motte, the former minister in Southampton.[29]

Besides their failure to consult the other churches which had financed Blier's education, the Southampton church was criticised not only for the precipitate promotion of the minister but also for its failure to follow the correct procedures. Candidates for the ministry were examined as to the conduct of their life and their religious doctrine, as well as delivering a practice sermon to the congregation. The minister was then presented to the congregation and received with prayers and orations together with the imposition of hands.[30] Blier had been presented to his chair but he had not received the imposition of hands which was seen as being contrary to the Discipline and the Word of God.[31]

The Colloquy which censured the church in 1606 recognised the church's need for a minister and allowed Blier to continue at Southampton as a temporary measure but Southampton's failure to operate through the Colloquy was strongly criticised.[32] However there was little that the Colloquy could effectively do and Blier even acted acted as the secretary for the 1606 Colloquy which censured the Southampton church. All the churches could do was to repeat that the appointment was only a temporary measure, no doubt especially because Philippe de la Motte remained in

Southampton and became a respected member of the local community, until his death in 1617.[33] However the French churches wreaked their revenge when they decided that having appropriated the minister, the Southampton church should assume responsibility for his widow and children if Blier's ministry continued in the town until his death.[34]

After 1572 and the gradual growth of the Reformed churches in the northern provinces of the Spanish Netherlands, appeals were frequently made to the exile churches for ministers to serve their newly-established churches. At the synod of Emden it had been agreed that 'when ministers who are native Netherlanders and who have entered the service of churches abroad are recalled, they should diligently seek to heed that calling. . . . Those who have no obligations should be exhorted to keep themselves free so that they can respond to a call'.[35] While the French churches in England were prevented from attending the synod, they would have been aware of the *actes* which were circulated among the churches.[36] Attempts were made by some of the more prominent churches to secure the services of particular ministers. Appeals were made through the Dutch church in London to persuade Adrian Saravia to return to the Netherlands and serve the community at Dordrecht in 1573 and 1576. Saravia was the former chaplain of William of Orange and may have been involved in the formation of the Belgic Confession of Faith in 1561. Although he had briefly served the church in Vlissingen in 1572, he was the Headmaster of the Grammar School in Southampton between 1572 and 1578 as well as probably being an assistant minister in the French church. Saravia returned to the Netherlands in 1578 to become a minister at Ghent.[37] Other assistant ministers in the exiled communities were also lured to the Netherlands, such as Michel de la Forest who left Southampton to be the pastor at Mechelen and Oudenaarde, and later died at the seige of Antwerp in 1585. Although de la Forest had been born in the Netherlands, he had trained and served as a minister in France.[38] The Walloon churches also secured the services of exiled French ministers, such as Jacob Tardif, the minister of Port-Audemer, Normandy who reluctantly responded to the call from the Netherlands and by 1577 was the minister at Tournai.[39]

The Walloon synods also appealed directly to the established ministers of the provincial churches to return to the Low Countries. Anthoine Lescaillet acted as a representative of the Walloon churches in England at the Walloon synods in the Netherlands, and on several occasions was called upon to return to the Netherlands. This was in spite of the his weak voice which it was considered would mean that he would be suitable to serve the persecuted churches only 'under the cross'.[40] The attempts to procure the services of Philippe de la Motte reveal something of the attitude of the exiled churches to the demands made by their continental brethren. He was called upon to serve the French-speaking church at Aachen in 1597. While the minister agreed to take up the post, the Colloquy of the French-speaking churches in England was less keen. They criticised the Walloon synod of Holland for its lack of consideration and decided to delay de la Motte's departure from Southampton for five months, until 1 September, so that they could find a replacement for him. Only then was the Colloquy prepared to provide de la Motte with a suitable testimonial as to his doctrine and personal conduct. However by April 1598, de la Motte still had not taken up his post at Aachen and the Walloon synod meeting at Zierikzee decided to write to Southampton to urge them not to delay de la Motte's departure. By September 1600, the church at Aachen was still awaiting the arrival of a minister. A more terse resolution was agreed in May 1601 which advised the church in Southampton to find a replacement for de la Motte so that he could take up a vocation at Delft within two months. However de la Motte failed to return to the continent and so the synod requested that he should write and inform them of the reasons for his failure.[41] There is no record of his reply, but it is possible that the ill-health which resulted in his retirement in 1604 had prevented his departure.

While the pressure for ministers to return overseas came mainly from the Netherlands, a few requests were also occasionally received from the Reformed church in France. In 1583 the Colloquy received a request for Mons. Morel to leave the church at Rye to go to Amiens. While the Synod of Vitré recognised the obligation that Jean Marie had to the church at Norwich, they urged the church there to allow him to continue his preaching in Normandy.[42]

The desperate keenness of churches in France and the Netherlands to secure the services of ministers from the exile churches was a direct consequence of the lack of well-qualified pastors at a time when sudden fluctuations in the military and political situation brought opportunities for rapid church-building. But the persistent attempts to employ de la Motte towards the end of the century obscure the fact that by this time the relationship between the churches had changed significantly. By the last decade of the century ministers were being delegated to serve the now ailing churches abroad by the established churches in the Netherlands. A minister had been directed to Southampton in 1585, while in 1597 the churches of Zeeland were urged to provide a minister for the Walloon church at Norwich. The Walloon synods however emphasised that such appointments were only temporary and that the ministers should return to the Netherlands when they were required. Ministers were also appointed for short periods of time. Daniel de Nielles was appointed to serve the Norwich church for six months and his replacement Jacques Polyander was also a temporary appointment.[43] There is also one instance of a minister being sent from France. A minister was sent from Dieppe to serve the church at Rye but the Colloquy of French churches in England were irritated that they had not been consulted about this.[44] By the 1590s there were even cases of refugee students being educated at the expense of the continental churches. Job du Rieu, the son of a Norwich refugee, was trained for the ministry, studying at Leiden, at the expense of the Walloon synods and became a minister in 1601. The church at Dieppe was offered the services of Nathaniel de Laune in 1599 on condition that it paid £20 per annum for him to continue his studies at Cambridge and then finance his education at Geneva. He became the pastor at Dieppe in 1604.[45]

By the end of the sixteenth century some of the provincial churches were experiencing severe financial difficulties. The minister at Canterbury, Samuel le Chevalier, protested to the consistory in 1596 that he was unable to live on his stipend of £4 per month and in 1603 asked the Colloquy to be discharged from the church because of his poverty.[46] However, the ministers' salaries probably compared favourably with the income of some of their English counterparts, particularly in the towns, where parishes were small and livings often extremely small. Five parishes in Canterbury had annual incomes of £5 or less in 1535 and there were a number of small parishes in towns such as Norwich and Winchester as well as London. The incomes of the urban clergy varied according to the types of parish they served and the sources of income available to them but testamentary evidence suggests that during Elizabeth's reign relatively few of these incomes kept pace with inflation.[47] Some indication of the relative prosperity of the exiled ministers can be seen in Southampton. Henry Hopkins who had become the Rector of All Saints, Southampton in 1589 left moveable goods worth £90 17s. 8d. when he died in 1600; his will makes no mention of any property. The moveable goods of another Southampton cleric, Thomas Hitchcock, were valued at £83 3s. 6d. in 1612. While the value of the moveable goods of Philippe de la Motte, the former minister of the French church, is unknown, he made bequests totalling £163 when he wrote his will in 1615. It should however be remembered that de la Motte had retired from the ministry in 1604 owing to ill-health but had then become involved in the cloth industry.[48]

The salary of the provincial ministers, however, did not compare quite so favourably with those of their London counterparts. Anthoine Lescaillet was granted a salary of £24 *per annum* by the Canterbury consistory in 1578.[49] However, the London French church had agreed to pay Nicholas des Gallars an annual salary of £50 in November 1560. Des Gallars's successor received only £30 per annum as well as a housing allowance. Jean Cousin complained 'that the money we [the consistory] give him is spent before the month is out and that nevertheless he makes as small cheer as possible, and sometimes must be content with but one egg to his dinner and that his office doth not deserve to be thus poorly maintained'.[50] When Adrian Saravia became the minister at Ghent in 1578 he received an income of £30, equal to that of a London minister. The States of Holland had established 300 Guilders (the equivalent of £30) as the minimum salary for ministers serving in the towns, although it is clear that stipends were in fact often badly in arrears. In a number of towns the ministers received more than this minimum salary; Saravia probably became one of the most highly paid ministers when he went to Leiden in November 1582, receiving a salary of 400 Guilders together with a housing allowance of 50 Guilders as well as a further allowance for his University preaching.[51]

The ministers of the foreign churches in England were paid from a fund administered by the deacons which was distinct from the funds used for poor relief. In some cases money was bequeathed for the maintenance of the ministry but the principal source of income was from regular collections. The records of the monthly house-to-house collections have survived for Canterbury for 1594–1604, in some cases listing the contributions made by each household.[52] The congregation were expected to contribute according to their means but the Colloquy considered the problem of those who failed to do so in 1586. They concluded that such people were to be rebuked and if this failed to be called before the consistory; if they still failed to contribute sufficiently the consistory could refer the case to the magistrates.[53] In Norwich two members of the congregation began to attend their parish church and refused to contribute to the maintenance of the ministry and the community's poor; this became an increasing problem for the church.[54] The refugee communities were also expected to make other financial contributions. The personal tithes paid to the English clergy in Canterbury and London had come to be raised as a tax upon house rents.[55] The Walloon congregation at Norwich was expected to contribute in the same way to 'all manner of dewties growenge to the preste and clarke of the same parrishe', and some members of the Southampton congregation appear to have contributed to the town's system of poor relief from which they could not benefit. These payments in addition to the demands of the exiled churches clearly placed a heavy burden upon the foreign congregations.[56]

The Southampton church appealed to the Colloquy and the Threadneedle Street church about its inability to finance its ministry in 1610, and similar appeals had been made by the congregation at Rye as early as 1583.[57] The church at Rye claimed that their financial difficulties were due to their inadequate means and their small size. Certainly by the end of the sixteenth century there was a gradual decline in the size of the stranger communities. The more settled situation on the continent not only resulted in fewer refugees joining the exile churches, but also caused some exiles to migrate to the United Provinces and France. The exiles who remained became increasingly integrated into their host communities, particularly amongst those who had been born in England. Marriages began to take place outside the French church in Southampton after 1588, and a similar trend can be seen at Canterbury.[58] The Southampton church was also decimated by plague in 1583–84 and about 150 lives, including whole families, were lost in 1604.

By 1596 there were only 296 aliens recorded in Southampton compared with 2,438 at Canterbury and about seven thousand foreigners (both French and Dutch-speaking exiles) in London.[59]

The decline in the size of some of the churches inevitably resulted in financial hardship and appeals to the Colloquy for assistance. The Colloquies called upon the other French congregations to contribute to assist the Rye congregation in 1583. A similar approach was taken in 1610 when the Southampton church pleaded its poverty. By 1615 the Canterbury church claimed to be too poor to assist Southampton, and the Norwich church also requested financial advice from the Colloquy in 1625. The Southampton congregation became increasingly dependent financially upon Threadneedle Street and this continued into the seventeenth century.[60]

The stranger churches and their ministers were therefore forced to adapt to changed circumstances. The church in Southampton had been forced to compromise earlier when the church had to survive for several months without a minister after the death of Walerand Thevelin in September 1584 until his successor Philippe de la Motte arrived in the town in May 1585. The celebration of the Lord's Supper was suspended but the religious life of the community was maintained by the consistory. The local vicar, Henry Hopkins, was responsible for conducting baptisms and officiating at one marriage during this period.[61]

The ministers were not immune to the gradual integration and assimilation into their host community. Intellectual contacts were evident from the first Elizabethan years when several London ministers established contacts with leading representatives of the forward tendency in English Protestantism.[62] These contacts were mirrored in the provincial communities. Philippe de la Motte borrowed books from Peter Caplin, whose library included the works of William Perkins, and received the works of Richard Greenham as a legacy from him.[63] Peter de Laune at Norwich was interested in the liturgy of the church of England which he translated into French.[64]

But by the end of the century the integration process had advanced considerably. De la Motte became a respected member of the town; five bequests were made to him, from people who were not members of his family, after he had retired from the ministry and which in some cases equalled bequests made to the incumbent minister Timothée Blier. De la Motte was clearly sufficiently well regarded in Southampton for all of the town corporation to attend his burial in 1617.[65] It is also interesting to note that de la Motte and Blier both received letters of denization, de la Motte in 1608 and Blier in 1616.[66] There is no evidence that any other French ministers applied for this, although a number of the second generation of ministers such as Pierre de Laune and Philippe Delmé were born in England and so technically would not have required them.[67]

Timothée Blier provides a more extreme example of integration. He had been educated at the expense of the French churches but gave up his post as the minister of the Southampton congregation to become the vicar of Titchfield in Hampshire. He may have been forced to move due to the financial difficulties that the church was experiencing, and the minister had a young family.[68] Unfortunately there are no surviving records concerning his appointment to the benefice, the advowson for which was in the hands of the earl of Southampton. As a result it is not possible to discover whether or not the appointment of a Calvinist minister to an Anglican benefice aroused any controversy or debate as to the validity of his ordination. Adrian Saravia had been presented to the rectory of Tatenhill by January 1588 and does not appear to have been reordained. In fact Saravia discussed the issue of reordination in his *Defensio tractationis* and concluded that ordination within the 'established' churches, i.e. the church of England and the Protestant churches of the continent, was valid. While he could attack the churches of the Channel Islands for behaving contrary to the church of England, the refugee churches in which Blier was ordained were seen to be an exiled part of the continental Protestant Church.[69] In 1620 the minister of the Italian community in London, Cesar Calindrini, was presented to the rectory of Stapleford Abbots and there were calls made for him to be reordained. However, these calls were rejected by the pro-Calvinist bishop Thomas Morton who was prepared to accept the validity of ordination within the stranger churches.[70] Blier was not, however, the sole example of this trend. His colleague Daniel Tuvel became the vicar of St Bartholomew the Less in London and Peter de Laune petitioned Charles I in 1628 to be presented to the rectory of Stamford Rivers. Nathaniel de Laune, who had been born in England, left the church at Dieppe to take up an English benefice.[71]

The gradual integration of the stranger communities, a process which in some cases included the ministers, meant that by the early seventeenth century the exile churches had become anachronisms. They no longer provided a refuge for a persecuted minority, nor did they serve as a model for their host community or as the religious arm of innovative economic communities. As a result the churches were vulnerable when they were challenged by Archbishop Laud in 1635. Ironically this attack established a degree of unity amongst the churches and probably delayed the schisms of the 1640s and the 1650s. These later disputes generally centred on the ministers and in some cases involved a conflict between the established second or third generation refugees and newcomers to the communities. In Norwich this was particularly clear in the struggle between the anglicised Pierre de Laune and the Presbyterian Pierre d'Assigny who had recently fled from the Channel Islands to Norwich.[72] The disputes in Southampton began much earlier in the 1620s and this was probably due to the small size and poverty of the community. Elie d'Arande came to Southampton after serving several Huguenot churches in France.[73] The comments that he made in his will in 1623 express something of the disillusionment that he felt:

> I doe alsoe protest in a good conscience and before god, that I have forced myselfe accordinge to my full power, to behave myselfe as a faythful pastor in the churches, where God hath binne pleased to be served by my ministry, as well by giveinge a pure and faythfull declaration of the Councell of God towards men for theire salvation as for the observinge of all the other dewties which doe binde those of our callinge to be faythfull laborers in the worde of the Lorde Our God. Itt is true that I have not seene soe much fruite of my ministry as I desired, nor such reste and advauncement of the said churches as I wished by the blessing of God uppon my faithfull labours, in regarde of the malignity of certaine personnes which perticularly in this ffrench church of Southampton have served as Instruments to the greate adversary to hinder the same. Itt is alsoe true that my imperfections may have binne in parte cause and perticularly in the defecte which I have allwaies perceaved in my selfe of sufficient science, ardur, prudence, constancy or wante of courage againste the difficultys and force of the maliciious and vigilency and dexterity toi breake the bad dessignes of the perverse. And as for the Offences which many and dyvers personnes have committed against me either through ignorance or mallice particu-

larly in this ffrench church of Sowthampton wherein many which
doe boaste themselves to bee the cheefest and mostlie apparente to
have pretexte and couver for their damnable Avarice, envy, hatred
of piety, ingratitude and malignity have layd to my charge stronge
impudente secrete affrontinge and perverse calumniations and have
troubled me by falce and secrete practices and have offended God
in divers waies moste cruelly in my personne.[74]

D'Arande's jaundiced reflections would be a sad epitaph if left to
stand as representative of the whole cadre of ministers who served
the Walloon exile churches. Inevitably strains occasionally
appeared between ministers and their congregations, not least
because their salaries were raised from levies on the income of
the congregation; the exile churches could rely on no parochial
endowment. But on the whole the ministers who served the exile
congregations may be seen as a talented and dedicated group; not
certainly the match of the elite group of scholars that Calvin
recruited at Geneva, but sufficiently capable for their services to
be eagerly sought by the new churches in their homelands in the
first generation after their establishment. The exile ministry placed
considerable additional demands on those who undertook it: not
merely meeting the needs of uprooted and dispossessed fellow
refugees, but also representing their interests to a sceptical and at
times hostile local population. The exile congregation had many
occasions to be grateful to those of their young scholars and fellow
refugees prepared to undertake these burdens.

Notes

I am grateful to Dr. A. C. Duke for his comments on an earlier version of
this paper. I would also like to acknowledge the support of Stonyhurst College.

1 A survey conducted in November 1572 at Rye recorded the refugees in
the town and the arrival of shiploads of refugees on 4, 7 and 9 November.
W. J. Hardy, 'Foreign Refugees at Rye', *Proceedings of the Huguenot
Society* [hereafter HS], 2 (1887–88), 568–75.

2 A. Pettegree, *Foreign Protestant Communities in Sixteenth-Century
London* (Oxford, 1986), pp. 139–42, 262–4, 279–82; Hardy, 'Foreign
Refugees at Rye', 576.

3 A. M. Oakley, 'The Canterbury Walloon Congregation from Elizabeth
I to Laud', in I. Scouloudi (ed.), *Huguenots in Britain and their French
Background* (London, 1987), pp. 56–8; F. W. Cross, *History of the
Walloon and Huguenot Church at Canterbury (Publications of the Hug-
uenot Society* [hereafter PHS], 15, 1898), pp. 63–4.

4 F. de Schickler, *Les Eglises du Refuge en Angleterre*, 3 vols (Paris, 1892), I, pp. 148–9; II, pp. 384–5. The names of Ursin Bayeux and Pierre Bence appear on both lists but have been counted only once.

5 *De Schickler, Les Eglises du Refuge*, I, pp. 198–200. Some of the names were also included on the 1568 lists.

6 Hardy, 'Foreign Refugees at Rye', 567; *Registre des Baptesmes, Mariages & Mortz et Jeusnes de leglise Wallonne . . . a Southampton*, ed. H. M. Godfray (*PHS*, 4, 1890), p. 8.

7 For example, Peter Baro became the Lady Margaret professor of divinity at the University of Cambridge. Adrian Saravia became a canon at Gloucester in 1591, after he had returned from the Netherlands: *Dictionary of National Biography* ed. L. Stephen and S. Lee (Oxford, 1917-), I, p. 1185; W. Nijenhuis, *Adrianus Saravia (c.1532–1613). Dutch Calvinist, first Reformed defender of the English episcopal Church order on the basis of the ius divinum* (Leiden, 1980), pp. 129–30.

8 *Discipline of the French Churches in England, 1588* in W. J. C. Moens, *The Walloons and their Church at Norwich, their History and Register, 1565–1832* (*PHS*, I, 1887–88), p. 286.

9 *Synodicon in Gallia Reformata*, ed. J. Quick, 2 vols (London, 1692), I, pp. 124–5; M. J. O. Kennedy, 'Jean Cousin, Minister of Threadneedle Street (c. 1562–1574) and his Congregation' *HS*, 22 (1970–76), 330–44.

10 De Schickler, *Les Eglises du Refuge*, I, p. 403; P. Collinson, 'The Elizabethan Puritans and the Foreign Reformed Churches in London', in his *Godly People* (London, 1983), pp. 250–2.

11 Pettegree, *Foreign Protestant Communities*, pp. 162, 256, 265, 266–7.

12 P. Beuzart, *Les Hérésies pendant le Moyen Age et la Réforme . . . dans le région de Douai, d'Arras et au pays de l'Alleu* (Le Puy, 1912), pp. 294–5, 447–8.

13 Archives Générales du Royaume, Brussels, Conseil des Troubles no. 6 fol. 229; P. Beuzart, 'La Reforme dans les environs de Lille specialement à Armentières, en 1566 d'après un document inédit', *BSHPF*, 78 (1929), 58–9; Stadsarchief Gent, Series 94 bis, reg. 9 fols 253–6v. I am grateful to Dr. J. Decavele for providing me with a photocopy of the latter source.

14 P. M. Crew, *Calvinist Preaching and Iconoclasm in the Netherlands 1544–1569* (Cambridge, 1978), p. 162.

15 H. Meylan, 'L'Eglise d'Anvers sous la terreur. Lettres inédites de Johannes Helmichius (1567)', in *Mélanges historique offerts à Monsieur Jean Meyhoffer, docteur en théologie* (Lausanne, 1952), pp. 73–85.

16 G. and J. Daval, *Histoire de la Reformation à Dieppe 1557–1657* ed. E. Lesens, 2 vols (Rouen, 1878), I, pp. 35, 45; de Schickler, *Les Eglises du Refuge*, I, p. 293.

17 Hardy, 'Foreign Refugees at Rye', 567–8.

18 An account of de la Motte's early life was written by a descendant, with some inaccuracies, in 1743. This is now in a private collection but a précis is included in S. Smiles, *The Huguenots, Their Settlements, Churches and Industries in England and Ireland* (3rd ed., London, 1869), p. 361; S. Stelling-Michaud (ed.), *Le Livre du recteur de l'acadé-*

mie de Genève (1559–1878), 6 vols (Geneva, 1959–81), IV, p. 603; *Livre Synodal contenant les Articles résolues dans les Synodes des Eglises Wallonnes des Pays-Bas*, 2 vols (The Hague, 1896), I, pp. 105, 110, 111; Nijenhuis, *Adrianus Saravia*, p. 60; British Library MSS Bibl. Egerton 868 'Delamotte Yearbook' fol. 8; *Registre* pp. 19, 104.

19 *Alumni Cantabridgiensis. A Biographical List of all Known Students Graduates and Holders of Office at the University of Cambridge . . . Part I From the Earliest Times to 1751* compiled by J. and J. A. Venn 4 vols (Cambridge, 1922–27), I, pp. 167, 253, II, p. 30; C. M. Dent, *Protestant Reformers in Elizabethan Oxford* (Oxford, 1983), pp. 153–4.

20 *Alumni Cantabridgiensis*, I, p. 289, 313, 331; Stelling-Michaud, *Le Livre du recteur*, II, p. 415, IV, p. 289; de Schickler, *Les Eglises du Refuge*, I, pp. 275–7, 291, 323, III, p. 151.

21 *Alumni Cantabridgiensis*, I, p. 253, II, p. 30; *Album Studiosorum. Academiae Lugduno Batavae MDLXXV-MDCCCLXXV* (The Hague, 1875), col. 70, 92.

22 *Les Actes des Colloques des Eglises Françaises, 1581–1654*, ed. A. C. Chamier (*PHS*, 2, 1890), pp. 4–5.

23 *Registre*, p. 133; City and Diocesan Record Office, Canterbury [hereafter Canterbury RO] U47/D Amount of money received and spent for students 1599–1601.

24 French Protestant Church of London Archives, Soho Square, AD/MS4 Actes du Consistoire 1589–1615, pp. 338, 344, 383.

25 *Actes des Colloques*, p. 45.

26 *Actes des Colloques*, pp. 13, 22.

27 *RCP* VI, pp. 80, 84, 120, 298–301, VII, 204–5; de Schickler, *Les Eglises du Refuge*, I, pp. 275–6.

28 *Actes des Colloques*, pp. 47, 48.

29 *Actes des Colloques*, pp. 48, 50; *Registre*, p. 92.

30 *Discipline of the French Churches in England, 1588*, p. 287.

31 *Actes des Colloques*, p. 50.

32 *Actes des Colloques*, pp. 47–8, 50.

33 *Actes des Colloques*, pp. 47, 50; *Registre*, pp. 111–12.

34 *Actes des Colloques*, p. 53.

35 *Livre Synodal*, I, p. 20.

36 *Actes du Consistoire de l'Eglise de Threadneedle Street, Londres Vol. II, 1571–77*, ed. A. M. Oakley (*PHS*, 48, 1969), p. 56; Pettegree, *Foreign Protestant Communities*, pp. 256, 269.

37 Nijenhuis, *Adrianus Saravia*, pp. 15–20, 26–7, 32–40.

38 De Schickler, *Les Eglises du Refuge*, III, pp. 370, 372, 373.

39 *Livre Synodal*, I, pp. 38, 42; Cross, *Walloon & Huguenot Church at Canterbury*, p. 74; de Schickler, *Les Eglises du Refuge*, I, pp. 198, 295.

40 Cross, *Walloon & Huguenot Church at Canterbury*, p. 71.

41 *Livre Synodal*, I, pp. 164, 166, 167, 175, 178, 179; *Actes des Colloques*, pp. 37–8.

42 *Actes des Colloques*, p. 5; Quick, *Synodicon*, I, p. 153.

43 *Livre Synodal*, I, pp. 110, 166, 167, 169.

44 *Actes des Colloques*, p. 21.

45 *Livre Synodal*, I, pp. 159, 161, 162, 165, 167, 171, 182; Daval, *Histoire de la Reformation à Dieppe*, I, pp. 164, 167. There may be some confusion over the name of the minister as the only Nathaniel de Laune recorded at Cambridge was admitted as a scholar in 1618. *Alumni Cantabridgiensis*, II, p. 29; Norfolk & Norwich Record Office, Mayor's Court Book 1615–24, fols 186, 187. I am grateful to Fr Raingard Esser for the latter reference.
46 Cross, *Walloon & Huguenot Church at Canterbury*, p.81; *Actes des Colloques*, p. 44.
47 M. L. Zell, 'Economic Problems of the Parochial Clergy in the Sixteenth Century', in R. O'Day and F. Heal (eds), *Princes & Paupers in the English Church 1500–1800* (Totowa, NJ, 1981), p. 35; C. Cross, 'The Incomes of Provincial Urban Clergy, 1520–1645', in ibid., pp. 66–7, 80.
48 Hampshire Record Office, Winchester, Wills: 1600 B 26 Henry Hopkins, 1612 Ad 51 Thomas Hitchcock; Public Record Office, London [hereafter PRO], Prerogative Court of Canterbury Wills, Prob. 11/130 1617 Philippe de la Motte; *Actes des Colloques*, p. 47. The only references to de la Motte's involvement in the cloth trade appear in the local records after 1604: Southampton Record Office, SC 6/1/28, SC 6/1/31, SC 6/1/32; *Court Leet Records*, ed. F. J. C. Hearnshaw 4 vols, (Southampton, 1905–08), Part III 1603–24, pp. 413–14, 480.
49 Canterbury RO, U47/A1 Actes du Consistoire 1576–78, p. 121.
50 *Actes du Consistoire de l'Eglise de Threadneedle Street, Londres, Vol. I 1560–1565*, ed. E. Johnston (*PHS*, 38, 1937), pp. xxi-xxii, xxxii, 17, 119.
51 Nijenhuis, *Adrianus Saravia*, pp. 43, 51–2; C. C. Hibben, *Gouda in revolt. Particularism and Pacifism in the Revolt of the Netherlands 1572–1588* (Utrecht, 1983), pp. 114–19.
52 Canterbury RO, U47/B Elders Accounts 1594–1604.
53 *Actes des Colloques*, pp. 9–10.
54 *Actes des Colloques*, p. 42; Moens, *The Walloons and their Church at Norwich*, p. 55.
55 Cross, 'The Incomes of Provincial Urban Clergy', p. 68; A. G. Little, 'Personal Tithes', *EHR*, 60 (1945), 76–7.
56 Moens, *The Walloons and their Church at Norwich*, pp. 60, 61, 255–6; Southampton Record Office, Poor Relief Collections: SC5/17/1, SC13/2/10, SC 10/1/3, SC10/1/4, SC10/1/7.
57 *Actes des Colloques* pp. 5, 52; Soho Square, p. 478.
58 *Registre*, p. 89; Canterbury RO U47/A2 fols 9v, 10, 10v.
59 *Registre*, pp. 102–4, 107–10; Southampton Record Office, SC 3/1/1; Oakley, *Canterbury Walloon Congregation*, p. 63; Pettegree, *Foreign Protestant Communities*, p. 293.
60 *Actes des Colloques*, pp. 5, 6, 52–3, 56, 58, 65, 67, 72; R. Gwynn, *A Calendar of the Letter Books of the French Church of London from the Civil War to the Restoration 1643–1659*, (*PHS*, 54, 1979), p. 24.
61 *Registre*, pp. 46, 88, 104, 127.
62 Collinson, 'The Elizabethan Puritans', pp. 265–7.
63 Hampshire Record Office, Winchester, Wills: 1609 A 15 Peter Caplin.
64 Gwynn, *Calendar of Letter Books*, p. 21.

65 PRO, Prerogative Court of Canterbury, Wills: Prob. 11/122 1613 Isaac le Gay, Prob. 11/125 1615 John Hersent; Hampshire Record Office, Winchester, Wills: 1609 A 15 Peter Caplin, 1611 A 19 Nicholas Caplin, 1611 A 28 John Cornish; *Registre*, pp. 111–12.

66 *Letters of Denization and Acts of Naturalisation, 1603–1700*, ed. W. A. Shaw (*PHS*, 18, 1911), pp. 12, 23.

67 *Returns of Strangers in the Metropolis 1593, 1627, 1635, 1639. A Study of an Active Minority*, ed. I. Scouloudi (*PHS*, 57, 1985) pp. 1–13; Hardy, 'Foreign Refugees at Rye', 579; Moens, *Walloons and their Church*, p. 232.

68 Hampshire Record Office, Winchester, 21M65 Visitation Books B1/27; *Registre*, pp. 54, 56, 58.

69 Nijenhuis, *Adrianus Saravia*, pp. 110–14.

70 O. P. Grell, *Dutch Calvinists in Early Stuart London. The Dutch Church of Austin Friars, 1603–1642* (Leiden, 1989), pp. 63–6.

71 *Alumni Cantabridgiensis*, IV, p. 280; Moens, *Walloons and their Church at Norwich*, p. 231; Daval, *Histoire de la Reformation à Dieppe*, I, pp. 198–9.

72 Gwynn, *Calendar of Letter Books*, pp. 8–25.

73 E. Haag and E. Haag, *La France Protestante* (2nd ed., Paris, 1886), V, cols 105–6.

74 Hampshire Record Office, Winchester, Wills: 1643 B 12 Elie d'Arande.

11

The implementation of Tridentine reform: the Passau Official and the parish clergy in Lower Austria, 1563–1637

Rona Johnston

Two contrasting quotations set the scene for this study of the post-Tridentine Roman Catholic clergy. The decrees of the twenty-second session of the Council of Trent (1545–63) stated:

> There is nothing that continually instructs others unto piety and the service of God, more than the life and example of those who have dedicated themselves to the divine ministry. For as they are seen to be raised to a higher position above the things of this world, others fix their eyes upon them as upon a mirror, and derive from them what they are to imitate. Wherefore clerics called to have the Lord for their portion, ought by all means so to regulate their whole life and conversation, as that in their dress, comportment, gait, discourse and all things else, nothing appear but what is grave, regulated and replete with religiousness; avoiding even slight faults, which in them would be most grievous; that so their actions may impress all with veneration.[1]

Sixty-six years subsequently the dean of Mistelbach wrote to the Passau Official in Vienna:

> About the priest in Ladendorff and his many crimes I cannot write enough ... and no improvement is to be hoped for ... in his outward gestures and clothes he resembles an impudent soldier more than a priest ... he celebrates mass poorly and on Sundays and Holy Days sometimes not at all ... if it is necessary during the week to bury the dead, to baptise children or to administer another sacrament then he is nowhere to be found, or drunk in the public inn ... about all of which the community complains greatly. He is a rough and tyrannical man, who strikes others, as can be proved ... he is a player with cards and dice ... he is a waster of church

possessions, within a short time he has used all of this year's wine and grain . . . about all this the village judge has complained to me in the name of the community, but has asked that his name not be made known, as the priest is threatening and would treat him badly.[2]

The implementation of the reform decrees of the Council of Trent in Lower Austria was neither a speedy achievement nor a straight-forward task.

By 1563, the Roman Catholic church had at last defined its response to the success of Protestantism. Reform of the parish clergy was central to the Counter-Reformation programme. According to the Catholic scheme the parish priest was the intermediary between laity and God, on whom his parishioners were dependent for their salvation; abuses by the parish priest could therefore damn his charges. Yet these representatives of the church at the local level had often borne the weight of the Reformers' criticism and where the traditional structure of the Roman Catholic church remained in place, the clergy – both regular and secular – were now a demoralised, undisciplined group often few in number and woe-fully deficient in training. It was therefore necessary not simply to restore worship according to the rites of the Catholic church, but also to redefine the role of the parish priest in his community, his relations with the local secular authority, and his position in the administrative structure of the church.

The decrees of the Council of Trent described the ideal Universal Church.[3] In assessing the impact of the Council the decrees on doctrinal matters have often been highlighted.[4] The Council's definition of such central points as the Eucharist and the means of Justification defined a Roman Catholic stance which was not reconcilable with Protestant theology. All hopes of compromise, at least between Lutheran and Catholic parties as successive Emperors had advocated, were at an end. Additionally, however, the Council produced at each session the 'decrees for reform', which laid out a comprehensive, if not always specific, programme for the correction of many of those abuses which had provided the Reformers with ammunition. These decrees, designed to 'restore ecclesiastical discipline, which is exceedingly relaxed, and to amend the depraved manners of the clergy', covered such items as the duties of the bishop in his diocese and the independence of the regular orders.[5] Additionally, much attention was devoted to the regulation of the secular clergy, who were responsible for the spiritual life of the majority of the laity.

The quality of spiritual provision in the parish was to be raised: the priest was to be of a suitable age; he was not to be forced to take orders; he was to dress appropriately; he was to administer the parish revenues well and present accounts to his bishop; he was to be of proven ability before being presented to the living and to be financially independent; he could not hold more than one benefice without permission; he was to be tied to one parish from which he could not absent himself without leave; his behaviour in the eyes of his parishioners was to be exemplary, both in the parish at large and in the church. He was to be well-educated – one of the most detailed clauses deals with the provision of a seminary in each diocese – and it was stressed that he should be able to explain the teaching and rites of the church to his parishioners and in particular that they should understand the meaning of the sacraments. The priest's duty to preach to the laity and explain Catholic doctrine was emphasised. Particularly relevant in the contemporary situation was the chapter which required the presence of a vicar in a parish when the incumbent was too ignorant to carry out these duties himself, although this would be avoided in future by the presentation of suitable candidates only. Whenever the living was vacant a temporary substitute was to be provided to ensure constant spiritual guidance in the parish.

Financial means which would enable the priest to carry out his duties were to be guaranteed. Reorganisation of parish boundaries and unification of beneficies were encouraged when this was necessary to provide sufficient income. Poorer parishes were to be supported directly from diocesan revenues. Beneficies were to be restored according to the details of their foundation; alienated church property was to be returned to the living; traditional tithes were to be paid. Church revenues were to be used only for the expenses of the priest and the upkeep of the church building and its functions. Neither patron nor any other secular authority was to interfere in internal church affairs.

Provision was also made for the supervision and disciplining of the parish clergy to ensure that they abided by Tridentine standards. This was the duty of the Ordinary.

> Whereas it is properly the office of bishops to reprove the vices of
> all who are subject to them, this will have to be principally their
> care – that clerics, especially those appointed to the cure of souls,
> be blameless, and that they do not, with their [i.e. the bishops']
> connivance, lead a disorderly life; for if they suffer them to be of
> evil and corrupt conversation, how shall they reprove the laity for
> their vices, when they themselves can be by one word silenced by
> them, for that they suffer clerics to be worse than they?[6]

All candidates for office were to be examined and approved by the
Ordinary, even nominees for benefices under lay patronage. The
bishop was also instructed to carry out visitations in the parishes
regularly, either in person or through his representatives:

> The principal object of all these visitations shall be to lead to sound
> and orthodox doctrine, by banishing heresies; to maintain good
> morals, and to correct such as are evil; to animate the people by
> exhortations and admonitions, to religion, peacefulness, and inno-
> cence; and to establish such other things as to the prudence of the
> visitors shall seem for the profit of the faithful according as time,
> place, and opportunity shall allow.[7]

A system of chastisement was also laid down, based on a series of
steps running from admonishment to deprivation of part of the
fruits of the benefice, to the forfeiture of all the income of the
living and temporary suspension, and finally to deprivation of all
benefices and offices. Excommunication was, however, to be used
sparingly and only as a final step when all other means of correction
had been unproductive.

The programme for the reform of the clergy was thus laid down at
Trent; its realisation was, however, neither quick nor easy. Just as
the course of the Reformation had varied according to the political
and religious traditions encountered in each territory, so too was
the form of the Counter-Reformation adapted to its context. In the
eighteenth century, the triumphalism of baroque demonstrated the
successful re-establishment of the Roman Catholic Church in the
Austrian Habsburg lands.[8] Yet this belied the very disparate nature
and timing of the movements which had made it possible. In each
area the re-establishment of Catholic worship had been tied to the
gradual growth of direct Habsburg authority. Habsburg absolutism
and the Counter-Reformation advanced hand in hand in a process

of mutual reinforcement.[9] The Tyrol and Inner Austria had been re-Catholicised by junior branches of the family: the former under Archduke Ferdinand II (1565–95) and the latter by Ferdinand of Styria (later Emperor Ferdinand II) after 1595. In Bohemia and Moravia, the failure of the estate-led uprising after 1618 led to a forceful re-Catholicisation at all levels of society; similarly in Upper Austria, rebellion which was associated with Protestantism provided the impetus for the re-establishment of Catholicism, but this was carried out by the Bavarian occupying force. Political circumstances in the Hungarian lands never made such a state-run Counter-Reformation possible and the result was the continuation of a far stronger Protestant tradition there than elsewhere in the Habsburg lands.

The framework for this study is provided by the independent course of the Counter-Reformation in Lower Austria, a further Habsburg hereditary province.[10] Lutheran teaching had been extensively adopted in the province among all social groups, but throughout the period covered here, between the final session of the Council of Trent in 1563 and the death of the arch-Counter-Reformer Emperor Ferdinand II in 1637, church institutions and laity were largely, if erratically, restored to the Roman Catholic church.[11] One aspect of this process was the regeneration of the parish clergy in the Lower Officialdom of the bishopric of Passau, covering most of Lower Austria. As Upper Austria also formed part of the bishopric of Passau, the ecclesiastical affairs of a large area of the Habsburg hereditary lands were in the hands of this 'foreign' bishop, for Passau was an independent province of the Empire.[12] The bishop of Passau's relationship with the Austrian Habsburgs was analogous to that of the archbishop of Salzburg, whose diocese also covered a large area of the Habsburg hereditary lands and whose independent policy was not always in agreement with that of the Emperor.[13] Parts of Lower Austria also composed the small Imperial foundations of Vienna and Wiener-Neustatt, created by Frederick III in the 1460s in an early attempt to counter the influence of foreign bishops in the lands he ruled directly.

The introduction of the Tridentine decrees into the Lower Officialdom through the ecclesiastical hierarchy highlighted the flaws present in the traditional structure by the second half of the sixteenth century. The Council had decreed that its tenets should be confirmed at provincial synods. The archbishop of Salzburg as

Metropolitan did not, however, convene his suffragan bishops until 1568; their decrees were in turn only confirmed by Rome in 1573.[14] The bishop of Passau then held a diocesan synod in 1576 and ordered synods to meet in the rural deaneries throughout his diocese immediately. In the Lower Officialdom three out of some ten deaneries did meet to discuss the decrees: all three synods were poorly attended and all disputed the advisability and feasibility of putting into effect the decrees of the provincial synod at Salzburg.[15]

In 1582 a further attempt was made to introduce the reforming spirit of Trent into Lower Austria by the Passau Official, Melchior Khlesl. The Passau Official, resident at the Passauer Hof in Vienna, was appointed by the bishop of Passau to oversee all matters concerning his ecclesiastical jurisdiction in Lower Austria.[16] Khlesl's *Rules for the Clergy* were based on the content and intentions of the decrees of the Council of Trent, reflecting his enthusiasm as a Jesuit-educated convert for the aims of the Counter-Reformation.[17] The *Rules for the Clergy* also contain, however, more detailed guidance concerning the daily work of the parish priest, concentrating on the priest's duties in the administration of the sacraments. Thus, for example, baptism was to be carried out in the church and not secretly in private houses; the priest was to be sober and to be careful to give suitable names; he should always be prepared to carry out emergency baptisms during the week.[18] Priests were to encourage parents to take their children to the bishop for confirmation, although the children must understand what they are doing. Confession and absolution were to be carried out individually; the secrets of the confession were not to be revealed; the correct form of absolution – in Latin – was to be administered, especially when giving absolution from heresy. The laity was to receive the Eucharist only after confession, and practical details were also given for the preparation of the communion wine and for communion of the sick. With matrimony, the couple was to be prepared beforehand and the priest was to ensure that there were no impediments to the marriage and that it was carried out at the correct time in the church calendar. Extreme unction was still to be administered and not largely ignored, as had recently been the case.

Although largely in line with the substance of the Tridentine decrees, the *Rules for the Clergy* were also specifically adapted to Lower Austrian circumstances. There is evident awareness of the lack of popularity of the clergy and of their teaching and that the priests had to win back allegiance to the Catholic church against the rival claims of neighbouring Lutheran preachers. As a result the need for modesty (*Beschaidenheit*) was repeatedly stated. Priests were to follow an exemplary lifestyle, dressing suitably, keeping fasts and holy days and staying away from activities which could harm their reputation. They were not to create unnecessary antagonism in the community. This is not the forceful, uncompromising Counter-Reformation spirit associated with re-Catholicisation elsewhere in the Habsburg lands. Rather, this was as far as the church could go when not guaranteed active secular support at local level.[19] In the same spirit, even greater stress than at Trent was put on the duty of the priest to explain the teachings and rites of the Roman Catholic church to the laity, especially the correct interpretation of the sacrifice of the mass. In particular in the countryside the people had lost the awareness of the way to righteousness and must be taught this again through the preaching of God's Word and through the Catechism – although the people should not be forced to remain in the church for so long that they become restless.

The *Rules for the Clergy* also demonstrate the need to balance the attempt to reintroduce specific Catholic practices with the extent to which this was a realistic aim. A clear differentiation from Protestant practices was made in some issues: godparents were to promise to bring up children in the Catholic faith and 'no other new teaching'; absolution was to be given to individuals and not in groups, 'as the sectarian preachers do' and priests were to avoid communion in both kinds, as 'true Catholic priests'. At the same time, however, when it was unavoidable, compromise was possible: the lay chalice was permitted when necessay, and specific instructions were given on how this should be done.

Thus by 1582 the Tridentine spirit directed at the improvement of Catholic provision in the parishes was clearly present in Lower Austria, emanating from the Passauer Hof in Vienna. It was, however, hindered and even halted in its progress by circumstances specific to Lower Austria. The Passau Official faced a longstanding distrust of independent action in Lower Austria by the bishop of Passau. The Tridentine decrees had immediately been seen as an infringement on the Emperor's authority and it was forbidden to issue them, although some items such as the chapter on matrimony had been published by 1637.[20] There was no natural alliance between Emperor and Roman Catholic church. Both Maximilian II (1564–76) and Rudolf II (1576–1612) were equivocal in their attitude towards Rome; Matthias's (1612–19) commitment to the Catholic cause was greater but hampered by his dependence on the Lutheran nobility; only the accession of Ferdinand II (1619–37) created a close alliance with the Roman Catholic church based on common cause. The Emperor was constantly concerned to prevent any action by the bishop or his representatives which could be seen as an incursion into his jurisdiction. In a legal system based so strongly on precedent, he could not permit anything which, although in line with his own intentions, might give Passau the edge in a dispute at a later date. The Passau Official in turn was charged on his appointment to defend Passau's traditional authority from rival claims.[21] That this was not always compatible with his duty to raise the standard of provision in the parishes was demonstrated in Khlesl's dispute with the Monastery Commission, a secular body established by Maximilian II in 1568. The Commission worked largely in line with the requirements of Trent in the incorporated monastery parishes and in the parishes to which the Emperor could nominate directly, examining candidates, carrying out visitations, and disciplining priests. Yet the Passau Official questioned its actions repeatedly on the grounds of conflicting jurisdiction, and after the settlement of this dispute in 1592 the Commission lost much of its authority and its enthusiastic reforming zeal was in turn lost to the cause of the Counter-Reformation.[22] Similarly the Passau Official questioned the right of the monasteries to present to their incorporated parishes – as well as the identity of these parishes – even when the candidate was clearly suitable but had not been presented to the Official for confirmation.[23]

Above all, however, parish reform could not be realised by the Official because many parishes had been effectively removed from his jurisdiction by Lutheran patrons. Although Protestant ideas had quickly moved south within the Empire and had found fruitful ground in Lower Austria, the visitation of 1544 still recorded that many parishes were in good Catholic hands.[24] The strength of the Lutheran party was, however, greatly enhanced as late as 1568 by the concessions granted by Maximilian II to the politically powerful Lower Austrian noble estates, giving them the right to worship according to the Confession of Augsburg. The

Concessions also specifically stated the right of a Lutheran patron to present in his patronage preachers who subscribed to the Confession of Augsburg – ignoring the bishop's theoretical right to reject any appointment. Until the political strength of the estates was broken, the clergy in these parishes were effectively outwith the jurisdiction, and discipline, of the Passau Consistory in Vienna.[25]

Nor was the impact of the Lutheran nobility restricted to political manoeuvring in the Landhaus in Vienna. The strength of their influence in rural Lower Austria must also be recognised. Some priests who arrived with great optimism in their new charge were driven from the living by the opposition of the local secular authority. In 1579 Georg Schneller applied for the parish of Münchreith an der Thaya, noting that the former preacher had died. With the support of the Monastery Commission he was presented by the Emperor and installed by the rural dean – but he was then driven out of the parish by the local lord, Adam von Püchheim, who instead installed a Lutheran preacher in the living. Events were repeated on the death of this new preacher in 1585.[26] Bating the local priest seems to have become a happy preoccupation of many local landowners. It was all too easy to forbid attendance at Catholic services, or to retain the vestments and vessels necessary for the Catholic mass, thus preventing the priest from being able to do anything other than preach – that is if he could get access to the church in the first place, since the local lord could have confiscated the keys, a very effective way of controlling worship. In Haselbach the church ornaments were retained by Wolf von Strein, despite orders to return them and he forbade his subjects from attending the Catholic mass. He also delayed the installation of the new priest in 1588 beyond Easter so that only the Protestant sacrament was available.[27] In the urban parishes this role was adopted by the town council which supported the activities of Lutheran preachers and strenuously resisted any attempts to replace them with Catholics.[28]

In the patchwork picture of Lutheran and Catholic parishes which was thus created throughout Lower Austria, the presence of a legitimate Lutheran preacher close at hand often hindered the Catholic priests in persuading the laity to attend their church. If Lutheran worship was not provided in a town or market, the citizens simply attended Protestant services in a local rural parish.

Some crossed the border into Hungary.[29] Household preachers for the rural nobility were often encouraged to extend their congregation into the surrounding areas. In 1571 the priest in Altpölla complained that the preacher in Franzen was usurping his jurisdiction over baptism, communion, and burials. According to the priest of Altpölla, the preacher had also been forbidden by his local lord to submit in any way to the jurisdiction of the Passau Official and the bishop.[30]

As the bishop was unwilling to call on secular support from the Emperor and unable to form an alliance with the Lutheran nobility, efforts to reform the secular clergy had to be implemented through the established ecclesiastical administrative hierarchy. Instructions were issued at the Passauer Hof in Vienna, and the rural deans responsible for a group of parishes functioned as the Official's principal local agents. This system was, however, too flawed to be able to enforce the Tridentine programme which was itself intended to revitalise the traditional structure. Trent required a self-regulating system of visitations and synods: these took place very rarely and usually at the instigation of the Emperor or the Lutheran party. In 1578 the dean of Traismauer appeared before the Consistory to answer why no congregation had been held: he replied that he had indeed called a synod but only five priests had attended; the others had either thrown the messenger down the stairs, not allowed him into the house, or answered that they had nothing to do with the Pope.[31] Nor, in any case, did such visitations achieve much other than painting a dismal picture of the quality of the Catholic clergy, both regular and secular.[32] The records of the Passau Consistory in Vienna under Khlesl between 1580 and 1600 are remarkable for the lack of evidence of a reforming spirit. They deal largely with cases of debt and disputed inheritance amongst the clergy and with matrimonial matters for the laity, and there is no mention of the disciplining of unruly clergy, decisions on presentations, the calling of synods, or the introduction of individual reforms.[33] The reforms of Trent were resisted not only by the laity, but also from within the church: the parish clergy opposed in particular Tridentine resolutions on clerical celibacy, celebration of the mass, and the establishment of a diocesan seminary. There was no general reform movement to support the initiative taken at Trent.

Many parishes remained vacant. Certainly there was a paucity

of candidates for a demoralised, unregarded profession. Many of
the priests under Khlesl whose background can be traced came
from outside Lower Austria. Others who had appeared suitable on
their introduction later adopted the Lutheran agenda, and in many
cases when apparently loyal Catholic priests converted to Lutheranism they simply retained the same parish living. Jakob Feucht-
inger, a priest from Carniola, was ordained in Passau in 1560 but
was a pastor preaching in the parish church in Fuglau after 1576.[34]
Above all, however, Lower Austria did not provide a seminary for
the training of candidates for the priesthood.[35] Although it had
been uniformly agreed at the synods held in the wake of Trent
that such an institution was desirable, the parish clergy repeatedly
claimed that they were unable to finance it on top of already
very high tax demands. Successive bishops of Passau showed great
interest in the establishment of some kind of training facility, but
could not find a method to support it. Urban of Trenbach, bishop
of Passau between 1561 and 1598, had proposed, with Khlesl's
support, the foundation of a seminary for six men in Vienna, to
be funded from diocesan revenues, but he faced the successful
opposition of the cathedral chapter in Passau.[36] The leading educational role was taken instead by the Jesuits. Their foundation in
Vienna, which was incorporated with the reformed University of
Vienna in 1623, and colleges established in Passau in 1612 and in
Krems in 1616 formed the backbone of their educational mission
to the province.[37] Within Lower Austria schools were also re-
established by the revitalised monasteries.[38] This was a gradual
development which gained momentum only fifty years after Trent;
additionally, Lutheran schools provided an attractive alternative
until 1627 when Protestant schoolmasters were banished from
Lower Austria. The failure to create an independent diocesan institution for Lower Austria remained a central concern for the leading
reformers throughout the period of the Counter-Reformation:
Khlesl left a grant in his will specifically for the funding of a
seminary in Vienna.[39]

The regulative system for the Roman Catholic church was, as
we have seen, not functioning efficiently, but on the other hand the
Lutheran estates had failed to exploit the tolerance of Maximilian II
and by his death in 1576 they had not established an independent
system of discipline for the Lutheran preachers in Lower Austria.[40]
In the light of this lack of control from above from either party,

local lay demands on the nature of spiritual provision in their parish could be very influential. It was possible for the 'Middle Way' (*Via Media*) which had characterised the early years of the Reformation in Lower Austria to continue, whereby priests adopted a position which incorporated aspects of both the Roman Catholic and Lutheran agendas. As late as 1600 in many rural parishes the battle lines had still not been clearly drawn. The term 'somewhat sectarian' was commonly in use; in 1590 the priest in Weisenalben was described as half-Lutheran, half-Catholic.[41] The Lutheran preacher whom we have seen installed in Münchreith an der Thaya complained before the Lutheran visitation in 1580 that his parishioners insisted on retaining saint's day holidays.[42] Priests considered loyal to Rome adopted some apparently specifically Protestant practices for several decades after 1563, without action being taken by Passau and, indeed, often with Passau's approval. Thus, as we have seen, the lay chalice could be given when unavoidable, and indeed was in common use. Many priests had married, having been given a licence to do so by their rural dean or even by the Official, and it was acknowledged that otherwise they might go to the local preacher to carry out the ceremony. Priests promised to submit to Passau's discipline if they could be allowed to retain their wives – or concubines as the church officially viewed them. Services were in German rather than Latin as Trent had required. Burials and marriages were carried out according to Protestant practices, on the basis that if the priest refused to do so, his parishioners would simply go elsewhere. In many instances of compromise, the priest was conforming to the demands of his parishioners, and the laity exploited the rivalry between neighbouring Lutheran and Catholic clergy to support these demands. The lay voice which had become so much louder with the initial success of the Reformation was also clearly heard within the Roman Catholic church.

Yet despite these inherent weaknesses in the nature of the Roman Catholic church in Lower Austria, a start in the re-Catholicisation process was made in the later sixteenth century, not least through the initiative of the Passau Official, Melchior Khlesl.[43] Khlesl has been acclaimed as the leader of the Counter-Reformation movement, and his main achievements dated to his time as Passau Official between 1580 and 1600. The explanation lies in his ability to bypass the problems listed above, through his personal commitment, enthusiasm, and involvement in the work of converting 'heretics'. Khlesl established close working relations with individuals of influence, ranging from Rudolf II's *Staathalter* for Lower Austria, Archduke Ernst (1576–94) and Archduke Matthias (1595–1609), to committed Catholic landowners and converted Lutheran nobility. He worked, however, as an individual, as Reformer General (an Imperial appointment) and Vicar General (appointed by Passau) rather than as Passau Official. With the support of Archdukes Ernst and Matthias he attended in person in the sovereign towns and markets which, despite their claims to the contrary, did not share in the concessions granted by Maximilian II.[44] He appeared in the parishes which the Emperor held directly and he preached, very effectively, in the parishes of sympathetic Catholic nobles.[45] The laity converted, he then tried to provide suitable parish priests. This method demonstrated that an alliance with the local secular authority was to be essential to the success of the Counter-Reformation; it did not answer the need to restore the parish clergy throughout the Officialdom.

Such individual action created pockets of Catholicism in a religiously diverse land and was the hallmark of re-Catholicisation in Lower Austria in the later sixteenth century. The Jesuits were established in Vienna after 1550 and in particular the preaching of Georg Scherer demonstated the impact such individual effort could have.[46] In 1590 the visitors in Waidhoffen an der Thaya recorded that 'Joachim Cörper maintains everything enthusiastically Catholic, although he himself seldom preaches, yet with his conviction and enthusiasm he has achieved more than many who preach frequently; this year he has 1,021 communicants'. Ten years later when Cörper left Waidhoffen, Catholic worship also declined. In 1615 the lay chalice was still in use.[47] Provision in incorporated parishes also improved as the monasteries were gradually revitalised during this period, often under the direction of a reform-minded prelate.[48] In the period between Khlesl's resignation as Passau Official in 1600 and the accession of Ferdinand of Styria as Emperor in 1619 further steps were taken in the Passau diocese to define the Catholic position – communion in both kinds was forbidden in 1602 and clerical 'concubinage' in 1605 – to be added to the reform programme drawn up by Khlesl in 1582. The problem of implementation remained, however, and was heightened by the loss to the Passau cause of Khlesl's personal zeal and by the further concessions granted to the Lutheran party in 1609 by Archduke Matthias in the course of the *Bruderzwist*, as he bargained with the nobility for support against his brother, Rudolf II. The achievement in the urban communities was fragile and in the rural parishes reconversions were even more limited. While the Catholic party could take heart from individual cases such as the conversion of the Liechtenstein family – which also brought the parishes in their patronage back into the Catholic fold – there was still no uniform policy of reconversion throughout Lower Austria.

This stalemate was broken, as the Lutherans had foreseen, by the election of Ferdinand II, whose reputation as the ruthless reformer of Inner Austria was well founded.[49] His personal wish to return all his subjects to the Catholic church was, however, realised only in conjunction with the outbreak of the Thirty Years' War, the fear it unleashed amongst the Lutheran estates, and above all Ferdinand's early successes against the rebellious Protestant estates in Bohemia and Upper Austria and their allies in Lower Austria. Protestantism was now equated with sedition and rebellion and the authority of the estates was directed instead to supporting the Emperor's cause. Although Ferdinand II had confirmed the concessions of the Lower Austrian noble estates and their members were not forcibly converted to Catholicism as elsewhere in the hereditary lands, the independent power of the Lutheran party based in the Landhaus in Vienna was broken by the alliance with Imperial Catholic interests. This was a first step in the move towards centralised Habsburg authority. For the first time the reformation by edict which had formed the basis of events elsewhere in the Empire could be executed in Lower Austria.

The first indirect step towards extension of Passau's influence into the Lutheran parishes was the seizure of the lands of those members of the nobility who had made common cause with the Upper Austrian and Bohemian rebels. These estates were passed into loyal Catholic hands, although the right of patronage was often retained by the Emperor. The decisive step for the Counter-Reformation in Lower Austria was the General Mandate, issued on 14 September 1627 at the height of Imperial military success in the Empire, which banished Protestant preachers and school-teachers from the Habsburg lands.[50] This was followed by an injunction to the Habsburg subjects to attend confession and mass and orders to the patrons of parishes to provide Catholic priests capable of the teaching which would bring about the genuine conversion of their restored parishioners. Patrons were required to state on oath their willingness to present a Catholic priest in their patronage. Attendance at a church not in the local parish was forbidden. For the first time there was no longer an alternative to the Catholic mass.

The Passau Official was now guaranteed secular support at both local and provincial level. The initiative for reform in the parishes passed into secular hands and, unlike Melchior Khlesl, the new Official, Karl von Kirchberg (1617–37), was willing to accept Habsburg involvement without the reservation that this could harm the bishop's independent status. The punishment of undisciplined priests, whether by fining, imprisonment, or removal from the living, was now carried out, often with the aid of secular agents, rather than remaining simply a threat. This new spirit is reflected in the protocol of the Passau Consistory where the notary now recorded – alongside still numerous cases of debt and infidelity – an active role for its members in the choice and installation of candidates, admonition and punishment of those who later lapsed from the required standards, and investigations of various complaints via the re-established system of rural deans. For the first time the Consistory can be seen to be initiating cases, rather than simply responding to events. Many more parishes were now covered by its active jurisdiction.[51]

Steps were also taken to improve the financial provision in parish livings. Khlesl had repeatedly recorded that a priest presented to a parish soon afterwards left his charge because it could not support him. Trent had countered this problem by declaring that the priest had to provide evidence of a private income and would therefore not be dependent on the stipend. Yet with the shortage of candidates this was a condition which neither Khlesl nor Kirchberg could afford to impose. After 1627, however, the situation was improved along Tridentine lines. Further edicts issued by Ferdinand II required the restoration of the possessions attached to the parish living, which had often been alienated during a vacancy or against the wishes of the incumbent, and several long-running disputes were settled in favour of the priest.[52] Poorer livings were united to create a joint charge which could support a priest, although this was usually intended to be a temporary measure. The payment to be made to the priest for individual services, in particular baptisms, weddings, and burials, had provided a source of disagreement between community and priest: claims that the priest's demands were too high had often been received at the Passauer Hof and had formerly provided a reason for turning instead to the local Lutheran preacher. Regulation of the *Stolgebühr* had been included in the decisions of the Salzburg Provincial Council in 1568; in the Lower Officialdom this was carried out after 1630 when the fee for each service was agreed upon in each parish in a settlement between priest and local secular authority.[53] Although individual disputes still occurred, this did regulate the position of the priest in relation to his parishioners, removing ammunition from both sides.

The flawed traditional system which Kirchberg had inherited as Passau Official could not, however, suddenly function smoothly in the new situation created by Ferdinand II's state-run re-Catholicisation programme.[54] The widely-held view that the revitalisation of the parish clergy was a prerequisite for the conversion of the laity was to prove misfounded: in many instances in Lower Austria the laity had been converted, at least outwardly, before suitable provision had been made in the local living, as the parishioners themselves often complained. Obermarkesdorf and Markersdorf which were confiscated from the Eitzing family in 1621 were united and the patronage given to a loyal Catholic family. Yet the first priest after 1621 was found guilty of misuse of the church income and sale of church ornaments which, as was pointed out at the time, had been preserved unscathed in the hands of the Lutheran Eitzing family. He was also accused of failing to hold mass, to preach, to keep the church clean, and to work to bring about genuine conversions.[55] He was removed in 1623, but only in 1630 was a more suitable priest in place. After 1627 many parishes, their Lutheran preacher banished, remained vacant for ten years and longer. Other parishes were filled in the rush to provide Catholic services after 1627 but proved to have unsuitable candidates who had to be repeatedly disciplined and even removed.[56] Priests continued to lack training and learning and were therefore inadequately equipped to perform their new role, to bring about by teaching and explanation true conversion and devotion to the rites of the Catholic church. This was a duty which the secular clergy often could not fulfil and as a result the regular clergy,

revitalised earlier, were able to adopt a role outside the monasteries, even in the non-incorporated parishes. The wealthy parish of
Raabs was, for example, supplied from the monastery of Geras from
1628 until 1668.[57] The need for such support was acknowledged by
Passau: in 1630 the Vice-Official had ordered the rural deans to
employ 'learned fathers' – whether Dominican, Jesuit, Franciscan,
Capuchin, or of another Order – to teach the laity how to make
the sign of the cross, how to pray and how to receive communion.
They were also to teach the Catechism and inspire the lay members
in order to bring about genuine conversion.[58] The result was the
distinctive nature of the Austrian Counter-Reformation which
included a very active role for the regular clergy in the daily
spiritual life of the laity.

Although visitations under Ferdinand III (1637–57) and even
later still demonstrated a stubborn attachment to Protestantism in
places and a resistance to the return to the Roman Catholic church,
the Lower Austrian Counter-Reformation had been defined and
largely run its course under Ferdinand II by 1637.[59] Yet the work
of re-Catholicisation had to continue, not simply as a response to
Protestantism but to ensure a higher standard within the church,
above all amongst the secular clergy. The community retained the
voice it had learned to raise when church discipline had been lax
and lay people were always ready to complain to the Passauer Hof
about the service provided in the parish. Complaints from the
community ranged from the failure of the priest in Landegg to
hear confession in Croatian to lists such as the allegations made
against the priest in Schrattenthal in 1642: that he was constantly
ill and insisted on being carried to the church in a chair, but would
attend a market day in local Retz with his housekeeper and their
children. Additionally he overcharged, despite the new regulation,
for burials, baptisms, and marriages.[60] Many features of the Tridentine model remained to be implemented after 1637: parish records
became standard only from the 1660s; examination of candidates
became regular only in the reforms of Joseph II in the 1780s.

Although the nature of the work and achievement of the
two Passau Officials Melchior Khlesl (1580–1600) and Karl von
Kirchberg (1617–37) were distinct, one strain was evident under
both men: the growth in ties, direct and indirect, with the secular
arm. This was clearly not in keeping with the Tridentine mood
which stressed the independence of the church. Yet, as both

Officials recognised, they were unable to implement any policy which faced opposition without the active support of other authorities, despite the concomitant loss of independence. The secular clergy, their allegiance still due to foreign Passau, were increasingly operating as a branch of the Habsburg bureaucracy. The loyal parish clergy provided a useful source of information as Archduke Ernst and Archduke Matthias recognised. In 1585, for example, parish priests reported on the presence of Lutheran preachers and on the use of the Old Calendar.[61] This was not a role which increased their popularity in the local community: on 6 January 1584 the Propst of Zwettl reported to Khlesl that he feared for his life having halted a Christmas service being held ten days late according to the Gregorian calendar.[62] Although Khlesl had rejected any secular involvement in church affairs where it could be avoided, Kirchberg was willing to act to a far greater extent as a functionary of the state. The traditional hierarchy was realigned in specific cases in which orders were issued not by the bishop (although with his acquiescence) but in the name of the Emperor. Thus in 1627 the parish clergy carried out a collection of prohibited books under orders received by the Official from Ferdinand II.[63] In 1630–31 statistics on precise numbers of Catholic and Protestant subjects were collected for the first time – by the parish clergy. In 1630 the priest in Speisendorf reported that his parish contained twenty-eight Catholic and fifteen Lutheran households.[64] This joint effort by secular and ecclesiastical bodies was evident in the nature and work of the Reformation Commissions. These were central to Ferdinand II's re-Catholicisation programme on the Inner Austrian model and were composed of members of the local clergy, proposed individually by the Official for their known abilities, working alongside secular officials and members of the regular clergy from neighbouring houses.[65] The members of the Commissions were also required to examine the financial basis of the living, a right which Trent had specifically reserved for the bishop alone.[66]

Habsburg relations with the foreign ecclesiastical jurisdiction in the hereditary lands have been discussed here in the light of the reform of the parish clergy. This highlights the complicated nature of the Habsburg role within the Empire (of which both Passau and Lower Austria were part) and the extent of the Habsburg writ. The development of a specifically *Austrian* identity under Ferdinand

II and his successors also had its effect on the parish clergy, who were so important to this Catholic Habsburg creation but owed allegiance to a foreign bishop. A series of measures was designed to control the potential independence of Passau. These reached from the election of three Habsburg bishops – Archduke Leopold (1598–1625), Archduke Leopold William (1625–62) and Archduke Charles (1662–64) – to the control of events at parish level through increased influence in the affairs of the secular clergy, tying them closely to Habsburg interests. Although this was a step contrary to Passau's desire to retain its traditional independence, it was a pragmatic necessity. And indeed the integration of the Passau clergy into the Austrian absolutist scheme established a *modus vivendi* which enabled the foreign bishop of Passau to continue to have such a large presence in Habsburg affairs until as late as the rationalisation of the Catholic church in Austria under Joseph II in the 1780s, when the lumbering, conservative, tradition-bound weight of the Passau diocese was finally removed from influence in internal 'Austrian' affairs.[67] In 1629, after fifty years of personal involvement in the work of re-establishing the Roman Catholic church in Lower Austria, Melchior Khlesl, now cardinal and bishop of Vienna had written to Ferdinand II, 'as your Imperial Majesty can see from all this, it is all dependent only on Your Imperial Majesty's resolution . . . to which I commend myself'.[68] This union of secular and ecclesiastical arms made possible the re-establishment of Roman Catholicism in Lower Austria, which the church alone could not have achieved and which rescued the secular clergy from impotence.

Notes

1 *The Canons and Decrees of the Council of Trent*, tr. J. Waterworth (London and New York, 1888), p. 162.
2 Vienna, Diözesanarchiv Wien (hereafter DAW), Reformation/Gegenreformation, 1585–1630, 2 November 1628.
3 On the Council of Trent, Hubert Jedin, *Geschichte des Konzils von Trient*, 4 vols (Freiburg i. B., 1949–75).
4 For example, G. R. Elton, *Reformation Europe 1517–1559* (London and Glasgow, 1963), pp. 195–7.
5 *Canons and Decrees of the Council of Trent*, p. 49.
6 Ibid., p. 111.
7 Ibid., p. 209.
8 For a discussion of the baroque style in its historical context, V.-L.

Tapie, *The Age of Grandeur*, tr. A. R. Williamson (London, 1960) chs 9–10; for individual examples, John Bourke, *Baroque Churches of Central Europe* (London, 1978).

9 On the nature of the Austrian Habsburg state in the seventeenth century, R. J. W. Evans, *The Making of the Habsburg Monarchy 1550–1700* (Oxford, 1985); Hans Sturmberger, *Kaiser Ferdinand II und das Problem des Absolutismus* (Munich 1957); Anna Coreth, *Pietas Austriaca* (Vienna, 1959).

10 Karl Gutkas, *Geschichte des Landes Niederösterreich*, 3 vols (St Pölten, 1957–62) especially vol. 2, *Von der Einigung des Donauraumes bis zu den Reformen Maria Theresias*; Theodor Wiedemann, *Geschichte der Reformation und Gegenreformation im Lande unter der Enns*, 5 vols (Prague and Leipzig, 1879–86); Friedrich Schragl, *Glaubensspaltung in Niederösterreich* (Vienna, 1973).

11 An overview of Protestantism in Lower Austria is provided in Grete Mecenseffy, *Geschichte des Protestantismus in Österreich* (Graz, 1956), pp. 9–186 and Gustav Reingrabner, *Protestantismus in Niederösterreich* (St Pölten and Vienna, 1977), pp. 3–24.

12 The bishopric of Passau was geographically the largest in the Empire: the greater part of the diocese was formed by the Habsburg lands of Upper Austria and most of Lower Austria, but it also encompassed part of Bavaria and the Hochstift Passau itself. In the period between 1563 and 1637 the see was held by Urban of Trenbach (1561–98), the last in a line of Wittelsbach-supported incumbents, by Archduke Leopold (1598–1625), brother of Emperor Ferdinand II, and by Archduke Leopold William (1625–62), brother of Emperor Ferdinand III.

13 Salzburg's failure openly to aid Imperial forces in the Thirty Years' War was a demonstration of the archbishop's ability to operate independently of Habsburg interests. On Salzburg see Hans Widmann, *Geschichte Salzburgs*, 3 vols (Gotha, 1907–14), III, pp. 1–346.

14 Salzburg was Metropolitan for Passau, Regensburg, Freising, and Brixen, and for four small *Eigenbistümer*: Seckau, Chiemsee, Gurk, and Lavant. For a detailed study of this synodial process in the Salzburg province, Gerhard B. Winkler, *Die nachtridentinischen Synoden im Reich: Salzburger Provinzialkonzilien 1569, 1573, 1576* (Vienna, Cologne, and Graz, 1988); also Josef Oswald, 'Das Bistum Passau und seine Beteilung am Konzil von Trient (1545–1563)', *Ostbairische Grenzmarken*, 3 (1959), 204–11.

15 Synods were held in the rural deaneries of Mistelbach, Krems, and Traismauer. Wiedemann, op. cit., II, pp. 271–5.

16 As a result of the long distance between Vienna and Passau and of the inferior standing of the Lower Officialdom to the Upper Officialdom, which comprised Passau, Upper Austria, and that part of the diocese which lay in Bavaria, the Passau Official was able to operate the Lower Officialdom largely independently of Passau. For the development of the administrative structure in the Passau diocese, Josef Oswald, 'Der organisatorische Aufbau des Bistums Passau im Mittelalter und in der Reformationszeit (Offizialats-, Dekanats- und Pfarreinteilung)', in Josef

Oswald (ed.), *Beiträge zur altbayerischen Kultur und Kirchengeschichte* (Passau, 1976), pp. 234–60.

17 DAW, Bistum Passau, bis 1650, *Verordnung an alle Decanos, Pfarrer..*, 1582. On Melchior Khlesl see below.

18 The priest was required to take particular care that male children were given boys' names and female children girls' names; the names themselves were not censored.

19 See below.

20 Wiedemann, op. cit., I, pp. 241–7.

21 DAW, Bistum Passau, General Vikariat in Wien: Instruktionen für Wolfgang Furtmayer (28 August 1548), Johann Grosthoman (7 August 1601), Damian Inama (14 Jänner 1644); also DAW, Bischofsakten, Kardinal Khlesl, Instruktion für Melchior Khlesl (2 Februar 1580).

22 On the Monastery Commission, Johann A. Sattek, 'Der niederösterreichische Klosterrat', (Vienna University dissertation, 1950). For a demonstration of the Commission at work see Floridus Röhrig, 'Protestantism und Gegenreformation im Stift Klosterneuburg und seine Pfarren', *Jahrbuch des Stiftes Klosterneuburg*, neue Folge, I (1961), 105–70. The dispute was also fuelled by the personal animosity between Khlesl and the President of the Commission, Wolf Unverzagt.

23 Such disputes were numerous and repetitive. See for example DAW, Pfarrakten, Traiskirchen to which the abbot of Melk nominated directly.

24 Vienna, Niederösterreichisches Landesarchiv (hereafter NÖLA), Klosterrat, Visitationsbericht, 5 März 1546.

25 For a survey of the *Ständestaat* in the hereditary lands, Herbert Hassinger, 'Die Landstände der Österreichischen Länder: Zusammensetzung, Organisation und Leistung im 16–18. Jahrhundert', *Jahrbuch für Landeskunde von Niederösterreich*, 36 (1964), 989–1035.

26 NÖLA, Klosterrat, Münchreith an der Thaya, 1579 and 1585.

27 NÖLA, Klosterrat, Karton 19, Haselbach, 3 Juni 1588.

28 The town council of Krems proved especially stubborn in resisting pressure to reintroduce Catholic priests. Anton Kerschbaumer, *Geschichte der Stadt Krems* (Krems, 1885).

29 In January 1586 Khlesl reported to Archduke Ernst: 'Although the town of Tulln . . . with the help of God and through the effort, troubles and work . . . of my dean has been brought to due spiritual obedience . . . Wolfgang Nussdorffer, a citizen of Stockerau, has secretly and wrongly . . . led many parishioners away again from the true Catholic religion.' DAW, Reformation/Gegenreformation, 1585–1630, 1586. Protestant sevices in Hungary remained an alternative even after Protestant preachers had been banished from Lower Austria in 1627. See for example the report from the priest of Dirnbach to the Passau Official, DAW, Reformation/Gegenreformation, 1630–1699, Nr 69.

30 Wiedemann, op. cit., II, p. 624.

31 Wiedemann, op. cit., IV, p. 137.

32 Robert Waissenberger, 'Die hauptsächlichsten Visitationen in Österreich ob und unter der Enns sowie in Innerösterreich in der Zeit von 1528–1580', (Vienna University dissertation, 1949).

THE REFORMATION OF THE PARISHES

33 DAW, PP 5 (1572–92).
34 Wiedemann, op. cit., I, p. 548.
35 Oskar Vasella, 'Über das Problem der Klerusbildung im 16. Jahrhundert', *Mitteilungen des Institutes für Österreichische Geschichtsforschung*, 58 (1950), 441–56.
36 The establishment of a seminary is repeatedly raised in correspondence between Passau and the Passau Official in DAW, Reformation/Gegenreformation, bis 1585; 1585–1630; 1630–99.
37 Bernhard Duhr, *Geschichte der Jesuiten in den Ländern deutscher Zunge*, 3 vols (Freiburg-Regensburg, 1907–21), II, pp. 318–27.
38 For example, Ignaz Franz Keiblinger, *Geschichte des Benediktinerstiftes Melk* (Vienna, 1851–69).
39 DAW, Bischofsakten, Kardinal Khlesl, 580.
40 The unsuccessful attempt to establish an organised Lutheran church in Lower Austria is described in detail in Victor Bibl, *Die Organisation des evangelischen Kirchenwesens im Erzherzogtum Österreich unter der Enns (1568–1576)* (Vienna, 1899).
41 The visitation of 1590 recorded that the priest in Weisenalben baptised in German, did not pray at the correct hours, accepted only the sacraments of baptism, absolution, and the Eucharist, and possessed many Lutheran books. *Geschichtliche Beilagen zu den Consistorial-Currenden der Diöcese St Pölten*, I, p. 193.
42 Wiedemann, op. cit., II, p. 571.
43 Melchior Khlesl (1552–1631), the son of a Lutheran baker in Vienna, had a career in which he became cardinal, bishop of Vienna and chief minister to Emperor Matthias, yet he lacks a recent study. See Joseph von Hammer-Purgstall, *Khlesls, des Cardinals . . . Leben*, 4 vols (Vienna, 1847–51). On Khlesl as Passau Official, Magdalena Lohn, 'Melchior Khlesl und die Gegenreformation in Niederösterreich', (Vienna University dissertation, 1949).
44 The creation of a Catholic party in the town council to provide a sympathetic local secular authority was a prerequisite for the reintroduction of a Catholic priest, as Khlesl recognised. The pressure applied from the Hofburg in Vienna was essential. See for example Richard Hübl, *Die Gegenreformation in St Pölten* (St Pölten, 1966), pp. 22–31.
45 Lohn, op. cit., pp. 52–145.
46 Duhr, op. cit., I. pp. 798–820.
47 NÖLA, Klosterrat, Waidhoffen an der Thaya.
48 See for example Günther Appelt, 'Georg Falb von Falberstein, Abt des Stiftes Göttweig (1578–1631)' (Vienna University dissertation, 1964); Gerhard Flossmann, 'Abt Caspar Hofmann von Melk (1587–1623)' (Vienna University dissertation, 1964); H. Riedl, 'Ulrich Hackl, Abt zu Zwettl' (Innsbruck University dissertation, 1936).
49 Karl Eder, 'Die Konfessionspolitik Ferdinands II', *Bericht über den dritten österreichischen Historikertag in Graz 1953* (1954), 12–25.
50 As the rights of the Lutheran members of the estates had been confirmed, the preachers and schoolteachers were banished on the grounds that they had adopted untolerated Calvinist practices.

51 DAW, PP 81 (1621–26; 1643–49); PP12 (1633–37).
52 DAW, Pfarrakten record the complaints of the parish priest and an increasing number of favourable settlements. In many cases, however, ecclesiastical possessions remained in dispute, based on conflicting claims over the terms of the original donation, often made centuries previously, and such disputes continued into the eighteenth century.
53 See lists contained in DAW, Konsistorialakten, Stolgebühr.
54 For example, the repeated demands made by Ferdinand II to the Passauer Hof that 'exemplary priests' be supplied for the restored parishes. DAW Reformation/Gegenreformation, 1585–1630, from 14 September 1627.
55 NÖLA, Klosterrat, Obermarkersdorf, 22 November 1622.
56 DAW PP12 (1633–37).
57 Wiedemann, op. cit., II, p. 568.
58 DAW, Reformation/Gegenreformation, 1585–1630, 28 März 1630.
59 On continuing Protestantism, Mecenseffy, op. cit., pp. 186–90.
60 DAW, Pfarrakten, Landegg, 1632; NÖLA, Klosterrat, Schrattenthal, 1642.
61 DAW Reformation/Gegenreformation 1585–1630, 23 Dezember 1585, Order from Archduke Ernst requiring Khlesl to investigate through the rural deans the use of the Old Calendar and the presence of Flacians.
62 DAW, Reformation/Gegenreformation, bis 1584, 6 Jänner 1584.
63 DAW, Reformation/Gegenreformation, 1585–1630, 20 April 1628.
64 Vienna, Haus-, Hof- und Staatsarchiv, Reichskanzlei, Religionsakten 3, 195r–196v.
65 The Passau Official proposed representatives of the bishop – usually the rural dean – as members of the Reformation Commissions in each area. DAW, Reformation/Gegenreformation, 1630–99, 14 Februar 1630.
66 DAW, Reformation/Gegenreformation, 1585–1630, 6 März 1630.
67 The Lower Officialdom was divided between the archbishopric of Vienna and the new creation of the bishopric of St Pölten; the Passau diocese in Upper Austria formed the new bishopric of Linz.
68 DAW, Reformation/Gegenreformation, 1585–1630, 8 Jänner 1629.

Index

239

INDEX

INDEX

wills, 45, 53, 124
Winchelsea, 195–6, 198
Winchester, 49, 204
Winghen, Godfrey van, 177
Winterthur, 69
Wittenberg, 7, 70
Worcestershire, 45
Württemberg, 88
Wybo, Joris, 177
Wycliff, John, 33

Yatton, 45, 48, 50, 52, 54

Zeeland, 175, 178, 200, 204
Zierikzee, 178, 203
Zoutermeer, 187
Zurich, 5, 9–10, 63, 65–71, 73–7, 80
Zwijndrecht, 179
Zwingli, Huldrych, 9, 63–70, 71, 75, 80
Zuttere, Pieter de, 179–80